Workers, Managers, Productivity

Akio Hosono • John Page • Go Shimada
Editors

Workers, Managers, Productivity

Kaizen in Developing Countries

palgrave
macmillan

Editors
Akio Hosono
JICA Research Institute
Tokyo, Japan

John Page
The Brookings Institution
Washington, DC, USA

Go Shimada
School of Information and
Communication
Meiji University
Tokyo, Japan

ISBN 978-981-15-0363-4 ISBN 978-981-15-0364-1 (eBook)
https://doi.org/10.1007/978-981-15-0364-1

This Palgrave Macmillan imprint is published by the registered company Springer Nature Singapore Pte Ltd.
The registered company address is: 152 Beach Road, #21-01/04 Gateway East, Singapore 189721, Singapore

Foreword

Development practitioners and researchers have long been confronted to the reality of a productivity gap between developed and developing countries. However, the role of management methods as an important determinant for quality and productivity outcomes has only surfaced in the recent past, and little is known about the effectiveness of initiatives that aim to increase managerial capital and improve productivity in the private or public sector in developing countries. *Kaizen*, as a model that has attracted much attention and captured imaginations from the 1960s on, and that has been adopted in many firms all over the world, provides an interesting lens to study the mechanisms at stakes. *Kaizen* can be defined as an inclusive and participatory approach to continuous improvement in quality and productivity, rooted in a distinctive philosophy and using specific tools and methods.

In 2015, the Japan International Cooperation Agency—Research Institute (JICA-RI) and the Global Development Network (GDN) felt that there would be high value in taking stock of the experiences of the various initiatives that disseminated and implemented *Kaizen* in different contexts and hence decided to join forces to document the adoption of *Kaizen* approaches.

This partnership was based on shared interests and strong complementarity. JICA-RI, the research arm of JICA, had invested much in private sector development. It was particularly interested in assessing how a now famous Japanese innovation, dating back to the 1960s and that it contributed to disseminate, can unleash innovation and productivity gains in developing country firms. GDN, a public international organization devoted to building research capacity in social sciences in developing countries, had supported research on productivity and industrial policies. It reckoned that a firm-based approach would provide both ample ground for capacity development and an opportunity to learn more about the driving forces underpinning the adoption of new managerial practices and their impact as a complement to research work on the conduct and impact of industrial policies.

This book is the product of this cooperation, which involved researchers from developing countries and *Kaizen* practitioners who worked on specific case studies and three co-editors, Akio Hosono, John Page, and Go Shimada who took the leadership in directing the book toward a coherent and meaningful object. It also involved researchers who advised research teams while they conducted their research, and we are grateful to Jocelyn Olivari, Aniceto Orbeta, and Tetsushi Sonobe for their comments and reviews. Because a book like this is more than a collection of individual studies, the contributors gathered several times in Tokyo, Nagoya, Bangkok, and Washington to discuss their research, identify commonalities and differences across context, and learn from the experience of each other. We hence hope to have planted the seed of a community of researchers in developed and developing countries interested in the dissemination and implementation of *Kaizen* approaches.

Through the voices of its co-editors, developing country researchers, and *Kaizen* practitioners, the book aims to present the diversity of *Kaizen* approaches in firms in developing countries and to address a number of a questions related to their effectiveness. Going beyond a traditional theory of firms, and by providing a deep dive into the intervention mechanisms used to introduce and sustain *Kaizen*, it also aims to put in the organizations- and countries-specific context the different experiences it describes. Such a book usually raises more question than it answers, but we hope it will provide the reader with an understanding of the mechanisms through which *Kaizen* initiatives may or may not work, how is *Kaizen* shaping the relations between workers and managers and the conditions for its adoption in a variety of firms from SMEs to Multinational corporations.

We would like to thank the book's chapter authors for their unerring dedicated involvement and the three co-editors Akio Hosono, John Page and Go Shimada for their invaluable analytical and editorial contributions.

We would also like to add here a special word for our colleague, Professor Nestor Raneses who led the work on Chap. 13 on the MPex Program in the Philippines and express our deep sadness at his passing before the publication of this book.

Global Development Network, New Delhi, India — Pierre Jacquet
JICA Research Institute, Tokyo, Japan — Izumi Ohno

ACKNOWLEDGMENTS

The editors are most grateful to the Global Development Network (GDN), Japan International Cooperation Agency Research Institute (JICA-RI), and the Brookings Institution, which provided efficient logistical support for our research, the organization of authors' workshops, and the preparation of this volume. The editors would like to extend their deepest gratitude to the President of GDN, Pierre Jaquet, and former and current directors of JICA-RI, Ichiro Tambo, Naohiro Kitano, Nobuko Kayashima, and Izumi Ohno, who all supported us during the process of conceiving, proposing, and carrying out the research project.

The editors would like to express their sincerest thanks to advisers to the research and writing of case-study chapters: Tetsushi Sonobe, the National Graduate Institute for Policy Studies (GRIPS), shared many valuable insights with us in the course of the project. The editors deeply appreciate valuable suggestions from Tsuyoshi Kikuchi, Japan Development Services Co., Ltd., Hiroyuki Tomita, JICA, and William Maloney, the World Bank.

The editors would also like to express special gratitude to several organizations that allowed us and the chapter authors to learn about the implementation, significance, and nature of *Kaizen* on site: Toyota Motor Corporation, Tahara Plant, Aichi, Japan, Denso (Thailand) Co., Ltd., Samrong Plant, Samutprakarn, Thailand, and Thai-Nichi Institute of Technology, Bangkok, Thailand. We appreciate the support of the JICA Offices in Bangkok, Nagoya, and Washington as well.

The editors and chapter authors would like to express their deep appreciation to those who supported the research and writing of individual chapters: members of the Malaysia Productivity Corporation (MPC), Petaling Jaya, Malaysia; Leo Guzman-Anaya, University of Guadalajara, Mexico; members of the Brazilian Development Bank (BNDES); members of the Institute of Applied Economic Research (IPEA), Brazil; members of the Inter-American Development Bank (IDB); Fekadu Nigussie Deresse, Agriculture Transformation Agency (ATA); Ethiopia; Girum Abebe Tefera, Ethiopian Development Research Institute (EDRI); Mekonnen Yaie, and Seblewongel Hargawin, Ethiopia Kaizen Institute (EKI); Nigusse Gebre Gebremedhin, Federal TVET Agency (FTA), Ethiopia; Gebeyehu Benti, Yasuto Kikuma, and Hiroyuki Tanana, JICA Ethiopia Office; Getafun Tadesse Mekonnen, Ethiopia; members of the Automotive Industry Development Centre (AIDC), Rosslyn, South Africa; Jocelyn Olivera, Universidad Alfonso Ibanez, Chile; Aniceto Orbeta, Philippines Institute for Development Studies, Philippines; members of the National Board for Small Scale Industries of Ghana; members of the JICA Ghana Country Office; the Samahan ng mga Rizaleño sa Sektor ng Agrikultura at Pagkain (SARAP), the Philippines; and members of the Department of Science and Technology and the Department of Trade of Industry, the Philippines.

The editors are especially grateful to Pierre Bertrand, Naotaka Yamaguchi, Eriko Sakamaki, Ritsuko Yamagata, and Kimiaki Jin for their continuous support of the research, authors' workshops, and other related meetings as well as for providing professional assistance during the preparation of this volume. Their tremendous support at different moments throughout the three years of this research project is greatly appreciated.

Contents

Notes on Contributors

Charles Godfred Ackah is a director of the Centre for Social Policy Studies and a senior research fellow at the Institute of Statistical, Social and Economic Research, University of Ghana. He is also an external research fellow at the Centre for Research in Economic Development and International Trade, University of Nottingham.

Johnson Appiah Kubi just finished his PhD in Development Economics from the University of Ghana (results published, formal award in July 2019). He is a research associate on two research projects in the University of Ghana and a consultant on one project elsewhere in Ghana.

Richmond Atta-Ankomah is a research fellow at the Institute of Statistical Social and Economic Research, University of Ghana. He received his PhD from the Open University, UK, in 2014. He has a research background in economics and development, particularly the economics of innovation, and poverty and inequality analysis.

Nelson G. Cainghog is Assistant Professor of Political Science at the University of the Philippines Diliman, Philippines. He was the Director of the Public Service Office that led to the development of a university-wide service reporting system. He completed his Master's degree in International Relations from the Australian National University.

Mauricio Canêdo-Pinheiro is a professor at Rio de Janeiro State University (UERJ) and in Getulio Vargas Foundation (FGV)—Brazilian School of Economics (EPGE). He worked at the Brazilian Ministry of Economy between 2001 and 2002 and was a researcher at the Brazilian

Institute of Economics (IBRE) of the FGV between 2004 and 2017. He holds a PhD in Economics from the FGV/EPGE. Canêdo-Pinheiro has written academic papers on topics related to industrial organization, regulation, economic development, industrial policy, and innovation.

Quang Hung Doan is a lecturer at Foreign Trade University, Vietnam, and a researcher at Development and Policies Research Center (DEPOCEN), Vietnam. He completed his Master's in Development Economics from the International Institute of Social Studies (ISS) at Erasmus University Rotterdam, Netherlands, and National Economics University, Vietnam, in 2015. He is now a PhD candidate at LUISS University, Italy. His research topics are social capital, innovation, and development economics. He has a strong background on data analysis and econometric models.

Kristine Mae C. Gotera is a research staff of the *Kaizen* and Innovation Makerspace in the Department of Industrial Engineering and Operations Research, University of the Philippines Diliman, Philippines. She is also an instructor in the Environmental Science Department at Ateneo de Manila University.

Toru Homma is a senior adviser on private sector development (Investment, Trade and Industry), Japan International Cooperation Agency (JICA), since 2010. He served as JICA Investment Promotion Advisor in the Myanmar government from 2014 to 2017, OECD Investment Policy Analyst at its headquarters in Paris from 2006 to 2009, JICA Project Formulation Advisor in JICA Indonesia Office from 2003 to 2006, JICA SME Development Expert in Indonesian government from 1999 to 2002, and other relevant assignments on private sector development, in particular industrial development, investment promotion, *Kaizen*, and others. He holds MSc in Industrial Strategy and Trade Policy and BEng in Administration Engineering.

Akio Hosono is a senior research adviser at the Japan International Cooperation Agency Research Institute (JICA-RI). He was a professor at the Institute of Policy and Planning Sciences, Tsukuba University; at the Research Institute of Economics and Business Administration, Kobe University; and at the National Graduate Institute for Policy Studies (GRIPS). He was a former director of JICA-RI.

Keiji Ishigame is the Director of Partnership Program Division, Yokohama Center, Japan International Cooperation Agency (JICA), Japan. He served as a senior representative of JICA in South Africa and an adviser of Private Sector Development Group and managed *Kaizen* projects in Africa and Latin America. He holds MA in International Development and Business.

Kimiaki Jin is a senior assistant chief, JICA Research Institute. He served as a chief representative of JICA in Ethiopia during 2013–2017 and in the UK during 2009–2013. He published a book titled *Applying the Kaizen in Africa* in 2018 as a co-editor. He served for two more periods with JICA in Ethiopia, during 1990–1993 and 2003–2006.

Keiji Katai is a director for Private Sector Development Group, Japan International Cooperation Agency (JICA). He is managing JICA's operation and strategy on private sector development in Latin America and the Caribbean, Africa, Middle East, and Europe. He received MIA from Columbia University and ME from Kyoto University.

Filipe Lage de Sousa is a senior economist at the BNDES and lecturer of Microeconomics at the Fluminense Federal University with 20 years of working experience. He holds a PhD from the London School of Economics, and his areas of expertise include productivity, innovation, and economic development.

Thi Tuong Anh Nguyen is an associate professor at Foreign Trade University, Vietnam, and a researcher at Development and Policies Research Center (DEPOCEN), Vietnam. She completed her Master's degree in Economics from the University of Birmingham, United Kingdom, in 2004 and her PhD in Economics at Foreign Trade University in 2012. Her research interests are firm's behavior, international economics, and foreign direct investment.

John Page is a senior fellow in the Global Economy and Development Program at the Brookings Institution, Washington, DC, and a non-resident senior fellow of the United Nations University World Institute for Development Economics Research (UNU-WIDER). He is a research associate at the Centre for the Study of African Economies, Oxford University, and the Oxford Centre for the Study of Resource Rich Economies.

Bernardo Pereira Cabral is a professor at the Faculty of Economics of the Federal University of Bahia. He holds a PhD in Economics from the Economics Institute of the Federal University of Rio de Janeiro. His works focus on innovation-related topics, and he specializes in qualitative research methods.

Nestor O. Raneses is Professor of Systems Thinking and Systems Dynamics at the Department of Industrial and Operations Research University of the Philippines Diliman. His academic and research interests are in total quality and productivity improvement, lean six sigma, operational excellence, and *Kaizen* methods. He is a practicing academic with extensive work experiences in process improvement and lean implementation in both industry and the public sectors.

Eriko Sakamaki was a deputy chief of Research Program Division of JICA Research Institute until March 2019. She has working experience in West African countries such as Benin, Burkina Faso, and Senegal. She holds a master's degree in Education and International Development from Institute of Education, University of London.

Go Shimada is an associate professor at Meiji University and a visiting scholar at Columbia University and Japan International Cooperation Agency (JICA) Research Institute. Prior to these, he was an associate professor at the University of Shizuoka, and worked for JICA for more than two decades as a senior research fellow, JICA Research Institute; a special assistant to the president, Office of the President; and a first secretary, Permanent Mission of Japan to the United Nations, New York. He holds a PhD from Waseda University.

Glaucia Estefânia de Sousa Ferreira is a research assistant from the Brazilian Economic Research Institute. She holds a bachelor's degree in Statistics from the National School of Statistical Sciences and a master's degree in Electrical Engineering from Catholic University in Rio (PUC-RJ). She has more than 10 years of working experience with large datasets for econometric models.

Momoko Suzuki is a senior deputy director of Private Sector Development Group, Industrial Development, and Public Policy Department of Japan International Cooperation Agency (JICA). She is leading the Africa *Kaizen* initiative which was launched together with the New Partnership for Africa's Development (NEPAD) in 2017. She holds a master's degree from Sussex University, Institute for Development Studies (IDS).

Mili-Ann M. Tamayao is an assistant professor in the Department of Industrial Engineering and Operations Research and Energy Engineering Program Faculty Fellow of the University of the Philippines Diliman. She is a visiting researcher at Chalmers University of Technology and holds a PhD in Engineering and Public Policy from Carnegie Mellon University.

Hoang Nam Vu is Associate Professor of Economics at Foreign Trade University, Vietnam. He completed his PhD from the National Graduate Institute for Policy Studies in Japan in 2008. His research interests include human capital, industrial cluster development, small- and medium-sized enterprise promotion, and economic development.

List of Figures

gained from someone outside their companies, such as their customers (such as the companies that order the surveyed companies to make products/components), their suppliers (such as the companies that supply material/parts for the surveyed company's production), and others listed in the (b) above. *Note 2*: The sample size was 262 except for the following: 922 for (3) and (4) and 786 for (5) and (6), because the 262 respondents were asked to list their multiple major customers/suppliers at maximum five (5). *Note 3*: In the items from (7) to (16), Type 1 refers to a company within the same province with the surveyed company; Type 2 means a company in a different province but within the same island with the surveyed company; Type 3 means a company on a different island as the surveyed company but within Indonesia; Type 4 means a company outside Indonesia; SOE means State-owned enterprise; and NGO/CSO means nongovernmental organization/civil society organization. *Note 4*: 5S is a working environment improvement methodology including *Seiri* (Sort/orderliness), *Seiton* (Set in order/tidiness), *Seisou* (Shine/cleaning up), *Seiketsu* (Standardize/cleanliness), and *Shitsuke* (Sustain/discipline) (Shimada et al. 2013). *Note 5*: This JICA-LPEM Survey inquires about *Kaizen* and 5S separately in some parts (such as the data used for Fig. 6.2(a)) and aggregately on *Kaizen* and 5S, and furthermore includes other types of management activities such as QC, ISO, and others in other part (such as the data used for Fig. 6.2(b)). This is because this survey was not necessarily designed for this chapter but for other purposes. However, the survey is still useful for discussions on *Kaizen* dissemination in Indonesia in this chapter. (Source: Processed by Author, data derived from JICA-LPEM Survey) 125

Fig. 6.3 Relationship between *Kaizen* engagement and labor productivity (*n* = 262). Note: IDR means Indonesian rupiah (Indonesian currency). (Source: Processed by Author, data derived from JICA-LPEM Survey) 126

Fig. 6.4 Stakeholders' roles and relations in *Kaizen* dissemination (possible standard model). (Source: Author) 132

Fig. 6.5 *Kaizen* dissemination path model: Paths of *Kaizen* dissemination in a country: (a) dissemination stage outline and (b) dissemination stages and stakeholders' major roles (Source: Author) 134

List of Tables

CHAPTER 1

Overview

Akio Hosono, John Page, and Go Shimada

1 Introduction

Productivity and quality are critical to success in international markets and, in particular, to entering global value chains (GVCs). Yet, despite a growing body of research on managerial capital, we still do not fully understand how to improve productivity and quality in the private and public sectors in developing countries. *Kaizen* is a widely adopted practice developed in Japan to improve productivity and quality, but empirical studies analyzing its effectiveness in developing countries—especially in Africa and South East Asia—are limited. This book presents a collection of essays on efforts to introduce *Kaizen* to developing countries and use it to enhance productivity and quality in both small and large firms. Our

A. Hosono (✉)
JICA Research Institute, Tokyo, Japan
e-mail: Hosono.Akio@jica.go.jp

J. Page
The Brookings Institution, Washington, DC, USA

G. Shimada
School of Information and Communication, Meiji University, Tokyo, Japan
e-mail: go_shimada@meiji.ac.jp

A. Hosono et al. (eds.), *Workers, Managers, Productivity*,
https://doi.org/10.1007/978-981-15-0364-1_1

objective is to give readers some new insights into how *Kaizen* can play a role in making developing countries more globally competitive.

The book is structured in the following way. Following this introductory chapter, Chaps. 2, 3 and 4 take up how *Kaizen* addresses three important issues in contemporary development policy—industrial policy and firm capabilities, creating a learning society and dealing with income inequality. The rest of this book consists of three parts: (1) introducing and implementing *Kaizen*; (2) the effectiveness of *Kaizen* in large companies; and (3) effectiveness of *Kaizen* for micro, small and medium enterprises. Part 1 presents three case studies of how *Kaizen* has been introduced and disseminated in developing countries. Part 2 addresses the impact of *Kaizen* on the performance of larger companies, including its role in efforts to upgrade firms' position in global value chains. The final part of the book consists of three chapters that assess the effectiveness of *Kaizen* in micro, small, and medium enterprises (MSMEs). Our introduction follows the same structure as the book.

2 Defining *Kaizen*

There is a consensus among experts, practitioners, and academics regarding a number of intrinsic attributes that define *Kaizen*. These central concepts shape our understanding of how *Kaizen* is conceived and how it is used.

2.1 Five Key Attributes of Kaizen

First, Kaizen *is an approach to continuous improvement.* This notion comes from the Japanese word *Kaizen* itself and is used by most of the leading institutions engaged in disseminating and implementing *Kaizen* activities such as the Asian Productivity Organization (APO) and the Japan International Cooperation Agency (JICA). Continuous improvement is a core concept of *Kaizen.*

Second, Kaizen *is about increasing quality and productivity.* When *Kaizen* was developed, Japanese companies introduced statistical quality control (SQC) in parallel with efforts to improve productivity. Because any reduction in defective products enhances yield rates (known in Japan as *budomari*), more effective quality control (QC) not only improves quality; it also increases productivity. Thus, the principal aims of *Kaizen* are improving quality and productivity at the firm level. Central to this objective are the elimination of *Muda* (waste), *Muri* (overloading), and *Mura* (inconsistency). These three elements—or "3Mus"—have become central concepts of *Kaizen*.

A defining characteristic of *Kaizen* is that it does not seek to improve productivity through investments in machinery. Rather it does so through reductions in costs—based on 3Mus—making it a low-cost approach to raising productivity, especially for smaller firms.[1] In addition, the elimination of 3Mus improves the safety of workers and reduces environmental burdens. Thus, *Kaizen* may be more comprehensively understood as the improvement of quality, productivity, safety, and sustainability.

Third, in Japan, *Kaizen* developed inclusive and participatory approaches to improving quality and productivity by aligning and adapting statistical quality control and productivity movement methods that were introduced from the United States to a higher level of worker participation. As Shimada argues in Chap. 4, the participatory approach developed in part to reduce confrontations between labor and management. The inclusive and participatory approach constitutes another core element of *Kaizen*.

Fourth, many *Kaizen* tools and methods have developed over the more than half a century of its dissemination and development in Japan. For example, 5S, quality control circles (QCC), and just-in-time (JIT) inventory are well-known *Kaizen* tools and methods, often used synonymously with *Kaizen*. The so-called *Kaizen* mindset, which places an emphasis on teamwork, communication, and learning attitudes—or the *Kaizen* philosophy—is essential for the effective application of the tools and methods.[2]

Fifth, as *Kaizen* has spread through firms, it has come to be referred to as total quality control (TQC) and total quality management (TQM). The Toyota Production System (commonly called TPS) is one of the most systematic and advanced Japanese TQC or TQM systems. TQM and TPS are not *Kaizen per se* but are management systems based on *Kaizen* (or that use *Kaizen*). Some systems that developed outside of Japan, like lean production, are based on TQM and TPS. The fact that *Kaizen* is the basis of such management systems is an important spillover. It has contributed to the design of new approaches in countries outside of Japan.

2.2 *The Definition of* Kaizen *Used in This Volume*

The first three of the five key attributes of *Kaizen* discussed above are its most important characteristics. With these in mind, we can give a basic, brief definition of *Kaizen*. Kaizen *is an inclusive and participatory approach to the continuous improvement of quality and productivity.*

Our brief definition, however, fails to reflect two of *Kaizen*'s other attributes. If we add them to the definition, we reach a somewhat longer but more complete one. Kaizen *is an inclusive and participatory approach to continuous improvement of quality and productivity, resting on its distinctive philosophy and tools/methods. It forms the basis of multiple management systems, including TQM and TPS, developed in Japan and adapted for use in other countries.*

3 *Kaizen* and Three Issues in Development

In this section, we draw on the three opening chapters and on the country-level research to explore how *Kaizen* addresses three major issues in economic development. The first is the role of *Kaizen* in industrial policy and the development of firm capabilities. The second issue is how *Kaizen* contributes to learning by individuals and institutions and to the capacity to learn in society more broadly. The third is how *Kaizen* can contribute to equitable growth. These issues are covered in detail in the essays in Chap. 2 by Page, Chap. 3 by Hosono, and Chap. 4 by Shimada. This section draws on key results from the country-level research to explore *Kaizen*'s contribution in each area.

3.1 Industrial Policy, Capabilities, and the Learning Firm

Chapter 2 by John Page analyzes the relationship between industrial policy, *Kaizen*, and firm capabilities—a key determinant of international competitiveness. He argues that industrial policy is finally reaching the development policy mainstream and that one of its major objectives in low-income countries should be to build knowledge in the firm. Traditionally, economists have viewed the firm as a black box, responding to changes in its external environment, as prices and incentives change. Recent work at the intersection between management studies and economics is beginning to pry open the black box and gives us greater insight into how workers and managers impact such critical outcomes as productivity and quality (Sutton 2012).

Productivity is one dimension of capability. The other is quality. Because *Kaizen* is "an inclusive and participatory approach to the continuous improvement of quality and productivity," it is intrinsically related to building firm capabilities. Page concludes that "*Kaizen* is a promising and uniquely Japanese approach to capability building," but he cautions that firms often fail to respond to opportunities to raise productivity and quality due to lack of perception or motivation. Competitive pressure must complement training initiatives, whether based on *Kaizen* or not. Moreover, *Kaizen* is not the only approach to training. Further evaluations of the impact of capability building efforts—ranging from collective action by private firms to structured training programs—will be essential to understanding the costs and benefits of industrial policies targeted at improving firms' performance.

Kaizen supports the learning of capabilities in firms by helping workers and managers to identify and resolve production and quality problems. In their studies of firms attempting to enter and move up the automotive value chains in Mexico and South Africa, Keiji Katai (Chap. 8) and Keiji Ishigame (Chap. 9) provide a number of examples of how *Kaizen* promoted capability building in medium- to large-scale firms. In Mexico, Katai found that in addition to making changes in the production lines targeted under the project, automotive firms expanded *Kaizen* activities to other production lines, leading to internal spillovers, evidence that they applied the knowledge gained to other areas of the enterprise. Katai also found evidence of knowledge spillovers between supplying and purchasing firms. The most successful Mexican suppliers were entering into longer-term partnerships with Japanese buyers that involved the transfer of knowledge to the supplying firm. Ishigame's surveys of firms in South Africa found that *Kaizen* contributed to learning not only in companies that participated fully in the project but also in companies that dropped out and failed to finish. He suggests that by giving workers greater voice, *Kaizen* encouraged learning. Managers noted that as firms implemented *Kaizen*, many operational staff began to identify problems in production and propose improvements in plant-level processes to solve them.

In Chap. 11, Vu Hoang Nam evaluates a *Kaizen* training program for MSMEs in garment production in Vietnam. One key finding of the evaluation was that in addition to the direct impact of training on targeted enterprises, there were important spill-over effects on learning by non-treated firms. The improved management practices that were adopted by participants were also acquired through an informal channel of networking among the proprietors of similar firms. Ackah, Atta-Ankomah, and Kubi evaluate the effect of *Kaizen* training offered to small manufacturing enterprises in Ghana in Chap. 12. Their results show that firms receiving *Kaizen* training had a statistically significantly higher probability of engaging in daily cleaning at the close of work, placing tools in the right place, having a *Kaizen* committee, and having a floor plan than firms that did not introduce *Kaizen*. Workers' suggestions to management for process improvements, employees' knowledge of the firm's sales targets or policies, and knowledge of the mission of the firm were significantly higher in treated firms. The Philippine experience outlined in Chap. 13 shows a number of similarities with the firm-level learning that took place in Ghana and Vietnam.

The case studies suggest that by including all members of the firm in the process of learning and problem-solving, *Kaizen* promotes the exchange of information between workers, managers, and engineers and helps to develop "learning organizations." However, they also point to a number of lessons with respect to sustainability. Katai and Ishigame conclude that in larger firms, leadership from top management is essential to keep workers and managers moving in the same direction. Among MSMEs, smaller size may promote closer engagement, but in Ghana and Vietnam, managers reported problems with the attitude to work and discipline of workers—the majority of whom had little prior organized work experience.

3.2 Kaizen *and the Learning Society*

Noman and Stiglitz (2017) argue that "perhaps the most important 'endowment' of a country [is] institutions and learning capacities that [are] embedded in local institutions." In Chap. 3, Akio Hosono examines the learning dimension of *Kaizen*, emphasizing that it differs from other approaches to achieving better quality and productivity because of its distinctive focus on inclusive and participatory learning. *Kaizen*, total quality management (TQM), and related approaches contribute to growth—and in particular to high-quality growth—by enhancing learning capacity, an essential endowment for industrial transformation.

Many *Kaizen* tools and methods have developed over more than half a century to address the three productivity dimensions of cost, quality, and speed. "The core concept of *Kaizen* is to eliminate *muri* (overloading), *muda* (waste), and *mura* (inconsistency) from the worksite through efficient utilization of labor, materials, and equipment" (APO 2015, 10). These approaches require participation and learning by all. Hosono argues that *Kaizen* differs from other approaches to achieving better quality and productivity—especially those based on monetary incentives or sanctions—due to its distinctive focus on inclusive and participatory learning.[3]

The case study evidence shows that *Kaizen* changes the mindset of managers and workers, fosters personnel who can think and act for themselves, and promotes teamwork by encouraging team-based problem-solving (JICA 2016). Ishigame's interviews with workers and managers of automotive suppliers in South Africa in Chap. 9 show that 88 percent of the respondents believed that *Kaizen* had a positive impact on learning. Respondents indicated that major changes took place with introduction of *Kaizen*. As operators participated in training, management and engineers encouraged them to express their opinions. Production workers learned to think for themselves and take the lead in improving factory operations. Managers and engineers, on the other hand, learned the importance of involving workers in quality and productivity improvements.

In Chap. 5, Jin also takes up the relationship between *Kaizen* and learning. He finds that the changes of mindset observed in workers in Ethiopia consisted of enhanced teamwork, communication, and learning attitudes. Jin argues that these changes are the result of collective activities of *Kaizen*, such as 5S, quality control circle (QCC), and *muda* elimination. He argues further that *Kaizen* addresses not only the development of the technical capacity of workers and management but also the development of "core capacity." Core capacity includes the ability to commit and engage, to identify needs and key issues, to plan, budget, execute, and monitor actions, and, most importantly, to acquire knowledge and skills.

Core capacity is closely related to employability. In Chap. 7, Suzuki and Sakamaki look at *Kaizen*'s role in employability training in Ethiopia and South Africa. They note that there is no unified definition of what specific skills are core employability skills, but that skills and abilities that consistently appear in employer surveys fall into four categories: learning to learn, communication, teamwork, and problem-solving. These skills are what many company managers expect from workers when implementing *Kaizen* activities.

In Chap. 10, De Sousa, Canêdo-Pinheiro, Cabral and de Sousa Ferreira suggest that in Brazil, *Kaizen* has played an important role in innovation. They find that both product and process innovation increases following the implementation of *Kaizen*. In their view, these innovations—with a lag of some years—eventually impact productivity. This is an important, but somewhat controversial finding. The relationship between *Kaizen* and innovation deserves special attention. We need to understand how *Kaizen* differs from the widely accepted notion of "innovation."

Masaaki Imai's view is well known and clearly highlights the main characteristics of *Kaizen*. He argues that effect of *Kaizen* is long-term and long-lasting but undramatic. "Innovation," on the other hand, is short-term and dramatic. *Kaizen* is based on group efforts and a systems approach; "innovation" is based on individual ideas and efforts. *Kaizen* requires little financial investment but great effort to maintain momentum, while "innovation" requires large financial investments (Imai 1986).

However, there are many definitions of innovation. Innovation can be incremental (JICA 2018, 9 of Part 1), and more recently some experts have associated *Kaizen* with incremental innovation (JICA 2018, 10 of Part 1). The *Kaizen* mindset and many *Kaizen* tools can be considered innovation inputs, enabling firms to take innovative actions, experiment, adopt new technology, and hence achieve innovation outputs.[4] The MIT Commission on Industrial Productivity notes that the cumulative effect of successive incremental improvements and modifications to established products and processes can be very large and may outpace efforts to achieve technological breakthroughs (Dertouzos et al. 1989).

3.3 Kaizen *and Equitable Growth*

Chapter 4 by Go Shimada analyzes the implications of *Kaizen* for inequality, one of the most important global issues we face today. This chapter draws on Japanese experience to argue "*Kaizen* is essential knowledge, a missing piece to achieve equitable growth." Japan introduced *Kaizen* at a time when labor relations were very conflictive. In order to secure worker participation in a process designed to improve productivity and quality, firms adopting *Kaizen* committed themselves to share the profits derived from such improvements equitably between labor and management. Several key features of the emphasis on equity, such as life-time employment and the growth of company-specific labor unions—most of Japan's labor unions are not organized by industry—increased employee loyalty to firms and strengthened firm-level competitiveness. The equity orientation of *Kaizen* was not a technological innovation. It was a social innovation that contributed to achieving economic growth and equality. Shimada argues that both developing and developed countries can adapt the social innovation embodied in *Kaizen* to address inequality.

As Shimada points out in Chap. 4, in most cases, productivity growth means that firms need fewer people to produce the same output. This is not the usual experience under *Kaizen*. Because *Kaizen* requires the long-term commitment of both managers and workers to implement behavior change, it has the potential to improve labor-management relations. In other words, *Kaizen* seeks to maximize long-term social return rather than short-term private return.

Our country studies paint a mixed picture of *Kaizen*'s impact on employment. In Ghana (Chap. 12), Ackah, Atta-Ankomah, and Kubi found that *Kaizen* firms increased average employment relative to non-*Kaizen* firms. Beyond the impact on the number of jobs, they also found managers reporting that workers' attitude toward work was more positive in treated firms. On the other hand, De Souza, Canêdo-Pinheiro, Cabral and de Sousa Ferreira (Chap. 10) found that in Brazil the employment impacts of *Kaizen* were mixed. Firms implementing *Kaizen* tended to hire more total employees, because production expanded compared to those not implementing *Kaizen*. More detailed analysis revealed, however, that *Kaizen* increased the total number of workers and the number of R&D-related workers, while reducing the number of workers on the production line. They also found that the expansion of employment was biased toward high-skilled workers.

Other case studies—Ethiopia, Mexico, the Philippines, South Africa, and Vietnam—do not address employment but give us some insights into how *Kaizen* impacts worker-management relations. It is a mixed picture. In Vietnam (Chap. 11), Nam et al. found high turnover rates and low worker commitment to be key problems. Set against that, managers reported not knowing how to motivate workers. In contrast the case study of the Philippines (Chap. 13) by Raneses et al. found that *Kaizen* empowered workers to assume a greater role in the operations of the firm. Managers promoted teamwork and introduced plant-level changes based on workers suggestions. In Ethiopia (Chap. 5), Jin observed that once workers were convinced of the usefulness of *Kaizen*, they used it even in their homes. His interviews of managers, however, found that workers participation in *Kaizen* represented a challenge to its sustainability. Ishigame in Chap. 9 finds similar difficulty with workers' attitudes and attributes the difficulty in changing mindsets among workers to the structure of labor-management relations in South Africa. Although it was a condition for firms to receive *Kaizen* support under the JICA project not to reduce the number of employees, workers refused to accept many proposed changes due to the perception that they would increase their burden of work.

How should we interpret this mixed picture? Japan's experience suggests that improving manager-worker relations takes a long time. Our case studies of Vietnam, Ethiopia, and South Africa show the same pattern. In each case, changing the mindset of managers and workers took time, but the change resulted in an improvement in labor-management relations. This improvement is essential for the sustainability of *Kaizen*, and if the change is successfully sustained, *Kaizen* will bring social innovation to the firm.

4 Introducing and Implementing *Kaizen*

Today, *Kaizen* is practiced in many countries. Part 1 of this volume focuses on case studies of how *Kaizen* was introduced and disseminated. Both the public and private sectors have introduced and disseminated *Kaizen*, sometimes working together. The country studies find that success in implementation depends on the development of specialized agencies, the level of industrialization of the economy, the presence of foreign firms, and the level of participation in global value chains (GVC).

In countries such as the United States and Japan, initiatives by the private sector were decisive. In Japan, manufacturing companies were strongly motivated first by the urgent necessity to become competitive in the world market after World War II (in the 1950s and 1960s) and later by the necessity to address challenges caused by the oil crises of the 1970s and 1980s.[5] In the US automobile industry, intense competition from Japan was one of the most important triggers to introduce new management systems, including total quality management and lean production, in the 1980s.

Among Southeast Asian countries, Singapore was the first to introduce *Kaizen*. The government led the process of nationwide introduction and dissemination of *Kaizen* in the 1980s. Later as public-private institutions directly charged with this process developed, the public sector's engagement diminished. In the other "ASEAN 5" countries (Indonesia, Malaysia, the Philippines, and Thailand), the introduction of *Kaizen* has been led by both public and private initiative, depending on the country context. Most other ASEAN countries have followed a similar trajectory. In North Africa, Tunisia and Egypt were pioneers in introducing *Kaizen* in the mid-2000s, while in sub-Saharan Africa, Ethiopia was the first country that promoted *Kaizen*, beginning in the late 2000s.

4.1 A Government-Led Process in Ethiopia

In Chap. 5, Jin analyzes how Ethiopia, a country at a very early stage of industrial development, introduced *Kaizen* from scratch. Ethiopia has few foreign firms and little participation of local firms in GVC. The Ethiopian case is relevant to understanding the process of introducing *Kaizen* when the concept is almost totally unknown. The process began with a pilot project, followed by sequential programs of scaling-up. In 2009, the Ministry of Industry created a *Kaizen* Unit with ten staff to test its effectiveness in the manufacturing sector. Once *Kaizen*'s effectiveness was established, the Unit expanded in 2011, to become the Ethiopia Kaizen Institute (EKI) with sixty technical staff. EKI provided training to 68,954 trainees and established 9658 *Kaizen* Promotion Teams (KPT)—a customized version of the quality control circle (QCC)—in 473 institutes in Ethiopia from 2012/2013 to 2016/2017.

As the EKI scaled up the introduction of *Kaizen* programs to a wider range of targets, it also communicated with sector-specific industrial development institutes (for example in the textile, leather, and metal industries) in order to mainstream *Kaizen* training. In 2014, the government established the National Kaizen Council chaired by the Prime Minister and started creating regional *Kaizen* institutes to strengthen dissemination across the country. In addition, the government incorporated mainstreaming *Kaizen* into its five-year national development plan, the Growth and Transformation Plan II. Recognizing that *Kaizen* could also play a role in the public sector, the government changed the supervising ministry of EKI from the Ministry of Industry to the Ministry of Public Service and Human Resource Development in 2015, and then to the Civil Service Commission in the Prime Minister's Office in 2018.

In more than half of the workplaces, the *Kaizen* methods taught were 5S, KPT, and Muda elimination, which are basic *Kaizen* tools that can target several bottlenecks in the production process. These activities do not require high-level technical skills, but the participation of people in all levels of management, supervisors, and workers is essential. Jin conducted interviews intended to analyze how practitioners in companies understood the impact of introducing *Kaizen*. More than half of respondents ranked: (i) changing the mindset of workers, (ii) improving the flow of materials, (iii) greater efficiency of machinery, (iv) better communication flow, (v) increased technical skills of workers, and (vi) leadership by management in descending order as the major impacts of introducing *Kaizen*.

Eighty-seven percent of the respondents chose "the mindset of workers" as the feature that most changed in the workplace. The most common three changes in mindset reported were better teamwork, communication, and learning attitudes, followed by self-confidence and activism.

Punctuality and obedience ranked relatively low. Jin concludes that the egalitarian approach of *Kaizen* was a major factor in its successful dissemination.[6] He concludes "people do not want to be treated like a disposable workforce by employers through a reform process. This point has critical importance in societies with limited dynamism in labor markets, such as Ethiopia, because it is difficult to find new job opportunities once people are dismissed. Workers don't appreciate any reform activities that affect their job security negatively, which is the other side of the coin of productivity improvement."

4.2 Diverse Dissemination Profiles in Southeast Asia

In Chap. 6, Homma describes how government, public-private organizations, and the private sector contributed to the introduction and dissemination of *Kaizen* in three ASEAN countries, Malaysia, Indonesia, and Myanmar. In Malaysia, *Kaizen* and associated approaches were introduced in 1983 through the National Productivity Center (NPC)—later renamed the Malaysia Productivity Corporation (MPC)—under the "Look East Policy," a government initiative to learn from the experiences of Japan.

Having introduced *Kaizen*, MPC/NPC adapted *Kaizen* tools to suit the Malaysian context; 5S was adapted and renamed "Quality Environment" and QCC "Innovation and Competitiveness Circle" (ICC). In Malaysia, *Kaizen* has generally been integrated into a comprehensive productivity improvement system, together with total quality management (TQM) and related approaches. Homma summarizes MPC's strengths as follows: (i) a strong mandate to lead productivity improvement in Malaysia, (ii) appropriate and timely adaptation of MPC's function to adapt to changing requirements, (iii) customization of foreign practices such as *Kaizen* to the Malaysian culture, and (iv) a wide variety of approaches designed to deliver services efficiently.

In Indonesia, the private sector played a significant role in introducing *Kaizen*, and it has been actively disseminating *Kaizen* mainly through two channels: (i) Japanese manufacturers have introduced local suppliers to *Kaizen* via their supply chain management systems and (ii) private sector organizations have implemented productivity- or quality-related programs and training. The Directorate General of Training and Productivity

Development under the Ministry of Manpower and Transmigration acts as Indonesia's National Productivity Organization, and has contributed to *Kaizen* dissemination as well.

The private sector has occupied a more central role in disseminating *Kaizen* in Indonesia than in Malaysia. The private sector supply chain (customer companies and supplier relationships) effectively disseminates *Kaizen* by providing information, services, and support. Homma finds that a company's engagement in *Kaizen* either on its own initiative or with information, services, and support from its customers through its supply chain increases labor productivity.

Myanmar, like Ethiopia, is a latecomer. *Kaizen* dissemination is still at an early stage, but there have been some attempts to introduce *Kaizen* in the private sector. The Myanmar Productivity Center (MPC) was created in 2016 as a small unit in the Union of Myanmar Federation of Chambers of Commerce and Industry (UMFCCI) with the support of the Japan Productivity Center (JPC).

Homma highlights two factors that help to determine whether government or the private sector takes the lead in the introduction and dissemination of *Kaizen*—the prominence of GVCs in the economy and the level of institutional quality. In Indonesia, a deep, long-lasting, and firmly established supply chain structure was already in place. Indonesia has the largest population in ASEAN and its market potential is huge. For that reason, almost all major Japanese automobile assemblers established factories under joint venture agreements and their presence provided impetus for *Kaizen* development along the supply chain. In Malaysia, a more centralized economy with stronger public institutions, the government under the Look East Policy took the initiative to develop a professional governmental body (Malaysia Productivity Corporation) which has become a leading productivity organization. Although Japanese car manufacturers contributed to *Kaizen* dissemination in Malaysia, they had less impact, in part due to the national car program.

4.3 *Developing the Employability of Youth Through* Kaizen

A new approach to introducing *Kaizen* is through training to enhance students' core capacities in vocational education and training (TVET) institutes or universities. In Chap. 7, Suzuki and Sakamaki assess the role of *Kaizen* in enhancing employability. Core employability skills fall into four broad categories: learning to learn; communication; teamwork; and problem-solving. These attributes are what many company managers expect from workers, and many Japanese companies use *Kaizen* to develop their workers' capabilities.

Ethiopia has expanded the number of TVET institutions from 17 in 1996/1997 to 505 in 2011/2012, and *Kaizen* has been incorporated into the Ethiopian TVET curriculum since 2012. The results of a survey conducted by Suzuki and Sakamaki confirmed that the *Kaizen* course fosters learning to learn (self-confidence, self-awareness, and willingness to learn) and teamwork. The survey also shows that *Kaizen* has had an impact on the mindset of students. Awareness toward learning to learn, especially self-awareness and willingness to learn, was higher for those students who had received *Kaizen* training in TVET.

South Africa has implemented Employability Improvement Training in universities to improve students' employability. JICA's Employability Improvement Project (EIP) uses *Kaizen* to address employability issues. Suzuki and Sakamaki surveyed a sample of recent graduates of the program and found positive results of the training on seven core employability skills. These included changes in critical/logical thinking, teamwork and communication, self-management, and identifying and solving problems. Students had more difficulty in demonstrating leadership and creativity, perhaps as a result of the structure of the training.

4.4 Summing Up

The experiences of Ethiopia and Myanmar suggest that an active government role is important when *Kaizen* is not widely known, FDI is limited, and local companies do not participate in GVCs. In other circumstances, a private sector-led process can be effective. In both cases, public and private collaboration can facilitate the introduction of *Kaizen*. An active government role may be particularly important when there is strong distrust between workers and employers regarding the distribution of benefits from any increase in productivity.[7] The main site of learning and implementing *Kaizen* has been at workplaces (factory floors), and the main pathway of introducing *Kaizen* has been training managers and employees and providing advice at site. More recently, the introduction and dissemination of *Kaizen* through formal education, such as TVET and universities, has proved effective in enhancing the employability of younger workers.

5 The Effectiveness of *Kaizen* in Large Companies

Initially pioneered in large manufacturing enterprises—where Toyota remains one of its foremost exponents—*Kaizen* spread through the manufacturing sector in Japan during the period of high economic growth after World War II. Many of *Kaizen*'s early adopters were larger firms. Today, as reflected in the studies in this book, *Kaizen* has found its way into training for micro, small, and medium enterprises (MSMEs) and even into the public administration in developing countries. In this section, we examine three country case studies of the impact of *Kaizen* on larger scale firms in middle-income countries.

5.1 Moving Up the Value Chain: Mexico and South Africa

The 1990s and 2000s witnessed an explosion of complex value chains spanning the globe. Labor costs drove many decisions about the location of production, but today only 18 percent of goods trade involves labor-cost arbitrage—defined as exports from countries with GDP per capita one-fifth or less than that of the importing country.[8] Lead companies in global value chains, however, still require suppliers to deliver high-quality inputs at competitive prices. Productivity and quality depend in turn on the knowledge possessed by the individuals who make up the firm. *Kaizen*'s goal is to help enterprises make higher quality products, reduce costs, and achieve timely delivery through continuous collaboration between managers and workers. Two of our country studies assess the effectiveness of *Kaizen* in helping domestic suppliers integrate into the automotive value chains of Mexico and South Africa.

Since the ratification of the North America Free Trade Area (NAFTA), Mexico has attracted major global carmakers, which use it as a base for export to the US market. In Chap. 8, Keiji Katai examines the effectiveness of a *Kaizen* training program designed to increase the integration of domestic Mexican suppliers into the automotive value chain. From 2012 until 2015, JICA supported supply chain development between Japanese automakers and domestic Mexican parts supplying firms. *Kaizen* experts with experience in the automotive industry conducted diagnoses of each firm, set targets for improvement in collaboration with buyer firms, and supported implementation for one year. Typical *Kaizen* interventions were 5S, reducing defective product ratios, improving job throughput, and reducing down time and inventory.

Twenty-seven domestic firms engaged in or wishing to enter the value chain received training. Katai examines the impact of the training on changes in the position of seventeen firms in the GVC and attempts to relate these changes to changes in their production capabilities. He defines the stages of participation in the value chain as ranging from the non-supplier stage (stage 1) to the level of global partner supplier (stage 6). Movement from stages 1 to 6 represents progress by domestic firms in upgrading their position in the value chain. Lead automotive firms rank suppliers based on quality, cost, and delivery (QCD). Higher level suppliers (stages 5 and 6) develop new products in collaboration with the buyer or collaborate with the Original Equipment Manufacturer (OEM) to supply and develop products for global markets.

Using information from both supplier firms and purchasing firms, Katai attempts to associate changes in lead firm's evaluations of suppliers before and after *Kaizen* training with measures of productivity and quality. He measures quality by changes in defective product ratios and productivity by reductions in mold-changing times. In the automotive industry, quality is assessed by the number of defective parts per million (PPM). After the intervention, the defect rate in firms receiving training declined substantially. Of fifteen firms, twelve firms reduced their defect rates to less than 100 PPM, lower than the average for domestic automotive parts makers in Mexico. He also finds that low defect rates are positively associated with lead firm's evaluations of quality.

Reduced mold-changing time enables firms to produce products with minimum machine stoppage and improve productivity. Each auto uses about 30,000 parts, and manufacturers carefully control assembly of each model to minimize inventory. Parts makers are therefore required to adjust production volumes of individual parts weekly. This creates frequent changes of molds, and each change can consume hours. The JICA project attempted to reduce mold-changing times. Katai does not find a clear and direct relationship between improved productivity, as measured by reduced mold-changing times, and buyer firms' evaluations of cost.

He does, however, find some evidence of a positive relationship between lead firms' evaluations of QCD levels after *Kaizen* training and the supplier firms' position in the GVC. Of seventeen supplier firms, eight (47 percent) improved their position in the supply chain, five (29 percent) maintained their position, and four (24 percent) experienced a deterioration. Further, there is a positive relationship between supplier firm positions in the GVC and business volumes. However, Katai's data are restricted to the treated group of firms and their corresponding lead firms. As he notes, without information on a control group or on the overall Mexican automotive parts industry, it is difficult infer a causal relationship.

In Chap. 9, Keiji Ishigame attempts to measure the impact of *Kaizen*—popularly known as the Toyota Production System (TPS) in South Africa—on the competitiveness of automotive suppliers. In doing so, he asks an important supplementary question: does the effectiveness of *Kaizen* differ among suppliers, and what factors contribute to these differences? In 2015, JICA launched an Automotive Industry Human Resource Development Project in South Africa. The purpose of the project was to enhance the capacity of human resources in the automotive industry and to improve the productivity and quality of domestic suppliers. The automotive industry is the largest manufacturing sector in South Africa. It is composed of six major vehicle assemblers, thirteen assemblers of heavy and medium commercial vehicles, and approximately 360 component manufacturers.

Under the project, two Japanese experts working with the South African Automotive Industry Development Center (AIDC) trained AIDC trainers and jointly with the AIDC trainers provided technical advice to local suppliers. Eight supplier firms were selected to receive *Kaizen* training. Because one of the goals of the project was to increase the capacity for *Kaizen* training in South Africa, Japanese experts visited the selected supplier firms five to ten days per year jointly with AIDC trainers. In addition, the AIDC trainers independently visited suppliers every two weeks on average. The training program itself consisted of a number of *Kaizen* tools associated with the Toyota Production System. The first stage taught suppliers to implement 5S.

An innovation of the project was that, contrary to normal practice, 5S was used in the initial stages of implementation, to create a foundation for other *Kaizen* activities. In the second stage, trainers and the supplier firms prepared a diagnostic to identify problems in the flow of information and materials. The third stage consisted of JICA experts, AIDC trainers, and the supplying firms jointly developing *Kaizen* activities to improve quality and productivity. The Japanese experts advised not only on 5S but also on the diagnosis of quality and productivity problems.

Ishigame presents three company case studies of impact. In the first case, a layout change significantly improved quality and productivity, with corresponding increases in sales and profits. The firm moved large machinery into correct positions and implemented one-piece flow, thereby shortening lead times. It achieved increases in quality by moving from batch production to one-piece flow, allowing operators to identify defects in the course of production. In the second case, a company producing textile-based automotive acoustic and trim components introduced gradual improvements to workflow and production processes, based on 5S. Over two years productivity and quality improved, costs were reduced by about US$1.6 million, and revenue increased by 25 percent with the same labor force. In the third case—a company making plastic injection molding parts—the introduction of a one-piece flow system produced improvements in quality and productivity and reduced production lead-time from 24 hours to 1 hour. With only a limited number of participating companies and no control group, however, there is insufficient evidence to determine whether the project made a meaningful change in the productivity and quality of supplying firms.

The results of the Mexico and South Africa studies are suggestive, but hardly definitive. Small sample size, lack of a control group, and the absence of benchmark data on the automotive sector make it impossible to answer the question of whether *Kaizen* increased the integration of domestic suppliers into complex global value chains. Some qualitative results provide grounds for optimism. One common thread among the successful cases was the level of commitment of senior management and engineering staff to *Kaizen*. Where managers were committed, implementation of such *Kaizen* tools as 5S and continuous flow led to substantial improvements in quality and productivity, and because *Kaizen* engages all members of the firm, it contributed to learning. The Mexico results further suggest that these are key elements enabling domestic firms to break into and move up the value chain.

5.2 *Shortening the "Left-Hand Tail" in Brazil*

Empirical microeconomic studies repeatedly find that there are large productivity differences among enterprises in quite narrowly defined industries. Even in rich countries, the magnitudes involved are striking. In the US manufacturing, on average a plant in the 90th percentile of the productivity distribution produces about twice as much output of the same product as a plant in the 10th percentile, using the same measured inputs (Syverson 2011).[9] While poorer countries have some firms that achieve world-class productivity levels, there is also a long "left-hand tail" of poorly performing firms.

In Chap. 10, De Sousa, Canêdo-Pinheiro, Cabral and de Sousa Ferreira evaluate whether *Kaizen* has improved firm-level performance in Brazil, using both quantitative and qualitative evidence. Put differently, they ask if *Kaizen* can shorten the "left-hand tail." They draw firm-level data from two sources—The Brazilian Innovation Survey (PINTEC) and the Annual Manufacturing Survey (PIA) and construct an unbalanced panel of firms. PIA surveys all manufacturing firms over thirty employees, on average around 30,000 firms annually. In PINTEC, the size threshold is much higher, 500 employees.

The researchers confront the considerable challenge of identifying *Kaizen* adoption. Neither data set includes questions on whether a firm has implemented *Kaizen*. However, the authors use the innovation survey to identify firms that have adopted management practices based on *Kaizen* principles. Examples of management practices using *Kaizen* tools are re-engineering, knowledge management, total quality control, training, and enterprise resource planning. The innovation survey also asks if the firm has introduced new methods to delegate responsibilities and decision-making to workers. Because in *Kaizen* participation by workers is central, the response to this question reflects a second *Kaizen* characteristic. A third strand of *Kaizen* is continuous improvement, which the authors argue should be reflected in continuous changes in management practice. Thus, they classify a firm answering all three questions affirmatively in repeated years as using a *Kaizen* approach. Using these criteria, the authors select a sample of 2541 firms of which some 63 percent are identified as having implemented *Kaizen*. As a counterfactual they choose firms that do not carry out innovations in management practices.

The authors use a number of econometric approaches to assess the impact of *Kaizen* on firm-level productivity, growth, and innovation. They find that *Kaizen* does not improve firm-level productivity, whether measured by labor productivity or total factor productivity (TFP). They do, however, find a robust positive relationship between *Kaizen* and the growth of the firm. Of greater interest is the finding of a positive impact on process innovation. To reduce potential selection bias, they perform a propensity score matching to restrict the group of untreated firms to only those similar to treated firms. Results using only matched firms in the control group indicate that the relationship between *Kaizen* and process innovation remains robustly positive. Comparing similar firms, *Kaizen* increases innovation in Brazilian manufacturing. Interpreting their results as a whole, the authors conclude that the channel in Brazil by which

Kaizen raises productivity may be through its impact on innovation. Because *Kaizen* is an incremental approach, they further conclude, it is possible that the time period between observations in the data is too short to observe this indirect effect.

5.3 Summing Up

The results of these studies of the impact of *Kaizen* on larger firms may disappoint its advocates. Small sample sizes and lack of counterfactual evidence limit what we can conclude from the Mexico and South Africa case studies. Clearly, *Kaizen* interventions were perceived by sponsoring managers and engineers as successful. There is also limited evidence of *Kaizen* contributing directly to improvements in quality and productivity. In both countries, the firms that persisted in the implementation of *Kaizen* appear to have moved up the value chain in the automotive sector.

Using a broader sample of firms, research in Brazil leads to similar ambiguity. It fails to find a significant relationship between the introduction of *Kaizen* and subsequent improvements in either labor productivity or total factor productivity (TFP). The authors speculate that this may be the result of observing the firm over too short a time period. More encouragingly, they find a strong relationship between *Kaizen* and process innovation. The firms that practice *Kaizen* in Brazil innovate more than similar firms.

Productivity is not the sole determinant of competitiveness, however. In fact, low wages can in some cases compensate for low productivity, but they cannot compensate for inferior quality. The Brazil surveys fail to tell us anything about quality. In the Mexico and South Africa cases, there is some evidence that quality was the capability most directly impacted by *Kaizen* methods.

6 Effectiveness of *Kaizen* for Micro, Small, and Medium Enterprises

The three essays in Part 3 measure the impact of *Kaizen* training on the performance of micro, small, and medium enterprises (MSMEs) in Vietnam, Ghana, and the Philippines. MSMEs are quite important to the economic growth of low-income countries (for example in Africa) since almost all firms in those countries are of this type. Of course, even in developed economies most firms are SMEs (small and medium enterprises). The number of large firms among all firms is just 0.3 percent in Japan, 0.3 percent in the United Kingdom, and 0.5 percent in Germany (Shimada 2017). This section summarizes the results of the country studies.

6.1 Rural MSMEs in Vietnam

In Chap. 11, Nam, Anh, and Hung analyze the impacts of a *Kaizen* management training program on the management practices and performance of small and medium sized enterprises in a rural village in Northern Vietnam. The research is interesting in two ways. First, as rural areas have more dense social capital, the training impact could spread through their social network. Second, the chapter examines whether *Kaizen* can have impact in rural settings. This latter point is important for countries attempting to achieve balanced economic growth while avoiding excessive urbanization.

Nam, Anh, and Hung choose to focus on the local trainers because the dissemination of *Kaizen* is often constrained by the availability of these resources. Even if a donor such as JICA sends foreign experts, the number of those experts is relatively limited, and the donor cannot continue sending those experts forever. As the authors correctly argue, the role of local trainers and how they can be trained are important unanswered questions. The JICA project sponsored Japanese experts to provide trainer training to five lecturers at Vietnam's Foreign Trade University. Of the five participants, two lecturers successfully completed the program.

The study site was a village, on the outskirts of Hanoi. The main products of that village are blankets, bed sheets, pillows, and bed mattresses, sold in the domestic market. The authors obtained a list of 816 enterprises from the local government office, and selected 195 bedding-related firms (59 registered, 136 unregistered). Applying a stratified sampling method, they randomly selected 32 formal enterprises out of the 59, and 68 out of the 136 unregistered firms. Because they could not collect complete data from three of the firms, the total number of final respondents was 97 enterprises. Firms were provided both classroom training and on-site training. Each local trainer was randomly assigned to the on-site training of treatment firms.

Since the sample size was small, the authors employed a pair-wise matching technique, following Bruhn and McKenzie (2009). The variables selected for matching were the gender of the owner, sales revenue, and the registration status of the enterprise. The treated enterprises increased the use of *Kaizen* practices significantly, and *ex-post* indicated greater willingness to pay for the management knowledge gained. The authors also found that the local trainers were successful in training micro, small, and medium sized enterprises. This suggests that it is feasible to scale up *Kaizen* training in the future through the use of local trainers.

An important result was that the *Kaizen* training had spill-over effects to non-treated enterprises. Discussion of *Kaizen* within the social network of the enterprise owners (family relatives, friends, and neighbors) in the village led to the adoption of good management practices by untreated firms. The findings are important because they show the possibility of scaling up and spreading *Kaizen* practices and tools to MSMEs in rural areas. Rural social networks may, in fact, encourage the dissemination of good management practices.

6.2 *Raising Manufacturing Productivity in Ghana*

Micro, small, and medium firms are the backbone of Ghana's manufacturing sector. In Chap. 12, Ackah, Atta-Ankomah, and Kubi evaluate a *Kaizen* project to raise productivity in MSMEs. The project has been implemented by Ghana's National Board for Small Scale Industries (NBSSI) in collaboration with JICA since 2012. It provides basic *Kaizen* training on principles and methods such as 5S, waste reduction and visualization, and basic accounting. The NBSSI's Business Advisory Centers (BACs) administer the training. To ensure the continuity and sustainability of the program, Japanese experts train local trainers who, in turn, assist firms independently.

Ackah, Atta-Ankomah, and Kubi focus their analysis on whether the project intervention had any impact on the performance of enterprises. They employ a Propensity Score Matching (PSM) method to examine the average treatment effect of the training (matching variables are educational background of the manager, subsector of manufacturing, age of the manager, and region and legal status of the enterprises). They also use random effects analysis to complement the PSM results. In total, they interviewed 184 enterprises (Treatment firms: 98, Control firms 86) from three administrative regions—Ashanti, Northern, and Brong Ahafo.

The empirical findings are twofold. First, *Kaizen* had a significant impact on the key performance indicators of these enterprises. Specifically, the authors found evidence of a statistically significant impact of the training on the number of workers, sales, profit, and output of the enterprise. Second, they observed significant differences in behavioral variables—such as workers' attitudes, daily cleaning practices, placing tools in the right places—and process indicators between the treated firms and firms that did not implement the training.

6.3 A Kaizen*-Like Intervention in the Philippines*

In Chap. 13, Raneses, Cainghog, Tamayao, and Gotera take up the case of a program implemented in the Philippines. Their case study is the government initiative known as the Manufacturing Productivity Extension Program (MPEX), which aims to increase the productivity of manufacturing firms by making their products more competitive in terms of price and quality. The MPEX program is a part of the Philippines Development Plan 2017–2022. Firms in the program cover a variety of sub-sectors such as agriculture and food processing, furniture, gifts and holiday decorations, information technology, materials science, metals and engineering, and microelectronics.

While MPEX is not *Kaizen*, the structural foundation of the program is based on *Kaizen* principles. The program aims to assist MSMEs in the manufacturing sector to get higher productivity through improvements in operations. Under the program, MPEX consultants examined major elements of firm operations such as manufacturing processes, materials management systems, and quality control systems. Based on their assessment, the consultants made recommendations in at least three priority areas. After two to three months, the consultants returned to each firm to see if the recommended improvements have been made.

Out of 300 MSMEs in the food manufacturing sector, 177 firms were selected and 64 firms were interviewed after the program. Using PSM, the authors analyzed the matched data using the difference-in-difference regression model. However, they did not find significant differences in the number of workers and sales per worker between treated and untreated firms. With a relatively small sample size there were not enough respondents in every category to give robust statistical results.

To supplement the quantitative work, the authors undertook two detailed case studies, one a bakery and the second a food products producer. In the bakery, the MPEX consultants provided a half-day training on 5S and hygiene methods to employees. One of the *Kaizen* practices introduced by the owner was promoting teamwork through team-based competitions. The firm also reduced unnecessary procedures in production, making the process faster. *Kaizen* brought a change in the mindset of the workers as well, making continuous improvements possible.

In the food products firm, the MPEX recommendations included changing layout, and contrary to *Kaizen* philosophy, purchasing new machines, which allowed the firm increase productivity and reach the hygiene standards required to access major supermarkets. These changes resulted in a tenfold increase in production and sales. Workers now process orders from clients independently from the owners and keep records. The authors conclude that successful implementation of *Kaizen* depends on the mindset of workers, the enthusiasm of the entrepreneur, and the managerial capital and time management skills of the owner.

6.4 Summing Up

As we have already seen, the evidence of the impact of *Kaizen* on large enterprises is mixed. It is the core principle for Toyota, one of the largest firms in the world, but the evidence in other chapters in this volume from Mexico, South Africa, and Brazil is inconclusive. The evidence is more persuasive with respect to micro, small, and medium enterprises. *Kaizen* works for MSMEs in developing countries. This is important not only for business performance but also for improvements in the living standards of workers. The cases of Vietnam and Ghana are of particular interest, because local trainers, initially trained by Japanese experts, conducted both programs successfully. They provide evidence that *Kaizen* can improve the performance of MSMEs and can be implemented by local human resources in a sustainable way.

7 Conclusions and Policy Implications

The country studies in this volume provide a fuller—but not a comprehensive—picture of *Kaizen*. This picture largely confirms the results of other research indicating *Kaizen* has the potential to make an important contribution to efforts to raise productivity and quality in poorer economies. We found evidence in both large and smaller firms that *Kaizen* resulted in productivity and quality improvements and in some cases, that it enabled firms to upgrade their position in global value chains. Our case studies gave multiple examples of *Kaizen*'s role in promoting learning.

Innovation is essential for an economy to grow, and recent literature suggests that *Kaizen* tools are innovation inputs, enabling firms to take innovative actions, experiment, adopt new technology, and achieve innovation. We also found that through its emphasis on continuous participation by all members of the firm—workers and managers alike—*Kaizen* has the potential to improve relations between workers and management. Our case studies and *Kaizen*'s history in Japan suggest, however, that it takes time to establish a win-win relationship between managers and workers through dialogue.

Managerial capital has recently become an object of interest of development scholars and practitioners. How does *Kaizen* fit into public policies directed at building managerial capital in developing economies? Traditionally, economists have viewed the firm as a black box—responding to changes in its external environment. The case studies in this volume take us some distance in opening up that black box. They show that productivity and quality depend on the knowledge and working practices possessed by the individuals who make up the firm, both managers and workers. Put in Anglo-American economic terminology, these are "firm capabilities." Improved capabilities increase the potential productivity of all firms. *Kaizen* is a promising and uniquely Japanese approach to capability building. Thus, it has a role to play in industrial policies directed at enhancing the performance of firms.

Beyond industrial policy, the research in this volume underlines the need for an active state. There is increasing recognition that market imperfections are widespread in low-income countries, and that many markets are incomplete and suffer from coordination failures. These are often reflected in barriers to learning. For that reason, government support is important when *Kaizen* is not widely known, where FDI is limited, and where local companies' participation in global value chains is not commonplace. An active government role may be particularly important when lack of trust between workers and employers regarding the distribution of benefits from any increase in productivity is strong.

Finally, workers are critical to the success of *Kaizen*. *Kaizen* makes them active participants in solving problems and pushes managers at all levels to listen to their suggestions for productivity and quality improvements. In that sense it contributes not only to better business performance; it is a social innovation that may help to reduce inequality through improvements of workers' living standards.

Notes

1. For a large firm, this distinction is less relevant than for a small firm.
2. See Chap. 5 by Jin, and Chap. 9 by Ishigame.
3. See for example World Bank (2015).
4. Regarding innovation inputs and outputs, see Cirera and Maloney (2017).
5. See Chap. 3 by Hosono.
6. See Shimada, Chap. 4.
7. As it was in Japan in the inception phase of the productivity enhancing campaign (see Chap. 4 by Shimada).
8. McKinsey Global Institute (2019).
9. The productivity differentials are even more striking in developing countries. See Hsieh and Klenow (2009).

References

Asian Productivity Organization (APO). 2015. *Handbook on Productivity*. Tokyo: APO.

Bruhn, Miriam, and David McKenzie. 2009. In Pursuit of Balance: Randomization in Practice in Development Field Experiment. *American Economic Journal: Applied Economics* 1 (4): 200–232.

Cirera, Xavier, and William F. Maloney. 2017. *The Innovation Paradox: Developing-Country Capabilities and the Unrealized Promise of Technological Catch-Up*. Washington, DC: World Bank.

Dertouzos, Michael, Richard Lester, and Robert Solow. 1989. *Made in America: Regaining the Productive Edge*. Cambridge, MA: MIT Press.

Hsieh, C.T., and P. Klenow. 2009. Misallocation and Manufacturing TFP in China and India. *Quarterly Journal of Economics* 124 (4): 1403–1448.

Imai, Masaaki. 1986. *Kaizen: The Key to Japan's Competitive Success*. New York: McGraw-Hill.

JICA. 2016. *Kaizen: Japan's Approach Towards Improved Quality and Productivity*. Tokyo: JICA.

———. 2018. *Kaizen Handbook*. Tokyo: JICA.

McKinsey Global Institute. 2019. *Globalization in Transition: The Future of Trade and Value Chains*. New York: McKinsey and Company.

Noman, Akbar, and Joseph E. Stiglitz. 2017. Learning, Industrial, and Technology Policies: An Overview. In *Efficiency, Finance, and Varieties of Industrial Policy: Guiding Resources, Learning, and Technology for Sustained Growth*, ed. Akbar Noman and Joseph E. Stiglitz, 1–20. New York: Columbia University Press.

Shimada, Go. 2017. "Inside the Black Box of Japan's Institution for Industrial Policy – An Institutional Analysis of Development Bank, Private Sector and

Labour". In Akbar Noman and Joseph Stiglitz, eds. *Efficiency, Finance and Varieties of Industrial Policy.* New York: Columbia University Press.

Sutton, John. 2012. *Competing in Capabilities.* Oxford: Clarendon Press.

Syverson, Chad. 2011. What Determines Productivity? *Journal of Economic Literature* 49 (2): 326–365.

World Bank. 2015. *World Development Report 2015: Mind, Society, and Behavior.* Washington, DC: World Bank.

CHAPTER 2

Industrial Policy, Firm Capabilities, and *Kaizen*

John Page

1 Introduction

Industrial policy is finally moving away from the longstanding but sterile debate between "picking winners" and "levelling the playing field." There is increasing recognition that the market imperfections on which theoretical arguments for industrial policies rest are widespread in low-income countries and that many markets are incomplete and suffer from coordination failures.[1] As Rodrik (2008) points out, today a strong case can be made for "normalizing" industrial policy in developing economies. Information failures, learning, and geography combine to underpin the case for policies to support industrial development and structural change.

As the consensus that well-designed industrial policies can contribute to improving economic outcomes has strengthened, new insights have also challenged the top-down model of economic policy-making. Traditionally, economists have viewed the firm as a black box, responding to changes in its external environment, as prices and other incentives change. Recent work at the juncture of management studies and economics is beginning to pry open the black box and give greater insight into how workers and managers impact such critical outcomes as productivity

J. Page (✉)
The Brookings Institution, Washington, DC, USA

A. Hosono et al. (eds.), *Workers, Managers, Productivity*,
https://doi.org/10.1007/978-981-15-0364-1_2

and quality. Using these insights, new initiatives in industrial policy have begun to focus on the role of management in industrial development.

This chapter considers how firm-level management training fits into industrial policy in low-income countries. Section 2 briefly summarizes the growing consensus that the debate over industrial policy has moved on from decades past toward recognizing that well-designed public policies can improve economic performance in low-income countries. Section 3 introduces the concept of "firm capabilities"—the knowledge and working practices used by firms in the course of production and in developing new products—and discusses how they are acquired and transmitted. Section 4 makes the case that *Kaizen* is a uniquely Japanese approach to capability building, based on the continuous interaction of workers and managers within the firm. Section 5 explores some arguments for capability building as a part of industrial policy, and Sect. 6 concludes.

2 The Case for Industrial Policy

The dominant view among Anglo-American economists during the past thirty years has been that industrial policy is a bad idea. Two lines of reasoning underpin this argument. The first is that the allocation of resources in an economy is too complex and too information intensive to be handled effectively by the public sector.[2] Where market failures are present, the mainstream view has been that policymakers should identify the distortions and then design taxes or subsidies to reduce the gaps between market prices and social costs or benefits. The second line of argument is that, even if governments could solve the information problem, rent-seeking behavior by private agents would undermine their well-meaning efforts. Governments should keep the private sector at arm's length, because it will lobby for actions that serve its own interests (Krueger 1974).

There has been pushback against both of these arguments. Rodrik (2009), among others, has argued for closer links between policymakers and the private sector. Industrial policy must, in practice, identify and respond to the need for public actions across a very broad front of industries and interventions. Because firms hold much of the information relevant to policy-making, he argues some form of structured engagement between the public and private sectors is essential. Stiglitz (2017) responds to the rent-seeking argument by noting that the incentives embodied in the price system often favor the interest groups that shape the institutions and regulations governing market transactions. Indeed, as he puts it: "not having an industrial policy—leaving it to the market, structured as it is by special interests—is itself a special interest agenda" (Stiglitz 2017, 24).

There has also been considerable rethinking of the theory underpinning the arguments for industrial policy in the last decade, and there is a growing consensus that market imperfections in low-income countries are widespread and impede structural change.[3] Many markets are incomplete and suffer from coordination failures. Collateral constraints combined with asymmetric information in credit markets limit investment, and there are potentially large spillovers associated with learning, not just among firms, but also among institutions. Imperfections in risk and capital markets mean that individuals, who should move from old to new sectors in low-income countries, cannot get access to the resources needed to make the shift; yet they have to bear the inevitable risks associated with the transition (Stiglitz 2017). In addition, the new economic geography has drawn attention to a major collective action problem—agglomeration (UNIDO 2009). Taken together, these arguments make a strong theoretical case for industrial policy.

3 Firm Capabilities

Empirical microeconomic studies repeatedly find that there are large productivity differences among enterprises in quite narrowly defined industries. Even in rich countries, the magnitudes involved are striking. In US manufacturing, on average a plant in the 90th percentile of the productivity distribution produces about twice as much output of the same product as a plant in the 10th percentile, using the same measured inputs.[4] In developing countries the differences in plant level productivity within well-defined industries are even larger. While poorer countries have some firms that achieve world-class productivity levels, they also have a much higher percentage of low productivity firms. There is a long "left-hand tail" of poorly performing firms in the productivity distributions of developing countries. In China and India, for example, average 90-10 total factor productivity (TFP) ratios are more than 5 to 1.[5] Large differences in productivity at the firm level reflect, in turn, profound differences in firm capabilities.

3.1 *What Are Firm Capabilities?*

Firm capabilities are the knowledge and working practices used by firms in the course of production and in developing new products. The term is relatively new, but management experts and businesspeople have known for a long time that firms differ markedly in the knowledge and working practices of both managers and workers. Productivity is one dimension of capability. The other is quality. To use Sutton's (2012) terminology, quality is a "demand shifter," shorthand for anything that moves the demand schedule outward at every price, including such things as after-sales service, or brand image. Used in this way, "quality" embraces a much wider range of characteristics than the technical excellence of the product itself.[6] Productivity, on the other hand, is a "cost shifter." Modifications in such things as the organization of production, reductions in wastage or better supervision of the workforce can lower unit production costs at every quantity level.

Globally, firms are competing in capabilities. The differences in the contributions of quality and productivity to international competitiveness are subtle, but important. To some extent, low productivity can be offset by low wages.[7] Shortfalls in quality on the other hand may make it impossible for firms to break into global markets. At some price-quality combinations, firms can succeed in entering a market, local or global; at others higher capability competitors will exclude them.

Productivity and quality depend in turn on the knowledge possessed by the individuals who make up the firm. In this respect, capabilities are fundamentally different from technology. Technology can be codified and purchased. Capabilities are mainly embodied in people and in working practices, so they are more difficult to codify and measure. They reflect the capacity of managers and workers to work effectively together within some framework of rules, routines, and tacit understandings that have been put in place or have evolved over time.[8]

3.2 Building Capabilities

Capability building takes place in two phases. The first phase involves the introduction of a higher level of capability into an economy, either because of the entry of new, more capable firms or as a result of learning by existing firms. Foreign direct investment (FDI) is one—and some would argue for countries at low levels industrial development the most important—way of introducing higher capability firms. The foreign investor brings the technology, managerial knowledge, and working practices it has developed elsewhere. A majority of researchers find that firms with foreign equity participation in developing countries typically have higher output per worker or higher levels of TFP than similar domestically owned firms.[9]

"Learning by exporting" is an example of how domestic firms build capabilities through learning. Two of the key mechanisms by which firms learn higher capabilities are:

- *Demanding Buyers.* In some industries—apparel and agro-based industry, for example—exchanges of information between suppliers and buyers with a reputation for high quality are well developed and add to the capabilities of supplying firms.
- *Repeated Relationships.* In many industries, there is a close and continuing contractual relationship between the buyer and the supplier, which often involves a two-way movement of technical and engineering personnel between their respective plants.[10]

Demanding buyers and repeated relationships are characteristic of global markets, spanning the range of industries from traditional manufacturing to tradable services and agro-industry. These inter-firm relationships are the means by which suppliers and purchasers exchange knowledge.

The empirical literature strongly suggests that exporting strengthens capabilities through improvements in working practices. One recent study of Vietnam, for example, found that the sources of productivity improvements differed markedly between foreign and domestic exporters (Newman et al. 2016). Foreign firms experienced an early surge of productivity growth upon entering export markets, attributable to increases in scale. Domestic firms on the other hand had longer-term productivity improvements, mainly from introducing process innovations. This pattern is consistent with the initial presence of higher capabilities in foreign firms and the greater opportunities for learning by domestic enterprises.

Once a higher level of capability has been introduced—say through a new foreign direct investment or through a newly successful export activity—its potential benefit to the host economy at large will depend on the extent to which the technical knowledge and working practices held by the firm are transmitted to other firms. Most of what we know about how capabilities are transferred comes from case studies or from econometric analyses of "spillovers" from foreign direct investment (FDI). Both types of evidence point in the same direction: buyer-seller relationships along the value chain are effective ways to transfer both technological knowledge and better working practices.

There is econometric evidence of positive productivity spillovers from foreign firms to domestic suppliers and from foreign suppliers to domestic firms. Surveys show that spillovers are often due to spin-offs by former employees of FDI firms and labor movements from foreign to domestic companies (Newman and others 2016). One-third of multinationals interviewed in Vietnam, for example, reported that employees left their company to set up local enterprises directly connected to the multinational, as customers or suppliers. Linked domestic firms reported that they, in turn, hired employees initially trained by the multinational companies.

3.3 *The Role of Management*

Intuitively, managers must largely be responsible for productivity and quality differences, either because of innate differences in their abilities or differences in management practices. Managers must be able to identify and develop new products, to organize production activity, to motivate workers, and to adapt to changing circumstances. Bloom and Van Reenen (2007) use interviews to score managerial practices from best to worst practice across a wide range of day-to-day operational management activities. They have by now undertaken surveys of more than 6000 firms in seventeen countries, including China, India, and Brazil.[11] They find that better management practices (measured by higher scores) are strongly correlated with several measures of productivity and firm performance, including survival. A particularly interesting finding is that China, India, and Brazil all have much lower average management scores than the higher-income countries in their sample.[12] This is due mainly to a very large left-hand tail of low scoring firms in the management practice distribution; a pattern that parallels closely the productivity distributions in these countries relative to higher-income countries.

One problem with the survey approach is that it is difficult to establish the causal direction of the relationship running from better management to higher productivity. To address this, Bloom, Van Reenen, and their associates (2013) randomly assigned a sample of large, multi-plant Indian textile firms to treatment and control groups. The treated firms received a month-long analysis of thirty-eight aspects of operational management followed by four months of intensive follow-up in the plant from a large international consulting firm. The control plants received only one month of diagnostic consulting. Within the first year, productivity increased on average by 17 percent in treated firms. In addition to increasing productivity, the intensive training led to significant improvements in quality and inventory control. The better-managed firms also grew faster and voluntarily spread the management improvements from their treated plants to other plants they owned.

4 Capabilities and *Kaizen*

Capabilities reflect two closely related elements. The first is technical knowledge or engineering expertise, the element that has been most studied by economists.[13] The second is improvement in "working practices." This has traditionally been the domain of management studies. Working practices are always critical to achieving high quality, but the relative importance of technological knowledge shifts as countries move into more sophisticated products. Engineering good practice is far more important in manufacturing pharmaceuticals or machine tools than in making t-shirts.

Kaizen—"continuous improvement"—while based originally on US principles of industrial engineering and quality management has a uniquely Japanese twist. It is incremental, continuous and involves all levels of workers within the firm, from top management to the factory floor (Imai 2012). *Kaizen* was mainly developed and spread through the manufacturing sector in Japan during the period of high economic growth after World War II, a period when Japanese productivity levels converged rapidly toward those in the United States. Initially developed in large manufacturing enterprises—Toyota remains one of its foremost exponents—through the efforts of the Japan International Cooperation Agency (JICA) *Kaizen* has found its way into training for large-scale firms, micro, small and medium enterprises (MSMEs) and even into the public administration in developing countries.

Imai (1997) defines *Kaizen* as a commonsense, low-cost approach to management. Its goal is to help enterprises attain higher quality products and services, lower costs, and achieve timely delivery by the continuous collaborative effort of managers and their workers (Imai 2012). It is a process-oriented approach based on the belief that "processes must be improved for results to improve" (Imai 1997, 4). Key *Kaizen* elements include:

- *Good housekeeping*: Tools and raw materials used at the workplace are put in good order.

- *Eliminating waste (muda)*: Wasteful processes and methods are reduced or eliminated throughout the firm.
- *Adopting Standards*: Small improvements in many processes are undertaken and gradually accumulate into "best practices."

Through these elements, firms are able to improve quality and productivity, cut costs, reduce lead times, and create a better work environment.

Kaizen often involves the so-called 5S system of seiri (sorting), seiton (setting in order), seiso (systematic cleaning), seiketsu (standardizing), and shitsuke (sustaining adherence to rules) to improve the efficiency and overall quality of the work environment. Experience indicates that it is not difficult for many enterprises to adopt the first three of the 5S. They will, however, revert to their original state unless efforts are made to institutionalize the behavioral changes learned. The fourth and fifth Ss are therefore focused on longer-term efforts to turn good housekeeping into habit.

Given their shared heritage in management studies, it is not surprising that *Kaizen* and capabilities are closely related. Imai (2012) stresses the concepts of quality, cost, and delivery (QCD). In his terminology, quality refers not only to the quality of finished products or services but also to the quality of the processes that go into those products or services. In the terminology of capabilities these are "working practices." Cost reflects the overall cost of designing, producing, selling, and servicing the product, and delivery means delivering the requested volume on time. All of these elements can be mapped into the quality and productivity dimensions of firm capabilities. Quality and delivery are "demand shifters," while cost is a "cost shifter." In fact, *Kaizen* is a Japanese approach to building firm capabilities.

Ethiopia provides a case study of *Kaizen*'s relevance to improving capabilities in larger firms. JICA provided *Kaizen* training to selected large manufacturing firms in Ethiopia from 2009 to 2011. The first part of the training was in the classroom and a second phase was onsite. Thirty large firms were selected by the Ethiopian government based on their ability to use the training effectively. Gebrehiwot (2013) compares the performance of these "treated" firms and 40 large comparator firms that did not receive training. Because the treated firms were selected due to their high growth potential, issues of bias cannot be ignored. Nevertheless, statistically significant increases in labor productivity, declines in production costs, and improvements in the quality of products were observed in treated firms.

JICA has invested significantly in *Kaizen* as a way to increase the capabilities of micro, small and medium enterprises, and a growing number of evaluations have been undertaken. Shimada and Sonobe (2017), for example, attempt to assess the impacts of *Kaizen* training on workers, using survey data collected from firms in eight countries in Central America and the Caribbean. *Kaizen* appears to have induced a number of important behavioral changes at the firm level. Managers in *Kaizen*-trained firms developed a greater understanding of the importance of sharing basic information with workers. Shimada and Sonobe also found that *Kaizen* improved employees' attitudes toward work, increased the number of productivity-enhancing suggestions from workers, and resulted in the introduction of more measures to prevent accidents. Better attitudes toward work were associated with more rapid wage growth. A majority of managers found *Kaizen* useful within three months, although some took considerably longer, and employees were initially more skeptical than management. Shimada and Sonobe conclude that the gradual pace of adoption reflects the fact that *Kaizen* is predicated on building a cooperative relationship among workers and between managers and workers, a process that takes time and validation.

In a recent contribution, Mhede et al. (2018) assess the durability of *Kaizen* training and provide some insight into its relationship with more standard MSME training curricula. Using a randomized controlled trial (RCT) of garment manufacturing firms in Dar es Salaam, Tanzania, the authors found that three years after the training intervention treated firms had adopted a statistically significantly larger number of good management practices than their untreated counterparts, and their business performance had improved. They found a slight difference in scale of adoption of *Kaizen* and non-*Kaizen* management practices, favoring the non-*Kaizen* practices, but they also found that the educational attainment of the owner was significantly correlated with which management practices were adopted. Non-*Kaizen* practices, such as planning and recordkeeping, were more likely to be adopted by better educated owners.

5 Some Implications for Industrial Policy

For the industrial transformation of low-income countries to succeed, industrial policy must address three objectives. First, while some firms in some countries are already sufficiently productive to be competitive internationally, a larger share of existing firms must become more productive.

Second, because the manufacturing sector in most low-income countries is quite small, governments need to create the conditions to attract new firms able to compete in regional and global markets. Finally, governments may wish to encourage firms to move into promising new areas of potential comparative advantage, what Rodrik (2009) has labeled "industrial policy in the large."

Of the three industrial policy objectives, management training falls most squarely into the first category, reducing differences in firm-level productivity. A change in management practices, for example, can increase the potential productivity of all firms. This is equivalent to shifting the entire productivity distribution uniformly to the right. With the growth of global value chains, it has become increasingly important for domestic firms to engage effectively with the multinational lead firms that drive them.[14] This means that management training also has the potential to contribute to the second industrial policy objective by attracting new value chains.

Placing management training in the broader context of industrial policy raises important questions regarding when and for which types of firms management interventions are appropriate. The mixed results of evaluations of management training interventions for MSMEs—whether *Kaizen* or other types of training—offer evidence that context is important. Not all firms may be able or willing to benefit from training. This in turn raises the question of why firms fail to adopt good management practices in the first place.

5.1 Why Do Firms Fail to Adopt Good Management Practices?

One of the central questions concerning management training is why managerial good practices are not taken up more rapidly. There are at least three answers to this question. First, incumbent managers may have problems of perception—they do not know they are ineffective. Second, managers may have problems of inspiration—they know they are ineffective, and do not know what to do about it. Third, managers may have problems of motivation—they know they are not effective; they know what to do; but they fail to act because of lack of competition or lack of incentives (Gibbons and Henderson 2012).

Interestingly, Bloom and his collaborators observed all three of these problems in their India case. Their evidence suggests that information constraints were the greatest impediment to better managerial practice.

Firms apparently did not believe that such basic practices as measuring quality defects or machine downtime and keeping track of inventory would improve profits. Owners claimed their quality was as good as that of other local firms, and because they were profitable, they felt they did not need to introduce a quality control process. Managers were often simply unaware of such common practices as daily factory meetings, standardized operating procedures, or inventory control norms. Competition in India was heavily restricted by high tariffs in the case of imports and in the case of new entry by lack of finance. Barriers to entry and the family structure of enterprises acted as a disincentive for firms to adopt better management practices.

5.2 Options to Improve Management Practices

Kaizen is not the only way in which governments can address the need to increase the productivity of existing firms. Organized efforts to acquire good management practices could take the form of collective actions by firms or a public-private partnership to seek out information on managerial good practices and make it available as a public good. In India, for example, the Confederation of Indian Industries, which is almost wholly funded by the private sector, provides services of this kind at fees that are within the reach of India's smaller manufacturing companies. The Fundacion Chile is another example of a public-private partnership for building capabilities. Its success in helping to establish Chile's world-class wine and salmon export industries has been widely documented. Initiatives of this type might be undertaken at lower cost, and with a greater share of the cost borne by the private beneficiaries, than training interventions. They also face a market test.

Management training of large-scale firms of the type offered in India by Bloom and his associates or in Ethiopia by JICA is another means of improving capabilities. The expertise of the international consultants certainly proved highly valuable to the firms trained. In addition to increasing productivity, the intensive training led to significant improvements in quality and inventory control. In the case of larger firms, however, care must be taken to put in place complementary policy changes to promote competition. In the absence of competitive pressure, firms may fail to recognize that improvements in management practices will be beneficial and any changes may be short lived.

Business training is one of the most common forms of support to micro, small and medium enterprises (MSMEs) around the world. There are a large number of programs offered by governments, aid donors, microfinance organizations, and NGOs. This is a very different target group for training than medium- to large-scale plants, and the results of most training programs have been disappointing (McKenzie and Woodruff 2012). The evaluations of *Kaizen* as a method of MSME management training are encouraging, but have not yet reached the point of being conclusive. Otsuka and Sonobe (2014) suggest that the reason for the disappointing results of evaluations of *Kaizen*—and of MSME training more generally—may be due to an excessively optimistic view of the types of firms that can benefit from training.

The literature on MSME often misses the fact that there is an enormous amount of heterogeneity among firms.[15] Recent research using nationally representative samples of MSME firms shows that there is a small but significant subset of MSME firms that have productivity levels higher than economy-wide manufacturing productivity (McMillan et al. 2017). These are the high capability firms in the MSME sector. Otsuka and Sonobe argue that these firms are the relevant target for management training. They further suggest that management training can be used to screen for promising entrepreneurs, because, if effective, it should produce visible changes in the way in which owners manage their firm.

6 Conclusions

Firm capabilities determine productivity and quality—the two key components of international competitiveness. Intuitively, they are closely related to management. Historically, economists have neglected management, preferring instead to focus on factors external to the firm. Recent work at the intersection of economics and management studies, however, very strongly points to the conclusion that management matters. Differences in management practice between firms and countries are responsible for much of the difference in measured productivity.

Building firm capabilities is a complex process. The capability transfer consists of both "hardware"—technological knowledge and engineering—and "software"—the working practices that are crucial to master technology and achieve higher quality. The relative importance of these two factors changes as countries move toward more complex, technologically sophisticated products. In low-income countries, for the time being, working practices are likely to be more important.

Capability building—including management training—is well within the mainstream of contemporary industrial policy. It is a means by which two of the major objectives of industrial policy in low-income countries—increasing the number of more-productive firms and attracting new firms along global value chains—can be pursued. *Kaizen* is a promising and uniquely Japanese approach to capability building, but it is not the only one. Further evaluations of the impact of capability building interventions, ranging from collective action by private firms to structured training programs, will be essential to understanding the costs and benefits of management interventions.

Notes

1. See Hausmann et al. (2007), Rodrik (2009) and Harrison and Rodriguez-Claire (2010).
2. See Pack and Saggi (2006) for a statement of the mainstream view.
3. See, for example, Stiglitz (2017), Cimoli et al. (2010), and Szirmai et al. (2013).
4. Syverson (2011).
5. Hsieh and Klenow (2009).
6. See Sutton (2012).
7. The low-wage advantage is limited because virtually all manufactured exports require some minimum amount of intermediate inputs sold at fixed international prices. Where—as in the case of trade in tasks—these comprise a significant share of total production costs the low-wage advantage erodes.
8. See Sutton (2005, 2012).
9. For a survey of the relevant literature, see Harrison and Rodriguez-Claire (2010).
10. Sutton (2005).
11. See Bloom and Van Reenen (2010) and Bloom and others (2010).
12. Bloom and Van Reenen (2010).
13. UNIDO in particular has had a long tradition of studying the role of technological knowledge in development. See UNIDO (2003) for an example.
14. The integration of domestic firms into global value chains is a particularly significant challenge in Africa, where there are few linkages between foreign and domestic firms. See Newman et al. (2016).
15. For the conventional view see La Porta and Shleifer (2014).

References

Bloom, N., B. Eifert, A. Mahajan, D. McKenzie, and J. Roberts. 2013. Does Management Matter? Evidence from India. *Quarterly Journal of Economics* 128 (1): 1–51.

Bloom, N., A. Mahajan, D. McKenzie, and J. Roberts. 2010. Why Do Firms in Developing Countries Have Low Productivity? *American Economic Review: Papers & Proceedings 2010* 100 (2): 619–623.

Bloom, N., and J. Van Reenen. 2007. Measuring and Explaining Management Practices across Firms and Countries. *Quarterly Journal of Economics* 122 (4): 1341–1408.

———. 2010. Why Do Management Practices Differ Across Firms and Countries? *Journal of Economic Perspectives* 24 (1): 203–224.

Cimoli, M., G. Dosi, and J. Stiglitz. 2010. *Industrial Policy and Development: Political Economy of Capabilities, Accumulation*. Oxford and New York: Oxford University Press.

Gebrehiwot, B.A. 2013. An Economic Inquiry into the International Transfer of Managerial Skills: Theory and Evidence from the Ethiopian Manufacturing Sector. PhD diss., National Graduate Institute for Policy Studies, Tokyo.

Gibbons, R., and R. Henderson. 2012. Relational Contracts and Organizational Capabilities. *Organizational Science* 23 (5): 1350–1364.

Harrison, A., and A. Rodriguez-Claire. 2010. Foreign Investment and Industrial Policy for Developing Countries. In *Handbook of Development Economics*, ed. D. Rodrik and M. Rosenzweig, vol. 5. Amsterdam: North Holland.

Hausmann, Ricardo, Dani Rodrik, and Charles F. Sabel. 2007. *Reconfiguring Industrial Policy: A Framework with an Application to South Africa*. Cambridge, MA: Harvard Kennedy School.

Hsieh, C.T., and P. Klenow. 2009. Misallocation and Manufacturing TFP in China and India. *Quarterly Journal of Economics* 124 (4): 1403–1448.

Imai, M. 1997. *Gemba Kaizen: A Commonsense, Low-Cost Approach to Management*. New York: McGraw-Hill.

———. 2012. *Gemba Kaizen: A Commonsense Approach to Continuous Improvement Strategy*. 2nd ed. New York: McGraw-Hill.

Krueger, A.O. 1974. The Political Economy of the Rent-Seeking Society. *American Economic Review* 64: 291–303.

La Porta, R., and A. Shleifer. 2014. The Unofficial Economy in Africa. In *African Successes: Government and Institutions*, ed. S. Edwards, S. Johnson, and D.N. Weil. Chicago: University of Chicago Press.

McKenzie, D., and C. Woodruff. 2012. What Are We Learning from Business Training and Entrepreneurship Evaluations around the Developing World? *Policy Research Working Paper 6202*. Washington: World Bank.

McMillan, M., J. Page, and S. Wangwe. 2017. Realizing Tanzania's Manufacturing Potential. In *Tanzania: The Path to Prosperity*, ed. C. Adam, P. Collier, and B. Ndulu. Oxford: Oxford University Press.

Mhede, E.P., Yuki Higuchi, and T. Sonobe. 2018. Medium Run Impact of Management Training: Evidence from a Randomized Controlled Experiment in Tanzania. Paper Presented at the 23rd REPOA Annual Research Workshop, Dar es Salaam.

Newman, C., J. Page, J. Rand, A. Shemeles, M. Söderbom, and F. Tarp. 2016. *Made in Africa: Learning to Compete in Industry*. Washington, DC: Brookings Institution Press.

Otsuka, K., and T. Sonobe. 2014. *Cluster-Based Industrial Development: KAIZEN Management for MSE Growth in Developing Countries*. New York: Palgrave Macmillan.

Pack, H., and S. Saggi. 2006. Is There a Case for Industrial Policy? A Critical Survey. *The World Bank Research Observer* 21 (2): 267–297.

Rodrik, D. 2008. Normalizing Industrial Policy. Paper Prepared for the Commission on Growth and Development. Washington DC: World Bank.

———. 2009. Industrial Policy: Don't Ask Why, Ask How. *Middle East Development Journal* 1 (1): 1–29.

Shimada, G., and T. Sonobe. 2017. *Impacts of Kaizen Management on Workers: Evidence from the Central America and Caribbean Region*. Paris: OECD.

Stiglitz, J.E. 2017. Industrial Policy, Learning, and Development. In *The Practice of Industrial Policy: Government—Business Coordination in Africa and East Asia*, ed. J. Page and F. Tarp. Oxford: Oxford University Press.

Sutton, J. 2005. *Competing in Capabilities: An Informal Overview*. London: London School of Economics.

———. 2012. *Competing in Capabilities*. Oxford: Clarendon Press.

Syverson, C. 2011. What Determines Productivity? *Journal of Economic Literature* 49 (2): 326–365.

Szirmai, A., W. Naudé, and L. Alcorta. 2013. *Pathways to Industrialization in the Twenty-first Century*. Oxford: Oxford University Press.

UNIDO. 2003. *Industrial Development Report 2002/2003: Competing Through Innovation and Learning*. Vienna: UNIDO.

———. 2009. *Industrial Development Report, 2009*. Vienna: UNIDO.

CHAPTER 3

Kaizen Toward Learning, Transformation, and High-Quality Growth: Insights from Outstanding Experiences

Akio Hosono

Kaizen is a Japanese word that literally means "improvement" but is also commonly referred to as "continuous improvement." Now a well-known concept worldwide, it normally refers to the Japanese approach toward improving quality and productivity. What distinguishes *Kaizen* from other approaches is that these goals are attained through its process—one in which learning and inclusiveness are essential. The sustainable development goals (SDGs) call on member states to promote sustained, inclusive, and sustainable economic growth and decent work for all. *Kaizen* can contribute to achieving the kind of growth characterized by these attributes. In this chapter, I begin by providing an analytical perspective and discussion of key issues related to *Kaizen* (Sect. 1). Based on this discussion, I then review the goals, tools/methods, and process of *Kaizen* (Sect. 2). In Sect. 3, I discuss the relationship between *Kaizen* and the targets of the SDGs as well as learning, transformation, and quality of growth. In Sect. 4, I analyze outstanding experiences of some countries that have

A. Hosono (✉)
JICA Research Institute, Tokyo, Japan
e-mail: Hosono.Akio@jica.go.jp

A. Hosono et al. (eds.), *Workers, Managers, Productivity*,
https://doi.org/10.1007/978-981-15-0364-1_3

introduced *Kaizen* or similar approaches to gather insights on the relationship. Finally, I provide some concluding remarks.[1]

1 Analytical Perspective and Key Issues

In recent policy debates on growth and development, increasing attention is being paid to the "quality" of economic growth.[2] In Asia and the Pacific region, APEC leaders at Yokohama in 2010 agreed on the "APEC Growth Strategy."[3] This strategy stresses that "the quality of growth" needs to be improved so that it will be more balanced, inclusive, sustainable, innovative, and secure. In 2015, the Japanese government announced the *Charter of Development Cooperation*. It stated that one of the most important challenges of development is " 'quality growth' and poverty eradication through such growth" while also stressing inclusiveness, sustainability, and resilience (Government of Japan, Cabinet Office 2015, 5–6). In that same year, the United Nations passed a resolution adopting "Transforming Our World: The 2030 Agenda for Sustainable Development" as its post-2015 development agenda. This outcome document sets out "The Sustainable Development Goals (SDGs)" and targets as integrated and indivisible, global in nature, and universally applicable (UNGA 2015). Among the 17 Global Goals and 169 targets, Goal 8 calls on member states to promote sustained, inclusive, and sustainable economic growth, full and productive employment, and decent work for all, while Goal 9 calls on governments to "build resilient infrastructure, promote inclusive and sustainable industrialization and foster innovation." As such, the SDGs—in particular Goals 8 and 9—largely overlap with the above-mentioned attributes of "quality growth."

Together with quality of growth, another feature of the SDGs is the importance placed on transformation. The above-cited United Nations 2030 Agenda declares that "We are determined to take the bold and transformative steps which are urgently needed to shift the world on to a sustainable and resilient path" (UNGA 2015, 2). Transformation-led growth is distinct from, for example, commodity price hike-led growth. Transformation-led growth could be high-quality growth and could generate further transformation. This implies that a virtuous circle of transformation and high-quality growth could take place. The ADB report on transformation (2013, 5) argues that, when structural transformation creates a virtuous circle, it leads to high growth and higher income per capita, and these induce further changes in the structure of the economy.

Regarding ways that such transformation can be achieved, there seems to be a growing consensus in the academic literature that structural transformation is closely related to changes of endowments or assets, changes in comparative advantage, and, finally, increasing innovation and technological progress. As Noman and Stiglitz emphasize, "the essence of development is dynamic. What matters, for instance, is not comparative advantage as of today, but dynamic comparative advantage" (Noman and Stiglitz 2012, 7). Lin, likewise, discusses "changing comparative advantage," arguing that "the more effective route for their learning and development is to exploit the advantages of backwardness and upgrade and diversify into new industries according to the changing comparative advantages determined by the changes in their endowment structure" (Lin 2012, 73).

Accordingly, endowments are extremely important for transformation based on changing or dynamic comparative advantage. In this regard, recent studies identified critical endowments for transformation. Drawing from many previous studies, Stiglitz and Greenwald (2014) present a systematic and holistic analysis of what constitutes a learning society, concluding that "the most important 'endowment' from our perspective, is a society's learning capacities." They further state that a country's policies have to be shaped to take advantage of its comparative advantage in knowledge and learning abilities, including its ability to learn and to learn to learn, in relation to its competitors and to help develop those capacities and capabilities further (26). Noman and Stiglitz (2017) reaffirm the importance of learning capacity, together with institutions: "Perhaps the most important 'endowment' of a country was assets that were not mobile—institutions and learning capacities that were embedded in local institutions. It was these that countries needed to take into account as they struggled to shape their long-term (dynamic) comparative advantage" (13).

Stiglitz and Greenwald also emphasize the relationship between learning capacity and inclusive growth. Inclusive growth has two interrelated aspects: all people participate in inclusive growth and, at the same time, benefit from it. But, from a "learning society" perspective, inclusive growth goes far beyond the above-mentioned aspects and has an intrinsic relationship with innovative growth. Growth can be really inclusive—and, at the same time, innovative—when such growth takes full advantage of the talents of all. Stiglitz and Greenwald (2014) state that "our argument for why inclusive growth is so important goes beyond the standard one that it is a waste of a country's most valuable resource, its human talent, to fail to ensure that everyone lives up to his or her abilities" (468). They suggest that policies to promote more inclusiveness may promote more learning (381).

1.1 Research Question and Structure of This Chapter

The overarching research question of this chapter is: what benefits can we expect from *Kaizen* and related approaches in terms of learning, transformation, and quality growth? The next sections discuss goals, tools/methods, and process of *Kaizen*, and their relationship to learning, transformation, and quality of growth. In order to obtain deeper insights into these relationships, we examine the experiences of several countries where *Kaizen* and related approaches/systems have been introduced.

2 Goals, Tools/Methods, and Process of *Kaizen*

2.1 Goals of Kaizen and Process to Achieve Them

Much of the literature on *Kaizen* concurs that the utmost goal of *Kaizen* is the improvement of quality and productivity. For example, JICA's brochure, "*Kaizen* as a 'Japan brand ODA,' " states that *Kaizen* is Japan's approach toward improved quality and productivity (JICA 2016). However, it should be emphasized that *Kaizen* is distinctive in its approach to improving quality and productivity and that there are other approaches to improving productivity. For example, employers typically turn to monetary incentives: performance pay, bonuses, or the threat of dismissal (World Bank 2015, ch. 7). Nevertheless, any increase in productivity resulting from these approaches over a short period is normally not accompanied by learning. Where *Kaizen* differs from these approaches is in its process for achieving better quality and productivity through its distinctive focus on inclusive and participatory learning. Stiglitz and Greenwald (2014) contend that "if it is true that productivity is the result of learning and that productivity increases (learning) are endogenous, then a focal point of policy ought to be increasing learning within the economy" (5–6). I will discuss the learning aspects of *Kaizen* in the next section.

2.2 Kaizen *Tools/Methods*

Many *Kaizen* tools and methods have been developed over more than half a century. They are essential for the process of achieving the goals of *Kaizen*. For example, the Asian Productivity Organization (APO) states that "*Kaizen* approaches employ various tools including 5S, quality control circles, total quality control, total preventive maintenance, just-in-time inventory, standard work, and automation, among others. These have all been useful in improving the three productivity dimensions of cost, quality, and speed. For example, the core concept of *Kaizen* is to eliminate *muri* (overloading), *muda* (waste), and *mura* (inconsistency) from the worksite through efficient utilization of labor, materials, and equipment" (APO 2015, 10).

Among typical *Kaizen* tools and methods, 5S and Quality Control Circles (QCC) are well known. 5S represents "Sort, Set in order (or *Systematic arrangement*), Shine (*or Sweep*), Standardize, Sustain," which corresponds to five simple actions that can be taken to obtain discernible results of *Kaizen* in a short period of time (JICA 2016; italics added by author). "Sort" refers to sorting necessary items from un-necessary items and tidying up any items that aren't needed. "Systematic arrangement" indicates the need to place items in their set positions so that they can be used immediately when needed (Kikuchi 2009). These activities are practiced with simple methods such as the tag method, color display, visual controls, and dividing lines. As such, 5S is an easy activity to start with and enables the participation of all.

Quality Control Circles (commonly called QC circles) are voluntary small-scale groups that solve onsite problems through teamwork (JICA 2016). This Japanese way of QCC was gradually consolidated when it was applied at the factory floor level. In QC activities, participants frequently collect data and identify the causes of defective products and possibilities for improving products or production methods based on information collected. The basic tools used to read various kinds of information from data are referred to as the seven tools of QC, which include Pareto diagrams, check sheets, histograms, scatter diagrams, control drawings, graphs, and cause and effect diagrams (Kikuchi 2009, 45).

Many other tools, especially those of easy application including "layout planning" based on transfer distance analysis and process proximity analysis, improvement of work/human hours balance, shortening of setup times, are implemented during the *Kaizen* process (Kikuchi 2009).

3 *Kaizen*, Learning, and Quality of Growth

3.1 Kaizen *as a Participatory and Inclusive Approach*

The APO explains that the inclusiveness of the *Kaizen* process is centered around improvement efforts through the participation of all. Its "Handbook of Productivity" asserts that "*Kaizen* means improvement and encompasses the concept of never-ending efforts to improve by all of the people working in an organization. Problem-solving in the *Kaizen* approach is cross-functional, systematic, and collaborative. It is a strategy that puts every member of the organization, from top management down, continuously on the watch for improvement options" (APO 2015, 9–10). JICA (2016) succinctly states that "*KAIZEN* is an incremental effort starting from small steps involving all individuals from top managers to those working on the factory floor. However, commitment from the top management is essential."

3.2 Kaizen *and Learning*

The next question concerns how *Kaizen* can facilitate learning. To answer this, we need to discuss determinants of learning and how *Kaizen* is related to them. Stiglitz and Greenwald (2014, 56–57) identified the following major determinants of learning: (1) learning capabilities; (2) access to knowledge; (3) catalysts for learning; (4) creating a creative mindset or developing the right cognitive frames; (5) contacts—people with whom one interacts—who can catalyze learning, help create the right cognitive frame, and provide crucial inputs into the learning process; and (6) the context of learning. They further mention that "Just as *knowledge* itself is endogenous, so is the ability to *learn*. Some economic activities (conducted in certain ways) not only facilitate learning, they may facilitate *learning to learn*" (50; italics in original).

Several studies on capacity development also refer to the two types of capacity. Capacity embodies not only specific technical elements, such as specific health care or road construction skills, but also so-called core capacities (Hosono et al. 2011, 180). They include generic and cross-cutting competencies and the ability to commit and engage, to identify needs and key issues, to plan, budget, execute, and monitor actions, and, most importantly, to acquire knowledge and skills (UNDP 1998; ECDPM 2008; JICA 2006, 2008).

Kaizen tools/methodology and process bear a close relationship to the determinants of learning and, in particular, learning to learn. As JICA (2016) emphasizes, the *Kaizen* process (1) changes the mindsets of managers and workers; (2) fosters personnel who can think and act themselves; and (3) solves problems as a team, thereby promoting teamwork. This learning process is most visible in the activities of QC Circles (QCC). According to Ishikawa (1990), father of QCC,[4] "The basic philosophy of QC circle activities carried out as part of companywide quality control activities is (1) to contribute to the improvement and development of the corporate culture, (2) to create cheerful workplaces that make life worthwhile and where humanity is respected, and (3) *to exercise people's capabilities and bring out their limitless potential*" (78–79; italics added). Here we find exactly what Stiglitz and Greenwald (2014) emphasized regarding the real meaning of inclusive growth, which is intrinsically innovative growth in the sense that "*it is a waste of a country's most valuable resource, its human talent, to fail to ensure that everyone lives up to his or her abilities*" (468; italics added).

3.3 Kaizen, *TQC/TQM, Organizational Learning, and Learning Firms*

The Japanese way of QC was gradually scaled up from the factory floor level to the whole company. At the same time, all company employees, including managers, engineers, supervisors, office workers, as well as frontline factory workers participated in QC. This holistic approach, developed in Japan, is referred to as the Japanese type of company-wide quality control (CWQC) or total quality control (TQC). The TQC practiced by Japanese companies evolved, with much refinement, to total quality management (TQM) in the late 1980s.[5] As such, TQM is a kind of management system and strategy based on CWQC or TQC, and is widely promoted in the 1980s in Japan.[6] However, the term TQM was first used in the United States when US companies learned TQC from Japan. In 1996, JUCE decided to substitute the TQC by TQM (Fujimoto 2003, 302). "The Handbook for TQM and QCC," edited by the Development Bank of Japan and the Japan Economic Research Institute, notes that "[TQM] includes a number of management practices, philosophies and methods to improve the way an organization does business, makes its products, and interacts with its employees and customers. *Kaizen* is one of those philosophies" (DBJ and JERI 2003, vii).

The Toyota Production System (commonly called TPS) can be considered one of the most systematic and advanced Japanese TQC or TQM systems. As Liker (2004), the author of *Toyota Way*,[7] stated, "Toyota invented 'lean production'—also known as 'the Toyota Production System' or TPS—which has triggered a global transformation in virtually every industry to Toyota's manufacturing and supply chain philosophy and methods over the last decade" (4). He further states that "TPS is often known as 'lean' or 'lean production', since these were the terms made popular in two best-selling books: *The Machine That Changed the World: The Story of Lean Production* (Womack et al. 1990) and *Lean Thinking* (Womack and Jones 1996). These authors make it clear that the foundation of their research on lean production is TPS and its development by Toyota" (Womack et al. 1990, 3–4; Liker 2004, 15).

In the 1990s, through the work conducted on the International Motor Vehicle Program (IMVP) by The Massachusetts Institute of Technology (MIT) and the above-mentioned bestsellers based on its research, the concept of "lean production" was discovered by the world manufacturing community (Liker 2004, 25). The study authors applied this term to what Toyota had learned a decade earlier: "through focusing on speed within its supply chain: *shortening lead time by eliminating waste in each step of a process leads to best quality and lower cost, while improving safety and morale*" (Liker 2004, 25; italics in original). The idea of shortening lead-time by eliminating waste in each step is related to the concept of just-in-time (JIT). "Simply put, JIT delivers the right items at the right time in the right amounts. The power of JIT is that it allows you to be responsive to the day-by-day shifts in customer demand, which was exactly what Toyota needed all along" (Liker 2004, 23).

Liker (2004) highlighted the importance of learning in TPS: "I believe Toyota has raised continuous improvement and employee involvement to a unique level, creating one of the few examples of *a genuine learning enterprise in human history—not a small accomplishment*" (xv; italics added). He further states: "The highest level of the Toyota Way is organizational learning. Identifying the root causes of problems and preventing them from occurring is the focus of Toyota's continuous learning system" (xvi). This concept of a learning enterprise is similar to the exploration by Stiglitz and Greenwald of the "learning firm" which, together with a learning macro-environment, constitutes critical aspects of learning architecture (2014, 88). The importance of the learning firm is emphasized by them because "so much learning occurs within organizations and because so much knowledge resides within firms."

3.4 Kaizen *and Sustainable Growth*

A core method of *Kaizen* is to eliminate *muri*, *muda*, and *mura* from the worksite through efficient utilization of labor, materials, and equipment. As such, the concept of environmental sustainability is intrinsically incorporated into *Kaizen*, TQM and related approaches from the beginning. Furthermore, these approaches have focused more on activities for energy conservation and measures for resource management in the post-oil crises period. In this regard, the "Total Energy Management Handbook" prepared in 2005 by the Energy Conservation Center Thailand (ECCT) and Energy Conservation Center Japan (ECCJ) puts stress on such items as motivation techniques, energy conservation attitudes, and small group activities (SGA) including TQM, all contributing to energy conservation through the participation of all the people working together (ECCT and ECCJ 2005, 4). The Asian Energy Efficiency and Conservation Collaboration Center (AEEC) was established by ECCJ in 2007. There have also been many initiatives to mainstream environmental sustainability in *Kaizen*, TQM, and so forth. For example, APO started to promote "green productivity" focusing explicitly on environmental improvement.

3.5 Kaizen *and Secure Growth*

The APEC growth strategy included "secure growth" as an attribute of the quality of growth and stated: "We seek to protect the region's citizen's economic and physical well-being and to provide the secure environment necessary for economic activity." Secure working conditions are explicitly and implicitly included among basic aims of 5S, elimination of *muri* and *mura*, as well as related approaches. As such, *Kaizen* aims to upgrade quality and productivity, improving the security and safety of workers at the same time.

4 Insights from Outstanding Experiences

4.1 *Experiences in Japan*

Much of the literature related to *Kaizen* acknowledges its significant contributions to industrial development in Japan. For example, APO (2015) emphasizes that "*Kaizen* is known as the single most important concept in Japanese management and it has been a key to the competitive success of

Japanese manufacturing industries." JICA (2016) notes that *Kaizen* is "the driving force of Japan's rapid growth." DBJ and JERI (2003) state that "The success of Japanese business in Canada, Latin America, and the United States as well as in Europe is attributable to TQM, a concept now widely practiced throughout Asia."

Only a few Japanese companies, such as Toyota, were aware of the importance of the US-derived statistical control of quality before Dr. William Edwards Deming came to Japan in 1947 and gave a series of lectures on the statistical process control of production and quality. Accordingly, the first step for many Japanese companies was the introduction of the statistical quality control (SQC) approach. The Japanese way of QC was gradually consolidated when it was applied at the factory floor level with the introduction of, among other things, *Kaizen* and QCC. The number of QCC could be considered as a kind of proxy indicator of the dissemination of *Kaizen*. The number of QCCs registered at the Union of Japanese Scientists and Engineers (JUSE) increased from 50,000 in the mid-1970s to 420,000 in 2001. The number of participants of QCCs increased from 500,000 to 3,200,000 during the same period (DBJ and JERI 2003, 59). As this shows, the large-scale dissemination of *Kaizen* has taken place since 1970s. It should be also noted that *Kaizen*—and in particular QCC—has been introduced not only into the manufacturing sector but also in various other sectors, such as the construction sector (since 1975), finance and insurance sectors (since 1981), and health care sector (hospitals) (since 1982) (DBJ and JERI 2003, 59).

According to a recent study on productivity gaps for Japanese and US industries by Jorgenson et al. (2015, 21–26), the total factor productivity (TFP) gaps of Japan compared to the United States were very large in both the manufacturing and non-manufacturing sectors in 1955. The gap for manufacturing productivity relative to the United States (US = 100) disappeared by 1980 and peaked at 103.8 in 1991. While it deteriorated somewhat afterward, the current gap is almost negligible. The motor vehicle industry, together with some other manufacturing industries of Japan, had a higher level of TFP than their US counterparts. As Japan's motor vehicle industry introduced *Kaizen*, TQM, and other related approaches ***much earlier and more intensively*** than the US motor vehicle industry (according to the MIT Commission on Industrial Productivity as discussed below), we could reasonably suppose that these approaches partly contributed to the impressive improvement of TFP level of the Japanese motor vehicle industry, particularly in the 1970s and 1980s.

It should also be highlighted that the widespread dissemination of *Kaizen*, QCC, TQM, and related approaches has contributed significantly to the sustainable growth of Japan since the 1970s. The extensive dissemination of these approaches coincided with the era following the first oil crisis. In Japan, public awareness of environmental issues gradually grew during the 1960s as air and water pollution worsened with accelerated industrialization. The subsequent 1973 oil shock was a major turning point in that it forced Japanese companies and the general public to take measures for improving energy efficiency. As DBJ and JERI (2003) emphasize, "One of the significant impacts of Japanese TQC/TQM is often explained through descriptions of the development of the car industry after the oil crises in the 1970s. During this period, TQC was extended to activities for energy conservation and measures for resource maintenance. It greatly impacted on various industries and became more securely established as a valuable quality framework for Japanese industrial development" (46).

According to *General Energy Statistics* published by Japan's Agency for Natural Resources and Energy (2005), energy efficiency in Japan improved 37 percent between 1973 and 2003. In this period, total energy consumption in the industrial sector has stayed at the same level (around 180 million kiloliters of crude oil equivalent), while real GDP doubled (from 250 trillion to 520 trillion yen). Japan is one of the most energy-efficient countries in the world. Japanese CO_2 emissions per GDP in 2005 were 0.24 kg of CO_2/US$ compared with 0.43 in the EU and 0.53 in the United States (based on exchange rates in the year 2000; IEA 2007). The Energy Conservation Law, incentives offered by the government, company investments in energy-saving equipment and technologies, as well as their efforts through *Kaizen*-based QC activities, TQM, and related approaches are likely to have enabled these achievements.

4.2 Experiences in the United States[8]

In the United States, comparative studies between US and Japanese industries were made in the 1980s. One of the most well known is "Made in America, Regaining the Productive Edge," a report issued by the MIT Commission on Industrial Productivity (Dertouzos et al. 1989, xiii). The findings showed that one area in which US firms often lagged behind their overseas competitors was in exploiting the potential for continuous improvement in the quality and reliability of their products and processes

(74). The report noted that "The cumulative effect of successive incremental improvements and modifications to established products and processes can be very large and may outpace efforts to achieve technological breakthroughs" (74). It further states that "In the long run, technological progress rests on a foundation of both incremental improvements and radical breakthroughs, and finding the right balance between them is a constant challenge. Lewis Branscomb (1987) has suggested that Japanese firms have been more effective in combining the two approaches" (74).[9]

Moreover, Womack et al. (1990), based on research from MIT's International Motor Vehicle Program (IMVP), concluded that:

> The auto industries of North America and Europe were relying on techniques little changed from Henry Ford's mass production system and that these techniques were simply not competitive with a new set of ideas pioneered by the Japanese companies, methods for which we did not even have a name… [T]he Western companies didn't seem to be able to learn from their Japanese competitors. Instead, they were focusing their energies on erecting trade barriers and other competitive impediments, which we thought simply delayed dealing with the real issue… [W]e feared that North America and Europe would seal themselves off from the Japanese threat and, in the process, reject the opportunity for the prosperity and more rewarding work that these new techniques offer. We felt that the most constructive step we could take to prevent this development from occurring would be to undertake a detailed study of the new Japanese techniques, which we subsequently named 'lean production', compared to the older Western mass-production techniques (3–4).

TQC/TQM and other management methods were gradually introduced into the US industries (DBJ and JERI 2003, 47). In this regard, Stiglitz and Greenwald (2014, 38) made an important observation in relation to the performance of the US manufacturing sector between the 1970s and early 1980s on the one hand and the late 1980s and 1990s on the other:

> Between these two periods, the annual rate of growth of U.S. manufacturing productivity rose by 2.0 per cent from 0.9 per cent to 2.9 per cent. The improvement coincided with a marked rise in U.S. real interest rates (normally associated with *less* investment in technology) and government deficits, a decline in U.S. research and development spending, and no detectable improvement in the performance of U.S. education (as measured by standardized tests). At the same time, it cannot be attributed to the availability

> of new technology. Such technology would have been equally available to other G7 economies. Over the period in question, the U.S. improvement in annual manufacturing productivity growth was 1.9 per cent higher than that of the other G7 countries. The improvement was thus a U.S., not a global, phenomenon. What seems to have changed in U.S. manufacturing was an intensified focus on improved operations management through the rigorous implementation of procedures like benchmarking, total quality management, and reengineering—in our language, an intensified focus on learning. America seemed to have learned how to learn (38).

Stiglitz and Greenwald (2014, 528) further noted that "interestingly, some of the learning involved learning from foreign firms, e.g., about quality circles and just in time production."

Regarding the car industry, the MIT's IMVP study referred to above found that the US companies improved car assembly productivity from 24 man hours/car unit to 20 between 1989 and 1993/1994, while Japanese companies improved from 16 man hours/car unit to 15 in the same period, confirming the catch-up process of the US car industry to its Japanese counterpart (Fujimoto 2003, 283).

These experiences confirm that the learning process has been closely related to approaches such as TQM, also seen in the United States. Together with experiences in Japan, this provides insights into effective approaches to create learning firms and learning societies, which are the main drivers of high-quality growth.

4.3 *Experiences in Singapore*[10]

Singapore was the first country in Southeast Asia to systematically introduce quality and productivity initiatives. According to former Prime Minister Lee Kuan Yew, "The shift to a knowledge-intensive industrial structure with strong international competitiveness is only possible through the human-resource development of 2.6 million people, the only resource Singapore has" (JPC 1990, 1).[11] Lee's concern was how to organize and motivate Singapore's workforce to make best use of the modernization of plants and capacity building. In April 1981, the Committee on Productivity was set up by representatives of enterprises, worker organizations, government officials, and academics.

The committee reviewed the experiences of productivity movements in Japan, another country without natural resources. It then presented a report to the president of the National Productivity Board (NPB) of Singapore, which had been designated as the main body for promoting productivity development in Singapore. In June 1983, the Singapore Productivity Development Project (SPDP) was launched with the support of the Japanese government.

Some 15,000 Singaporean engineers, managers, and other professionals participated in the project. About 200 engineers, managers, and other professionals from Singapore took part in training courses in Japan, and more than 200 Japanese experts were dispatched to Singapore. In addition, more than 100 textbooks and other training materials were prepared specifically for the project. During the period of SPDP and beyond, labor productivity in manufacturing industries improved by an annual average rate of 5.7 percent (1981–1986), 3.0 percent (1986–1991), and 4.8 percent (1991–1996). In 1990, when SPDP ended, 90 percent of workers in the country were involved in productivity development activities, compared with 54 percent in 1986. In 2001, 13 percent of the total labor force was participating in quality control circles (QCC), in comparison with 0.4 percent in 1983, when SPDP started.

Experiences in Singapore have proven the effectiveness of *Kaizen* and related approaches for the transformation from unskilled labor-intensive industries to skilled labor-intensive or knowledge-intensive industries, strongly inspired by the country's leader Lee Kuan Yu. In this regard, JICA (2014) concludes that "the *Kaizen* Project laid the groundwork for Singapore's growth, contributing to upgrading the country's industrial structure" (4).

4.4 Experiences in Thailand

In 1995, Thailand's annual automobile exports were less than half a billion US dollars, well below exports from India and Malaysia. In 2008, exports approached 28 billion US dollars, making Thailand the largest automobile exporter in the ASEAN region, and by 2012, Thailand was the seventh largest exporter in the world. It was estimated in 2010 that there were about 690 first-tier parts makers, 30 percent of them Thai-majority joint venture companies, with 23 percent of them pure Thai companies. There were also 1700 second- and third-tier parts makers, most of them locally owned small and medium enterprises (SMEs), supporting the automobile industry in Thailand (Natsuda and Thoburn 2011, 8). At present, the automobile industry is the principal engine for growth in Thailand's economy. "The Detroit of Asia" envisaged once by the Thai government is now a reality. As Athukorala and Kohpaiboon (2011) point out, "the automobile industry has been the target of industrial development in many countries as a driver of growth—a source of employment, technological expertise, and a stimulus to other sectors through backward linkages.... But only a handful of developing countries have managed to develop an internationally competitive automobile industry." Thus, Thailand successfully achieved a transformation of its industrial structure.

In this process, "Japanese assemblers played a crucial role in the development of automobile production and supporting industries" (Techakanont 2015, 204). For example, the Toyota Production System (TPS) has been introduced:

> Toyota facilitated interfirm knowledge-sharing through supplier associations, knowledge-transfer consultants and small-group learning teams (Dyer and Nobeoka 2000). Toyota created the Toyota Cooperation Club (TCC) and established a training center in 1982, when they had around thirty-five suppliers. This number increased to more than 160 members (as first-tier suppliers) in 2014. The TCC organized activities to increase capabilities in the TPS. It shared explicit and tacit knowledge on its System through company visits by Toyota's trained consultants. As a member, suppliers received free consulting services. Experts at Toyota Thailand also provided TPS training to parts manufacturers in other ASEAN countries. Another initiative was the coordination of learning activities in small groups, intended to encourage suppliers to learn and share specific tacit knowledge with each other (Techakanont 2015, 205).

One of the largest public-private supplier development efforts, apart from private initiatives such as Toyota's, was the Thailand Automotive Human Resource Development Project (AHRDP) for first-tier and second-tier suppliers, which ran from 2006 to 2010. It was implemented with the support of JICA and four Japanese companies, including Toyota, which provided TPS training. In total, 233 SMEs and 7151 workers participated in AHRDP. According to Techakanont (2015), a poll of 200 case studies conducted by the Thai Automotive Institute (TAI) on the results of the AHRDP revealed that, on average, suppliers were able to improve productivity by 30 percent to 50 percent, reduce work-in-process inventory by 25 percent to 75 percent, and free up 30 percent to 50 percent of factory space (206–207).

Beginning in 2012, the Automotive Human Resource Development Institute Project (AHRDIP) conducted a five-year program with the aim of providing a higher level of technological content. The specific goals of the AHRDIP were, among other aims, to instruct 1000 trainers who would then train 255,000 personnel in manufacturing, to teach 200 trainers and 30,000 personnel in testing, and to teach 100 trainers and train 15,000 personnel in R&D (Techakanont 2015, 208).

4.5 *Experiences in Tanzania and Other African Countries*

Tanzania became a pioneer in introducing *Kaizen* and total quality management (TQM) in hospitals.[12] Building on the inspiration gained from Sri Lankan best practice and witnessing the visible changes in the first pilots at Mbeya Referral Hospital (MRH), the Ministry of Health and Social Welfare (MoHSW) officially adopted the 5S-*Kaizen*-TQM approach to provide the core of the national quality improvement program as part of the National Health Sector Strategy. With many specific initiatives of MoHSW, this approach has started to take root in a number of hospitals in Tanzania.

This approach has, first of all, been officially designated the foundation of all quality improvement (QI) approaches in Tanzania. As of September 2012, some fifty-six hospitals—including all national, specialized and regional referral hospitals as well as a number of municipal and district hospitals—have established quality improvement teams (QITs) and have implemented 5S. Of these hospitals, thirteen have moved to the second step of *Kaizen*: evidence-based participatory problem-solving actions for service quality improvement. Through the cascade approach, well over 5000 health workers have been trained in 5S. Some of the achievements through *Kaizen* include reductions of overstocked inventory, reductions in waiting time for patient consultations (down to one-third from forty-six minutes to fifteen minutes), and increases in hospital income through better processing of insurance claims (Honda 2012, 117–119; Takizawa 2013). This experience demonstrates effects of the *Kaizen* approach in improving quality and productivity of health care services.

Over five years of continuous efforts have made Tanzania a center of excellence in quality improvement of hospital care through application of 5S-*Kaizen*-TQM in Africa. JICA is working in partnership with Sri Lanka in applying this approach to improve hospital management in over fifteen countries in Africa (Takizawa 2013, 259). Several countries have mainstreamed or are in process of mainstreaming the approach in their strategies and framework of quality assurance for health services. As such, Tanzania emerged as a pivotal country in this approach by providing an example for other African countries to emulate (Honda 2012, 119–120).

5 Concluding Remarks

The case studies of experiences presented here illustrate the application of *Kaizen* in a variety of contexts with significant impact. As *Kaizen* and related approaches do not demand large investments, they enabled the Japanese manufacturing industry to improve productivity and competitiveness during the post-war period, when the availability of funds for investment was severely limited. During the post-1973 oil crisis era, a time when Japanese companies were seriously affected by energy price hikes, *Kaizen* and related approaches were introduced very widely—not only into manufacturing industries but also into finance, insurance, construction, health care, and other sectors. In the United States, improved operational management systems, including TQM, were widely introduced to manufacturing industries.

In Singapore and Thailand, where *Kaizen* was introduced—at least into some of the sectors that are leading their economic growth—the increase in productivity was crucial to the transformation of their industrial structure. In Singapore, *Kaizen* and related approaches contributed to the transformation from unskilled labor-intensive industries to skilled labor-intensive or knowledge-intensive industries. In Thailand, scaling-up of supporting industries for automobile industry was facilitated by the development of small and medium parts industries that benefited from, among other things, *Kaizen* and related approaches such as TPS. The competitive automobile industry contributed to the transformation of the industrial structure of the country.

Experiences in the hospitals of Tanzania and other African countries clearly demonstrate the possibility of introducing *Kaizen* and related approaches to sectors other than the manufacturing industry, as has occurred in Japan and other Asian countries.

These diverse experiences provide evidence of some other important features of *Kaizen* and related approaches. For example, they are inexpensive without the need for much investment and are easily applied. The sizable dissemination of QCC in the 1970s and 1980s in Japan was possible because of these features.

In short, *Kaizen*, TQM, and related approaches were able to contribute to growth—and in particular to high-quality growth—by increasing productivity through learning. It also enabled transformation through enhancing learning capacity, especially learning how to learn ("learning to learn" in terms of Stiglitz and Greenwald 2014), the essential endowment for industrial transformation. These approaches are intrinsically inclusive, because they are approaches in which participation by all and their learning are essential. They are also able to contribute to sustainable growth because they reduce use of materials and improve energy efficiency by eradicating *muda*. Such approaches improve security and safety for workers as well through elimination of *muri*, *mura*, and so forth. Therefore, *Kaizen*, TQM, and related approaches can contribute to the achievement of Goal 8 of SDGs by facilitating directly and indirectly sustained, inclusive, and sustainable economic growth, full and productive employment, and decent work. However, it should be recognized that there are challenges to fully implementing these approaches in the many diverse contexts of developing countries and that further in-depth studies are needed to address these challenges effectively.

Notes

1. This chapter draws partly on the author's previous works such as Hosono (2009, 2015a, b, 2017).
2. For a literature review and discussion on the quality of growth, see Haddad et al. (2015) and Hosono (2015a).
3. "The APEC (Asia Pacific Economic Cooperation) Leaders' Growth Strategy" was agreed on November 14, 2010. It is referred to as the "APEC Growth Strategy."
4. Dr. Kaoru Ishikawa, ex-Rector of the Musashi Institute of Technology (recently renamed Tokyo City University), is considered to be the "founder of quality control in Japan," as well as the father of the QC circle, as a result of the important theoretical and practical contributions he made. His book, *Introduction to Quality Control*, first published in 1954 (Ishikawa 1954), is one of the most widely read books in Japan in this field. The third edition (1989) was translated into English and published in 1990 (Ishikawa 1990). There are also a large number of well-known engineers and managers who have promoted quality activities in many Japanese companies. One of the most prominent is Mr. Taiichi Ohno, ex-Vice President of Toyota Motor Company. He is one of those who consolidated the Toyota

Production System (TPS). Another prominent Japanese engineer who contributed substantially to quality activities is Dr. Shigeo Shingo, a consultant for Toyota and Panasonic, among others. In recognition of his work, Utah State University created "The Shingo Prize." Mr. Masaaki Imai, who once worked for the Japan Productivity Center in Washington DC, founded the Kaizen Institute Consulting Group in 1986 and, in the same year, wrote *Kaizen: The Key to Japan's Competitive Success.*

5. For example, Toyota's TQM comprises the integration of three main points that must be present in order for the company to succeed: focus on customers, continual improvement, and participation by all employees (DBJ and JERI 2003, 3, 7).
6. This explanation of the relationship between CWQC, TQC and TQM is based on DBJ and JERI (2003, 2).
7. According to Liker (2004), "The Toyota Way" can be briefly summarized through the two pillars that support it: "Continuous Improvement" and "Respect for People." Continuous improvement, often called *Kaizen*, defines Toyota's basic approach to doing business: "challenge everything." Liker states: "More important than the actual improvements that individuals contribute, the true value of continuous improvement is in creating an atmosphere of continuous *learning* and an environment that not only accepts but actually *embraces* change. Such an environment can only be created where there is respect for people—hence the second pillar of the Toyota Way. Toyota demonstrates this respect by providing employment security and seeking to engage team members through active participation in improving their jobs" (xi-xii; italics in original).
8. This part heavily draws from Hosono (2017).
9. In this regard, Imai (1986) compares *Kaizen* and "innovation." These concepts correspond, respectively, to "incremental improvement" and "breakthrough" in terms of Dertouzos et al. (1989). According to Imai, *Kaizen* is of long-term and long-lasting effect, with small steps, with the involvement of everybody, based on conventional know-how and state-of-the-art practices that require little investment. "Innovation," on the other hand, is of short-term but dynamic effect, with big steps, with involvement of a selected few "champions," based on technological breakthroughs, new inventions and new theories, and requires large investments (Imai 1986, 25).
10. This part draws heavily from Hosono (2015b).
11. Comments made by the Prime Minister during his visit to Mr. Kohei Goshi, honorary President of the Japan Productivity Center (JPC) in June 1981 (JPC 1990, 1).
12. This paragraph draws mainly from Honda (2012).

References

Agency for Natural Resources and Energy. 2005. *General Energy Statistics*. Tokyo: Agency for Natural Resources and Energy.

Asian Development Bank (ADB). 2013. *Key Indicators for Asia and the Pacific: Asia's Economic Transformation: Where to, How, and How Fast?* Manila: ADB.

Asian Productivity Organization (APO). 2015. *Handbook on Productivity*. Tokyo: APO.

Athukorala, Prema-Chandra, and Archanun Kohpaiboon. 2011. Thailand in Global Automobile Networks. Paper Submitted to Study for the International Trade Center, Geneva.

Branscomb, Lewis. 1987. Towards a National Policy on Research and Development. Conference Sponsored by the Council on Research and Technology (CORE-TECH) and the Conference Board, MIT, October 8 (Cited by Dertouzos et al. 1989.).

Dertouzos, Michael, Richard Lester, and Robert Solow. 1989. *Made in America: Regaining the Productive Edge*. Cambridge, MA: MIT Press.

Development Bank of Japan (DBJ) and Japan Economic Research Institute (JERI). 2003. *Handbook for TQM and QCC*. Washington, DC: Inter-American Development Bank (IDB).

Dyer, Jeffrey H., and Kentaro Nobeoka. 2000. Creating and Managing a High-Performance Knowledge-Sharing Network: The Toyota Case. *Strategy Management Journal* 21 (3): 345–367.

Energy Conservation Center Thailand (ECCT) and Energy Conservation Center Japan (ECCJ). 2005. *The Energy Management Handbook*. Bangkok and Tokyo: ECCT and ECCJ.

European Center for Development Policy Management (ECDPM). 2008. Capacity, Change, and Performance: Study Report. *Discussion Paper 59B*. April. Maastricht, Holland: ECDPM.

Fujimoto, Takahiro. 2003. *Nouryoku Kouchiku Kyouso: Nihon no Jidousha Sangyou wa Naze Tsuyoinoka?* [Competition of Capacity Building: Why is the Japanese Car Industry Strong?]. Tokyo: Chuo Koron Sha.

Government of Japan, Cabinet Office. 2015. *Development Cooperation Charter*. Tokyo: Cabinet Office.

Haddad, Lawrence, Hiroshi Kato, and Nicolas Meisel, eds. 2015. *Growth is Dead, Long Live Growth: The Quality of Economic Growth and Why it Matters*. Tokyo: JICA Research Institute.

Honda, Shunichiro. 2012. Inspired by Sri Lankan Practice: Scaling-up 5S-KAIZEN-TQM for Improving African Hospital Service. In *Scaling Up South-South and Triangular Cooperation*, ed. Hiroshi Kato, 107–127. Tokyo: JICA Research Institute.

Hosono, Akio. 2009. Kaizen: Quality, Productivity and Beyond. In *Introducing Kaizen in Africa*, ed. GRIPS Development Forum, 23–37. Tokyo: National Graduate Institute for Policy Studies (GRIPS).

———. 2015a. Industrial Transformation and Quality of Growth. In *Growth is Dead, Long Live Growth: The Quality of Economic Growth and Why it Matters*, ed. Lawrence Haddad, Hiroshi Kato, and Nicolas Meisel, 267–300. Tokyo: JICA Research Institute.

———. 2015b. Industrial Strategy and Economic Transformation: Lessons from Five Outstanding Cases. In *Industrial Policy and Economic Transformation in Africa*, ed. Akbar Noman and Joseph Stiglitz, 53–101. New York: Columbia University Press.

———. 2017. Industrial Strategies Toward a Learning Society for Quality Growth. In *Efficiency, Finance, and Variety of Industrial Policy: Guiding Resources, Learning, and Technology for Sustained Growth*, ed. Akbar Noman and Joseph Stiglitz, 306–352. New York: Columbia University Press.

Hosono, Akio, Shunichiro Honda, Mine Sato, and Mai Ono. 2011. Inside the Black Box of Capacity Development. In *Catalyzing Development: A New Vision for Aid*, ed. Homi Kharas, Koji Makino, and Woojin Jung, 179–201. Washington DC: Brookings Institution.

Imai, Masaaki. 1986. *Kaizen: The Key to Japan's Competitive Success.* New York: McGraw-Hill.

International Energy Agency (IEA). 2007. *CO2 Emissions from Fuel Combustion 1971–2005.* Paris: IEA.

Ishikawa, Kaoru. 1954. *Hinshitsu Kanri Nyumon* [Introduction to Quality Control]. Tokyo: JUSE Press.

———. 1990. *Introduction to Quality Control.* Tokyo: 3A Corporation.

Japan Productivity Center (JPC). 1990. *Singapore Productivity Improvement Project.* Tokyo: JPC.

JICA. 2006. *Capacity Development: What Is CD? How JICA Understands CD, and How-to Concepts for Improving JICA Projects.* Tokyo: JICA.

———. 2008. *Capacity Assessment Handbook: Managing Programs and Projects toward Capacity Development.* Tokyo: JICA.

———. 2014. The Kaizen Project: Laying the Groundwork for Singapore's Growth. JICA's World, January 2014. Tokyo: JICA.

———. 2016. *Kaizen: Japan's Approach Towards Improved Quality and Productivity.* Tokyo: JICA.

Jorgenson, Dale W., Koji Nomura, and Jon D. Samuels. 2015. A Half Century of Trans-Pacific Competition: Price Level Indices and Productivity Gap for Japanese and U.S. Industries, 1955–2012. RIETI Discussion Paper Series 15-E-054. Tokyo: Research Institute of Economy, Trade and Industry (RIETI).

Kikuchi, Tsuyoshi. 2009. JICA-Supported Project for Quality and Productivity Improvement in Tunisia. In *Introducing Kaizen in Africa*, ed. GRIPS Development Forum, 39–54. Tokyo: GRIPS.

Liker, Jeffrey K. 2004. *The Toyota Way*. New York: McGraw Hill.

Lin, Justin Yifu. 2012. *New Structural Economics: A Framework of Rethinking Development and Policy*. Washington, DC: World Bank.

Natsuda, Kaoru, and John Thoburn. 2011. Industrial Policy and the Development of the Automotive Industry in Thailand. *Working Paper No. 11(5)*. Ritsumeikan Center for Asia Pacific Studies (RCAPS).

Noman, Akbar, and Joseph Stiglitz. 2012. "Strategies for African Development." In *Good Growth and Governance for Africa: Rethinking Development Strategies*, edited by Akbar Noman, Kwesi Botchwey, Howard Stein, and Joseph Stiglitz, 3–47. New York: Oxford University Press.

———. 2017. Learning, Industrial, and Technology Policies: An Overview. In *Efficiency, Finance, and Varieties of Industrial Policy: Guiding Resources, Learning, and Technology for Sustained Growth*, ed. Akbar Noman and Joseph E. Stiglitz, 1–20. New York: Columbia University Press.

Stiglitz, Joseph, and Bruce Greenwald. 2014. *Creating a Learning Society: A New Approach to Growth, Development, and Social Progress*. New York: Columbia University Press.

Takizawa, Ikuo. 2013. Toward Universal Health Coverage in Africa—Achieving MDGs with Equity, and Beyond. In *For Inclusive and Dynamic Development in Sub-Saharan Africa*, ed. JICA Research Institute, 247–266. Tokyo: JICA Research Institute.

Techakanont, Kriengkrai. 2015. Supplier Development Programs in the Automotive Industry in Asia. In *Rising Concentration in Asia-Latin American Value Chains: Can Small Firms Turn the Tide?* ed. Osvaldo Rosales, Keiji Inoue, and Nanno Mulder, 183–214. Santiago: UN-ECLAC.

United Nations Development Program (UNDP). 1998. Capacity Assessment and Development in a Systems and Strategic Management Context. *MDGB Technical Advisory Paper 3*. New York: UNDP.

United Nations General Assembly (UNGA). 2015. *The 2030 Agenda for Sustainable Development*. New York: United Nations.

Womack, James, and Daniel Jones. 1996. *Lean Thinking: Banish Waste and Create Wealth in Your Corporation*. New York: Free Press.

Womack, James, Daniel Jones, and Daniel Roos. 1990. *The Machine that Changed the World: The Story of Lean Production*. New York: Macmillan.

World Bank. 2015. *World Development Report 2015: Mind, Society, and Behavior*. Washington, DC: World Bank.

CHAPTER 4

Why Is *Kaizen* Critical for Developing Countries?: *Kaizen* as a Social Innovation in the Era of Global Inequality

Go Shimada

1 Introduction

One of the most important global issues we face today is rising inequality in both developed and developing countries (Piketty 2014). Even if the inequality between countries has converged with the economic growth of emerging states, domestic inequality has worsened (Milanović 2016), so the global economy today faces convergence and divergence at the same time. In regional terms, even if the overall economic gap has lessened, African countries still lag behind those in other regions. To change this situation, industrial sector development is certainly important, but to catch up, what African countries need to do is twofold. The first is to move their production possibility frontier (PPF) outward (movement of the PPF curve itself). For this, the best performing firms need to develop technological and/or production innovations. They can also introduce new technology and/or production methods from developed countries. These moves will allow their production possibility frontier to expand.

G. Shimada (✉)
School of Information and Communication, Meiji University, Tokyo, Japan
e-mail: go_shimada@meiji.ac.jp

A. Hosono et al. (eds.), *Workers, Managers, Productivity*,
https://doi.org/10.1007/978-981-15-0364-1_4

The second way is to assist average firms to reach their production possibility frontier using existing technology (movement toward the frontier). A number of researchers (Baily and Solow 2001; Baily et al. 1992) have discovered that most firms operate well below their optimum level, compared with the best performing firms in the same industry. In other words, there is a huge and persistent difference in productivity between the leading and average firms in an industry (Stiglitz and Greenwald 2015). And, internal technological breakthrough innovation does not occur very often. Rather, most firms adopt proven technologies and try to catch up to the leading firms.

Both the movement of the PPF itself and the movement of individual firms toward the frontier can accelerate the economic growth of Africa and reduce the economic gap with developed countries. However, these changes may not be enough to tackle the issue of rising inequality in each country. We cannot expect the benefit of industrial development or firm growth to easily trickle down to the poor. Then, how can we make industrial development work for the poor? More precisely, can *Kaizen* contribute to solving the issue of inequality for each country? This chapter tries to answer this question looking back at Japan's experience.

2 In the Era of Declining Labor Share in GDP: Toward Social Innovation

Innovation is the source of economic growth. The Nobel Laureate Robert Solow (1956, 1957) showed that technological progress is the source of economic growth, rather than capital accumulation and increases in labor. Leapfrog innovation is important. We, however, need to remember that most of the innovations are small and incremental changes. These changes include both technological and production processes. These are not dramatic, but they are fundamental to the everyday operation of firms. It is also important to grow in the long run, not just enjoy short-term growth from innovation. That is why, Kenneth Arrow analyzed technological progress as focusing not only on research and development (1962a) but also on learning by doing (1962b).

As Stiglitz and Greenwald (2015) discussed, although technological and production innovations are important, they often increase just private returns, not social returns. There are reasons for this. First, the large firms in developed countries are more able to produce innovations compared with small and medium enterprises (SMEs) and firms in developing countries. This is because they have more financial resources. Since their market is bigger than that of the SMEs, there are economies of scale for large firms in innovation.

Second, the first innovators, which are often large firms as discussed, can enjoy a monopoly over this new technology under strict intellectual property regimes (e.g., WTO/TRIPS [World Trade Organization/Trade-Related Aspects of Intellectual Property Rights]). As is well known in respect of monopolistic competition, firms produce less than the social optimum and increase the price whenever they can. This happens to many pharmaceutical drugs, which are essential for the lives of people in developing countries but are not affordable for the poor.

Third, under monopolistic competition, R&D investment in the area is often reduced. New innovations may be created based on existing technology, but without access to the technological information, it is hard to make investment within firms, especially in small and medium enterprises and firms in developing countries. Thus, future production will be smaller than the socially desirable level. In this contest, *Kaizen* can bring production innovation for firms without cost, and has very large spillover effects from the methods of production it advocates across sectors (institutional spillover). While the costs include more than just investment cost, there are no patent use costs as *Kaizen* is not patented.

As Fig. 4.1 shows, to increase productivity two types of innovation are required: production innovation and technological innovation. For a firm

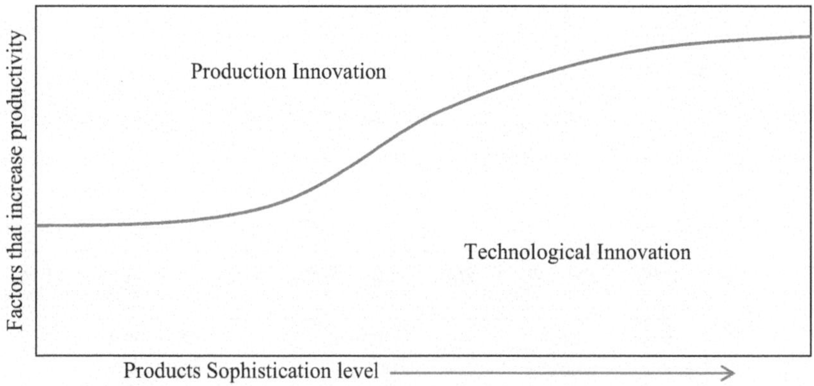

Fig. 4.1 Factor to increase productivity and types of innovation. (Source: Author)

producing basic products, changes in production processes are required for an increase in productivity. As the sophistication level of products goes up, technological innovation becomes more important. In other words, *Kaizen* is more important for many small and medium firms that produce relatively less sophisticated products, allowing them to improve their productivity.

However, productivity growth is a double-edged sword. This is because, on the one hand, although it improves a firm's performance, on the other, it means firms can operate with fewer workers (Shimada 2015a, 2017a, 2018a, 2019; Shimada and Sonobe 2018; Higuchi and Shimada 2019). Further, since most technological innovations tend to be labor saving technologies, productivity growth could have negative consequences on the lives of workers if they lose their jobs. It is important to consider the distributional aspect of productivity growth. Figure 4.2 shows the share of labor compensation in gross domestic product (GDP) over the last two decades for selected countries. As is shown, there is declining trend. This means that the share of income distributed to workers in GDP is decreasing, and this is a global trend. In the age of rising inequality, the distributional aspect of productivity growth thus becomes very important.

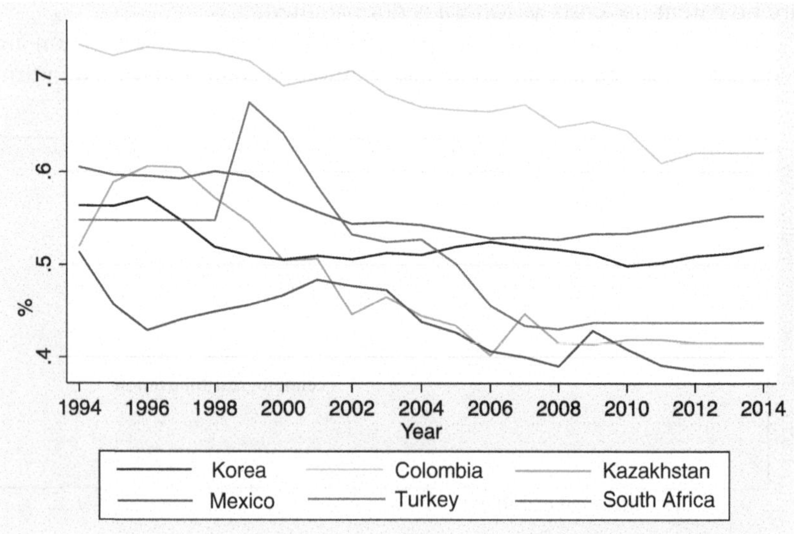

Fig. 4.2 Share of labor compensation in GDP at current national prices. (Source: Author, based on Penn World Table 9.0)

Then, the question comes into mind could *Kaizen* contribute to this? The next section will examine this, analyzing how *Kaizen* worked in Japan when it was introduced, and paying special attention to its impact on labor.

3 US Aid to Japan: Japan's Experience Introducing *Kaizen* to Create Social Innovation

Japan introduced *Kaizen* in 1955 with assistance from the United States. As we will see in detail, there were three different aims for that introduction by each stakeholder: Japanese firms; the United States; and labor (Shimada 2015a, 2017a, 2018a, b, 2019; Shimada and Sonobe 2018; Higuchi and Shimada 2019). First, for Japanese firms, the main objective was to increase production with less labor. Because of World War II, the production capacity of Japanese firms was much lower than in the pre-war period. At the same time, the labor movement using confrontational methods such as strikes was very active. Under this condition, it was difficult for Japanese firms to meet market demands. So, for firms, there was a huge demand to increase productivity.

Second, for the United States, there were two objectives. Initially, after World War II the main objective was to democratize Japan, dismantling large enterprises and, at the same time, promoting small and medium enterprises and the labor movement (Shimada 2018a). After the start of the cold war though, the objective changed toward keeping labor unions on-side and away from the Soviet bloc. Third, for labor unions, when US aid was decided, they were against the productivity movement, because they feared that their jobs would be lost with increasing productivity. However, as they kept negotiating with employers, they started to secure wage increases, which raised their living standards considerably.

In the next section, we will examine why Japan introduced *Kaizen* from these three different perspectives. We will also examine what kind of impact this had on Japanese society. To begin this analysis, we start by looking at the situation existing soon after World War II.

3.1 Economic Policy During the United States' Occupation of Japan: The GHQ Policy Toward Economic Recovery

GHQ policy had a huge impact on how Japan recovered from the devastation of World War II, not just in the short term, but over the long term until today. The GHQ, especially the GS (Government Section), had a clear policy to transform Japan from the old regime to a democratic, non-autocratic and non-militarized country. The GS was the hub for making these policies. A lot of the *New Dealers* who participated in the New Deal program of US President Roosevelt worked in the GS,[1] and the occupation policies strongly reflected their political and economic views. Further, it had strong influence on industrial policies in Japan, as we will review in the next section. GS personnel were very radical, and in his memoir, former Prime Minister Yoshida Shigeru even called them "radical elements," and mentioned that they used Japan as a laboratory for testing their theories.[2]

The old systems that GHQ considered necessary to change were: (1) political system and bureaucracy; (2) conglomerates (*zaibatsu*) which were controlled by family-owned holding companies; and (3) landlordism. These were considered to have supported Japan's militarism during the war. Based on notions of democratic reforms, the GHQ launched a series of policies to: (a) purge leaders and public officials who were responsible for the war; (b) abolish the internal security law, giving freedom of expression to the mass media, political parties and organizations, such as labor unions; (c) dissolve conglomerates and trusts; and (d) reform land ownership.[3] These policies changed the political balance between the existing old regime and the leftist political parties, small and medium enterprises, and the labor movement (Tsunekawa 2010), and had a huge influence on industrial policy, which will be discussed next as the essence of Japan's inclusive economic growth in the post-war period.

3.2 The Necessity to Improve Productivity for Recovery After the War[4]

3.2.1 Hyperinflation

After the war, Japan suffered very serious hyperinflation. There were two reasons for this: first, Japan's production capacity was totally destroyed by bombing during the war, as Table 4.1 shows.[5] Due to this, supplies of almost all goods were affected by shortages. To be more precise, almost no products were available at the regulated market price, and prices went up in the black market; second, the money supply was increased to monetize the huge stock of war debts to victorious countries. This very rapid money supply increase was another reason for hyperinflation. One of the policy priorities for the Japanese government, therefore, was to increase

Table 4.1 Indices of industrial production, 1946–1947

Period	*SCAP index (1930–1944 = 100)*	*United nations index (1937 = 100)*
1946	31.8	19
January	17.7	11
August	35.9	22
December	38.1	23
1947	38.8[a]	25
January	33.6	20
August	40.0	25
December	–	27

Source: Japanese Economics Statistics, GHQ, SCAP (Supreme Commander for the Allied Powers), September 1947, 7–9; and Monthly Bulletin of Statistics, United Nations, February 1948, 26 (Bisson 1949)

[a]First eight months only

production to bring basic food and necessary goods to people and to stabilize inflation.[6]

During the same period, the dissolution of the conglomerates was implemented. Bisson, the top economic analyst of the GS at GHQ, thought that during the war Japanese cabinets were largely controlled by conglomerates and industrial capitalists (Schonberger 1980). In 1947, the GHQ required the stock owned by the conglomerates' holding companies to be sold to the public.[7] At the same time, the GHQ adopted policies to promote SMEs as a counter force to the former conglomerates' larger firms. Policies such as the establishment of an SME agency to support new SMEs and help them compete with the erstwhile-conglomerate companies; the enforcement of anti-monopoly laws in 1947; and the establishment of the Japan National Finance Corporation for SMEs in 1953 to support SMEs financially were introduced. These SME-related policies made Japan's industrial policy more inclusive, as we will see later.

3.2.2 *Labor Movement*

Other than hyperinflation, there was another reason underpinning the necessity for productivity increases. While increase in production was the policy priority in Japan at this time, the labor movement also became very active soon after the war. This was also related to the GHQ policy mentioned above. The GHQ released communist political leaders such as *Tokuda Kyuichi* from prison as a part of its policy to give freedom of expression to mass media, political parties, and organizations. As soon as they were released, they attracted popular support.[8] At the same time, Article 28 of the Constitution of Japan promulgated in November 1946 guaranteed the three rights of work (the right of workers to organize, to bargain, and to act collectively).

Against the GHQ's intentions however, the labor movement became too active and radical.[9] With the establishment of the People's Republic of China in 1949 and the start of the Cold War between the United States and the Soviet Union, the GHQ changed its stance on the labor movement and tried to repress it.[10] However, the labor movement continued to spread all over Japan. As the labor movement became stronger, conflict between the government and labor movement increased day by day. In 1950, the GHQ started its red purge of government and journalism, as well as private companies (for a detailed discussion on this topic, please refer to Shimada 2018a). Finally, private companies were under pressure to increase production to tackle the shortage of all kinds of goods from basic food to steel in the market and to increase productivity with less labor because of the strong labor union movement. Otherwise, the shortage of labor would impede any production increase.

3.2.3 Cold War

As described above, there was strong incentive for private companies to increase productivity. At the same time, during this period the United States was enthusiastic about transplanting the productivity movement not only to Japan but also to war-torn Europe through their aid programs such as the Marshall Plan and the Point Four Program.[11] The main objective for the United States was to influence labor unions, keeping them as social democrat and not allowing them to become communist (Sovietization). Therefore, it was natural for the US government to support the productivity movement in Japan, as Japan was strategically important in East Asia. In 1951, a plan was drafted in Japan to establish a productivity organization with support from the FOA (Foreign Operation Administration) of the US government (Shimada 2015a, 2017a, 2018a, 2019; Shimada and Sonobe 2018; Higuchi and Shimada 2019).[12]

3.2.4 Creating Social Innovation

The plan to introduce the productivity movement met fierce opposition from labor unions (through the *Sohyo* or General Council of Trade Unions of Japan). The unions feared that with increased production, jobs could be cut, and work intensified for employees. So, in 1955 they declined to participate in the US-assisted productivity movement. However, as it was suggested by the United States that there be three partners (government, private companies, and labor), labor was essential for the country to receive aid from the United States. As the aid plan was stalled, long negotiations between the three sides were held. Finally, as a compromise, the JPC (Japan Productivity Center) issued three guiding principles for the productivity movement, influenced by the Philadelphia declaration of the ILO (International Labor Organization) of 1944. Based on this, labor agreed to participate in the movement, stressing the importance of "industrial democracy." With this agreement, many bureaucrats and business personnel studied productivity improvement with support from the United States. This significantly helped Japan's manufacturing sector to grow, and the Toyota Production System (TPS) or *Kaizen* was born from the productivity movement and spread all over Japan.

The principles are as follows:

1. Expansion of employment

In the long term, improving productivity should lead to expanding employment. However, from the standpoint of the national economy, a public-private partnership is essential in formulating valid policies to prevent the unemployment of surplus personnel through job relocations or other measures.

2. Cooperation between labor and management

Labor and management must cooperate in researching and discussing specific methods to improve productivity in consideration of specific corporate circumstances.

3. Fair distribution of the fruits of productivity

The fruits of productivity should be distributed fairly among labor, management, and consumers in line with the state of national economy.

There were dual aims. One was to enhance competitiveness to expand markets by utilizing resources effectively and scientifically, while at the same time reducing production costs. The other was to boost employment and to enhance real wages and the standard of living. The expansion of employment and wages was very important to improve living standards in

Japan. This also changed the nature of labor-management relations from combative to collaborative. Without this collaborative partnership between labor and management, high economic growth may not have occurred. In 1960, Prime Minister Hayato Ikeda also announced a plan to double the income of the Japanese people in ten years. This collaborative relationship between employers and employees was the basis of the inclusive economic growth of Japan.

4 Impacts on Wage: *Kaizen* as Social Innovation

Then, what were the impacts on labor, especially on wage and living standards? Figure 4.3 shows the labor compensation in Japan's GDP by firm size. As it is clear from the figure, labor share has been steadily increasing in both large firms and SMEs since the 1960s in Japan. This is in sharp contrast with the current global trend seen in Fig. 4.1, which shows a declining trend in labor share.

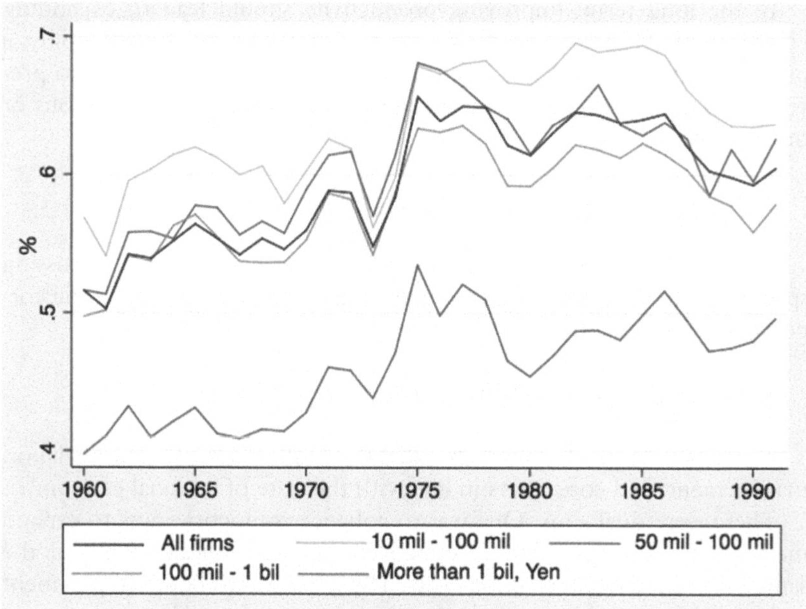

Fig. 4.3 Share of labor compensation in Japan's GDP by firm size. (Source: Author, based on Penn World Table 9.0)

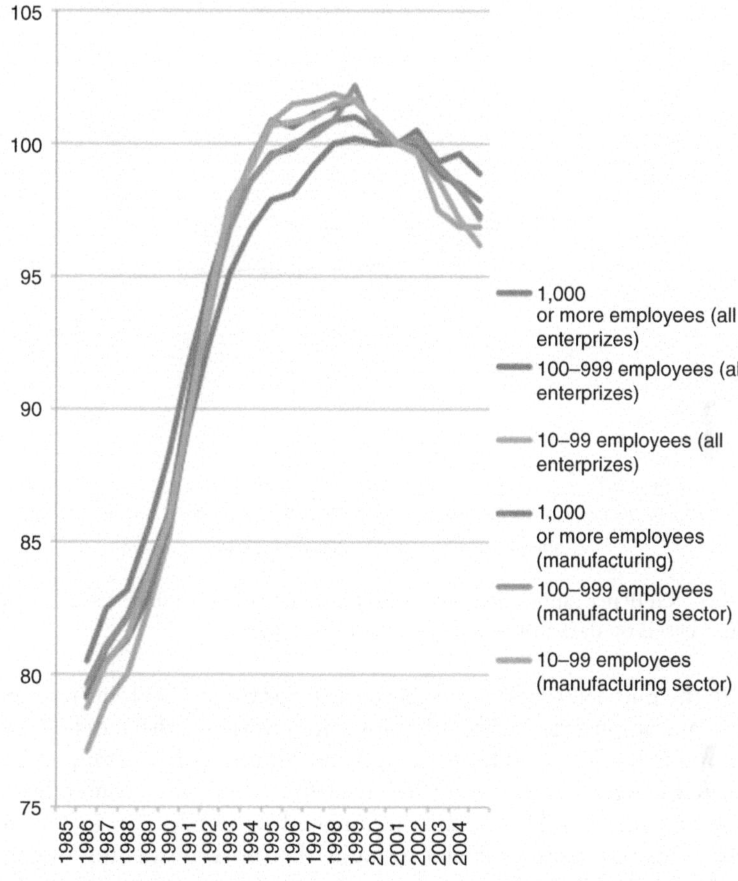

Fig. 4.4 Wage rate index of scheduled cash earnings and bonus in number of months by industry and by size of enterprise (1985–2004). (Source: Author, based on information from the Statistics and Information Department, Minister's Secretariat, Ministry of Health, Labor and Welfare)

Figure 4.4 also shows that the wage rate index by industry and by size of enterprise increased at the same rate not only for large companies but also for micro and small enterprises. As wages increased, living standards have improved in Japan.

As shown in Fig. 4.5, as GDP per capita increased, the ratio of households on welfare rapidly decreased from around 40% in 1952 to around

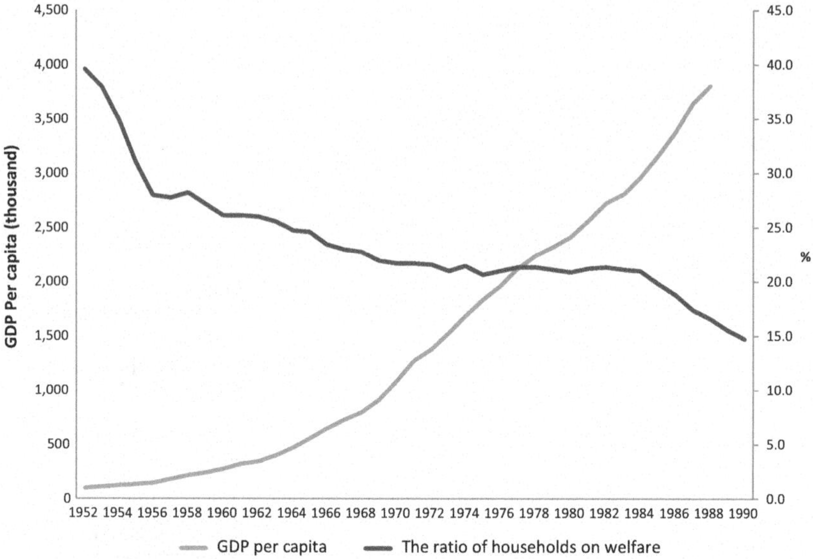

Fig. 4.5 GDP per capita and households on welfare of Japan since 1952. (Source: Author, based on data from the Government of Japan)

20% in the mid-1970s. We used this measure as there is no long-term time series data on poverty in Japan because there was no official definition of the poverty line until 2009. Although the Ministry of Welfare published estimated poverty rates from 1953 to 1965 based on a comprehensive survey of living conditions, they terminated its publication in the mid-1960s. This was because it was thought that poverty was no longer an issue in Japan. Therefore, instead of the poverty ratio, this chapter uses "the ratio of households on welfare" as, even if this data is technically not very precise with respect to the poverty ratio, at least it can show us the trend of poverty over time. The ratio of households on welfare dropped to less than 15% in the early 1990s. Therefore, it appears that Japan's economic growth was pro-poor growth, especially during the rapid growth period from the 1960s to the 1980s.

East Asia including Japan is known for its record of high and sustained economic growth, as the World Bank (1993) discussed. This was also characterized by highly equal income distributions (Birdsall and Sabot 1993).[13] To develop its economy, soon after World War II, Japan developed an industrial policy called the *priority production system* and made huge investments in infrastructure. Both of these policy measures were the basis for Japan's high economic growth. These policies, however, do not explain why Japan's economic recovery after the war was inclusive. Economic growth does not necessarily become inclusive. The keys to understanding the inclusiveness were the tension with the labor union and the introduction of the productivity movement (later called *Kaizen* because of this tension). The introduction of *Kaizen* made Japan's economic growth inclusive (Shimada 2015b, 2017a; Shimada and Motomura 2017).

5 Conclusions and Policy Implications

As we have seen in this chapter, Japan created a social innovation through the process of conflict and negotiation between labor and employers to share the profits equitably. This innovation not only improved the lives of people but also strengthened the competitiveness of firms. This is because employees became loyal to the firms they belong to with life-time employment and company-specific labor unions (most Japan's labor unions are not organized by industry). Under life-time employment, the prospect of wage increases raises labors' motivation to work. This is not technological innovation, but an innovation to boost firm performance and, hence, economic growth. This win-win situation, achieving economic growth and equality, was a social innovation. Developing countries as well as developed countries need this social innovation to tackle the issue of inequality in the age of globalization and rapid economic growth. As we have seen in this chapter, *Kaizen* is essential knowledge, a missing piece, for both developed and developing countries to achieve equitable growth.

Notes

1. These include Courtney Whitney (Chief of the Government Section), Charles Louis Kades (Chief and Deputy Chief of the Government Section), and Thomas Arthur Bisson (Top Economic Analyst).
2. Mr. Yoshida singled out T.A. Bisson for special criticism (Schonberger 1980).
3. Land was confiscated in 1946 and 1947. This land reform reduced income inequality and expanded the middle class a lot.

4. For details of the discussion of this section, please see Shimada (2017b, 2018a).
5. The official SCAP index is based on the low 1930–1934 levels of production output. Bisson (1949, 104) mentioned that the UN index is a better measurement since Japan needed to reach at least the 1937 level of production to become economically self-supporting.
6. Following the hyperinflation, Japan was forced to adopt austerity measures, called the Dodge Plan, by the United States.
7. Bisson regarded the hyperinflation Japan suffered during this period as a result of conscious and deliberate policies of the conglomerates and bureaucrats. The various taxes against big stockholders became meaningless with a devalued yen. Further, he argued the inflation raised stock valuation of those companies, generating more gains (Schonberger 1980)
8. Bisson (1949, 44) mentioned that: "The Communists were the one group that could point to a consistent record of opposition to Japanese militarism and the war. This factor helped them to muster popular support as soon as their leaders were released from prison."
9. Bisson (1949, 74) recalled that: "….the occupant authorities became increasingly disturbed by the `left-wing` character of the programs sponsored by the new political parties. And after the first election in April 1946, the emphasis of occupant policy was placed on controlling rather than encouraging the growth of the popular movement."
10. Because of this change in policy, as Dower (2000) described, communist leaders, such as Tokuda, were embarrassed. Because of this, when they were released in October 1945, he read "Appeal to the People" that said: "We express our deepest gratitude that the occupation of Japan by the Allied forces, dedicated to liberating the world from fascism and militarism, has opened the way for the democratic revolution in Japan." Later, the communists were forced to justify his statement, saying that the reference to "Allies" included the Soviet Union.
11. With the aid from the United States, productivity centers were established all around Europe: UK (1948), Denmark (1949), Turkey (1949), Austria (1950), West Germany (1950), Netherlands (1950), Trieste (1950), Belgium (1951), Italy (1951), Switzerland (1951), Greece (1953), Sweden (1953), France (1954), among others (Shimada 2018a).
12. This is one of precursor organizations to the USAID (United States Agency for International Development).
13. Some academic papers have estimated the poverty rate. For instance, Otake (2003) estimated that the Gini coefficient very rapidly improved, especially in the 1960s. The coefficient was 0.31 in 1963, and it had become 0.25 by 1971.

References

Arrow, Kenneth J. 1962a. Economic Welfare and the Allocation of Resources for Innovation. In *The Rate and Direction of Inventive Activity: Economic and Social Factors*, ed. R. Nelson and National Bureau of Economic Research, 609–629. Princeton, NJ: Princeton University Press.

———. 1962b. The Economic Implications of Learning by Doing. *Review of Economic Studies* 29: 155–173.

Baily, Martin Neil, Charles Hulten, David Campbell, Timothy Bresnahan, and Richard E. Caves. 1992. Productivity Dynamics in Manufacturing Plants. *Brooking Papers on Economic Activity: Microeconomics* 23: 187–267.

Baily, Martin Neil, and Robert M. Solow. 2001. International Productivity Comparisons Built from the Firm Level. *Journal of Economic Perspective* 15 (3): 151–172.

Birdsall, N., and R.H. Sabot. 1993. Virtuous Circles: Human Capital Growth and Equity in East Asia. *Background Paper for The East Asian Miracle*. Washington, DC: World Bank, Policy Research Department.

Bisson, T.A. 1949. *Prospects for Democracy in Japan*. New York: Macmillan.

Dower, John. W. 2000. *Embracing Defeat: Japan in the Wake of World War II*. Kindle ed. W. W. Norton & Company.

Higuchi, Yuki, and Shimada Go. 2019. Industrial Policy, Industrial Development and Structural Transformation in Asia and Africa. In *Paths to the Emerging State in Asia and Africa*, Emerging-Economy State and International Policy Studies, ed. Keijiro Osuka and Kaoru Sugihara. Singapore: Springer.

Milanović, B. 2016. *Global Inequality: A New Approach for the Age of Globalization*. Cambridge, MA: Harvard University Press.

Otake, F. 2003. Was There the Expansion of Income Inequality? In *Income Inequality and Social Hierarchy in Japan*, ed. Y. Higuchi and The Ministry of Finance. Tokyo: Nihon Hyoronsha.

Piketty, T. 2014. *Capital in the 21st Century*. Cambridge, MA: Harvard University Press.

Schonberger, H. 1980. Thomas Arthur Bisson and the Limits of Reforms in Occupied Japan. *Bulletin of Concerned Asian Scholars* 12 (4): 26–37.

Shimada, Go. 2015a. The Economic Implications of Comprehensive Approach to Learning on Industrial Development (Policy and Managerial Capability Learning): A Case of Ethiopia. In *Industrial Policy and Economic Transformation in Africa*, ed. Akbar Noman and Joseph Stiglitz. New York: Columbia University Press.

———. 2015b. The Role of Social Capital after Disasters: An Empirical Study of Japan based on Time-Series-Cross-Section (TSCS) Data from 1981 to 2012. *International Journal of Disaster Risk Reduction* 14: 388–394.

———. 2017a. A Quantitative Study of Social Capital in the Tertiary Sector of Kobe—Has Social Capital Promoted Economic Reconstruction since the Great

Hanshin Awaji Earthquake? *International Journal of Disaster Risk Reduction* 22: 494–502.

———. 2017b. Inside the Black Box of Japan's Institution for Industrial Policy—An Institutional Analysis of Development Bank, Private Sector and Labor. In *Efficiency, Finance and Varieties of Industrial Policy*, ed. Akbar Noman and Joseph Stiglitz. New York: Columbia University Press.

———. 2018a. The US Aid Strategy for Productivity Improvement in Japan after World War II with a Focus on Labor Unions: Japan's Experience as a Recipient Country. *Journal of International Development Studies* 27 (2): 69–84.

———. 2018b. *United States' Aid to Japan in the Postwar Era for Improving Productivity—From Recipient Country to Donor Country*. Tokyo: JICA Research Institute.

———. 2019. Does Environmental Policy Make African Industry Less Competitive?—The Possibilities in Green Industrial Policy. In *The Quality of Growth in Africa*, ed. Ravi Kanbur, Akbar Norman, and Joseph Stiglitz. New York: Columbia University Press.

Shimada, Go, and Miki Motomura. 2017. Building Resilience through Social Capital as a Counter-Measure to Natural Disasters in Africa: A Case Study from a Project in Pastoralist and Agro-pastoralist communities in Borena, in the Oromia Region of Ethiopia. *Africa Study Monograph*. Supplement Issue No. 53: 35–51.

Shimada, Go, and Tetsushi Sonobe. 2018. Impacts of Kaizen Management on Workers: Evidence from the Central America and Caribbean Region. *JICA-RI Working Paper* (173).

Solow, Robert M. 1956. A Contribution to the Theory of Economic Growth. *Quarter Journal of Economics* 70: 65–94.

———. 1957. Technical Change and the Aggregate Production Function. *Review of Economics and Statistics* 39 (3): 312–320.

Stiglitz, Joseph, and Bruce C. Greenwald. 2015. *Creating a Learning Society: A New Approach to Growth, Development and Social Progress*. New York: Columbia University Press.

Tsunekawa, Keiichi. 2010. State-Building, Economic Development, and Democracy: The Japanese Experience. *World Development Report 2011 Background Case Note*. Tokyo: JICA Research Institute.

World Bank. 1993. *The East Asian Miracle—Economic Growth and Public Policy*. Oxon: Oxford University Press.

PART I

Introducing and Implementing *Kaizen*

CHAPTER 5

Kaizen Promotion in Ethiopia: A Role of the Government and Change of Mindset of People

Kimiaki Jin

1 Introduction

1.1 Background

The Ethiopian government began piloting *Kaizen* in 2009 and scaling it up in 2011 in Ethiopia. Following its satisfiable results of *Kaizen* promotion from 2011 until 2014, the government incorporated *Kaizen* dissemination into the country's five-year development plan (2015–2020). In the meantime, several international media[1] have covered *Kaizen* promotion in Ethiopia as a part of stories related to its good economic performance, epitomized by a decade of double-digit growth of the gross domestic product (GDP) from mid-2000s till early 2010s. Many African countries and regional organizations, such as the New Partnership for Africa's

Kimiaki Jin works for the Research Institute and the Private Sector Development Group, Industrial Development and Public Policy Department, Japan International Cooperation Agency (JICA), Japan.

K. Jin (✉)
Research Program Division, JICA Research Institute, Japan International Cooperation Agency (JICA), Tokyo, Japan
e-mail: Jin.Kimiaki@jica.go.jp

A. Hosono et al. (eds.), *Workers, Managers, Productivity*,
https://doi.org/10.1007/978-981-15-0364-1_5

Development (NEPAD), have also shown a strong interest in adopting *Kaizen*. Nowadays, *Kaizen* in Africa is attracting considerable interest from policymakers, practitioners, researchers and students.

Several key factors may have contributed to its rapid progress in Ethiopia. One factor in the supply side of *Kaizen* services may be the proactive role of the government guided by the then prime minister Meles Zenawi, as this chapter illustrates. However, the question is whether any method will generate good results when a government shows strong commitment. Also, assuming that this is not, by itself, a sufficient condition, we would need to consider what other key factors may have contributed to the promotion of *Kaizen* in Ethiopia. A factor which we would focus on in this chapter is how *Kaizen* creates changes on the ground as the nature of the approach itself brings benefits to its practitioners.

1.2 Framework of the Analysis

In order to deepen our understanding of the factors behind *Kaizen* promotion, this research focuses on the intrinsic character of *Kaizen* and analyzes how its application has contributed to the development of various capacities of practitioners within companies and organizations. To analyze the benefits for these practitioners, the "framework of capacity assessment" developed by UNDP (2008) and JICA (2008) is used. According to capacity assessment methods, capacity can be stratified into individual capacity, organizational capacity, and enabling environments.

It is also categorized into technical capacity in the form of techniques and particular knowledge and core capacity (capacity to address core issues in individual and organizational levels), which utilizes technical capacity to independently solve issues, including will, attitude, and leadership. Hosono et al. (2011) define core capacity as generic and crosscutting competencies and the ability to commit and engage, to identify needs and key issues, to plan, budget, execute, and monitor actions, and to acquire knowledge and skills. They point out that the challenge is how to enhance effectively such crosscutting core capacity.

In considering a framework of *Kaizen*, its tools and methods have dimensions focusing on issues related to technical/scientific aspects which can be calculated and controlled, and dimensions of human aspects of workers/management which cannot be calculated and controlled in the exact meaning (Jin 2018). Based on these categorizations, capacities can be divided, as shown in Table 5.1, for use in the research framework for

Table 5.1 Categorization of capacities

	Technical Aspects (measurable)	Human Aspects (difficult to measure)
Enabling Environment	Economic growth, regulatory system of business, and foreign exchange	Social norms, religious and cultural aspects, and mutual aid in a society
Organizational Capacity	Organizational structures, machinery & equipment, information technology, and resource allocation	Decision making systems, labor management systems, incentive system, (and corporate culture)
Individual Capacity	Technical capacity (sector specific technologies, skills and knowledge management)	Core capacity (discipline, will, motivation, learning attitude, leadership of individuals)

Source: Author, based on UNDP (2008) and JICA (2008)

further arguments. Core capacity, such as motivation, self-discipline and communication skills, is also characterized as a "non-cognitive" skill (Joshi 2014). And it has common elements with "socio-behavioral skills" such as aptitude for teamwork and empathy pointed out by the World Bank (2019).

One hypothesis of this research is that *Kaizen* may be accepted by the companies and organizations in Ethiopia because it addresses development of not only their technical capacity but also the core capacity of workers and management, which can be distinguished by using the framework of capacity assessment. Improvement of core capacity provides a means of stimulating the participation of workers, motivating learning and acceptance of changes for streamlining production systems in the company.

1.3 Structure and Methods of Analysis

In Sect. 2, this chapter illustrates how the government of Ethiopia has been promoting *Kaizen* in the country as a case study. The section first provides an overview of the government's strategies and actions to promote reforms since the current ruling party took power in 1991. This helps to provide a historical context regarding the role of *Kaizen*. It also explains, through focusing on developmental policy, why the government has shown strong commitment to implementing *Kaizen* across the country. The section further reports inputs and outputs of *Kaizen* promotion based on the government data.

In Sect. 3, the chapter describes changes resulting from the introduction of *Kaizen* into the companies/organizations where the staff became its actual practitioners. Major parts of this section depend on interviews and a questionnaire survey conducted with the practitioners. The structured survey questions, with a range of possible choices, were as follows: (1) what kind of *Kaizen* tools are being applied in the company, (2) what kind of positive changes are being created, and (3) do you want to proceed to a higher level of *Kaizen*. Because *Kaizen* covers a very broad range of tools and technologies at different levels, as shown in Table 5.2 (Sugimoto 2018), it is important to identify the tools applied for the assessment of capacity development as outcomes. Questions also covered challenges to the sustainability of the activities. Key questions made and results of the survey are found in the Appendix.

The chapter finally discusses possible implications in Sect. 4 followed by concluding remarks in the Sect. 5.

Table 5.2 Comprehensive features of *Kaizen* tools and technologies

Levels		Target* of technology: Quality	Productivity	Cost	Delivery	Others
Advanced *Kaizen*		Taguchi method Experimental design Quality function deployment Reliability	TPS: JIT Jidoka Leveling SMED TPM: Planed maintenance	Economic engineering NPV Target costing Activity-based costing	Decoupling point APS	
Intermediate *Kaizen*		TQM: Policy management Daily management Statistical quality control Verification	TPS: Kanban Poka-yoke TPM: Autonomous maintenance OEE Cell production TOC (Theory of constraint) IE: Multiple activity analysis	Value engineering Value analysis Standard costing	Cell production MRP Pull production	Value stream mapping SWOT analysis Five forces analysis Value chain analysis Ergonomics
Basic *Kaizen*	Fundamental technology	Control chart Process capability index OC process chart	IE: Process analysis Motion study, Time study Work analysis Work sampling Line balancing, Layout	Direct costing Cost accounting		
	Common** *Kaizen* tech.	•5S, •7 QC tools, •New 7 QC tools, •Why-why analysis, •Brain storming, •TWI •Visualization, •Muda elimination, •QC circle, •Cross functional team, •Suggestion system				
Meta *Kaizen* technology***		•PDCA, •SDCA, •QC Story, •Problem solving procedure, •Task achieving procedure ◎Project management				

* Target means purpose of each *Kaizen* technology.
** Common *Kaizen* technology is one that has several targets.
*** Meta *Kaizen* technology means ones that apply other *Kaizen* technologies according to situation.
• shows essential technologies to be learnt in the basic level. ◎ shows necessary technology to be learnt in the intermediate level.

Source: Sugimoto (2018)

2 Policy and Actions Taken by the Government of Ethiopia

2.1 Reforms Apart from Kaizen *in Ethiopia*

Ethiopian production systems have generally been characterized by low levels of productivity and inconstant quality of products compared with industrialized countries. The decision-making process in organizations is generally portrayed by strong top-down processes, but its implementation on the ground is often disorganized and not very efficient. Chanie (2001) argues that this is partly due to the low capacity of the civil service to cope with prevailing social, political and economic difficulties, as well as management innovations.

Cognizant of these facts, since the current ruling party assumed power in 1991 after defeating the former socialist government, reforms have been introduced across political, economic and social spheres. From 1996 until 2009, the Public Sector Capacity Building Program (PSCAP) was initiated to bring about comprehensive civil service reform, focusing on (1) expenditure management and control, (2) human resource management, (3) enhancement of the top management system, (4) improved service delivery and quality of service, and (5) ethics and judicial reform. The outcome of PSCAP was satisfactory (World Bank Group 2013).

Several other reform approaches were also attempted. Business Process Re-engineering (BPR) was implemented in parallel with PSCAP, commencing in 2004, because service delivery by public institutes was very slow, costly and non-responsive to the needs of customers (Gebrehiwot 2010). The concept of BPR emphasizes the fundamental reconsideration and radical redesign of organizational processes to realize a drastic increase in performance, particularly by eliminating the work that does not add any value for customers.

However, some evaluation reports on BPR (Debela 2009; Setegn et al. 2013; Kebede and Abetwe 2017) concluded that BPR had failed to bring about drastic change and contributed only limited improvement in the Ethiopian civil service delivery. In addition, there was dissatisfaction among workers at the organizations because BPR puts greater emphasis on processes that benefit the organizations than it does on human resources development. Absence of alternative employment or safety net schemes to absorb laid-off manpower resulting from the change process gave rise to negative perceptions of the process that severely hindered and eventually undermined the sustainability of BPR.

Furthermore, as part of the ongoing civil service reform that the government is undertaking, a balanced score card (BSC) has been under implementation since 2011. It is an approach that integrates strategic planning, implementing and measuring the performance of all actors involved in the realization of the goals and objectives of the country (MoCS 2013).

The Ethiopian government has a strong policy orientation toward the developmental state, as Meles Zenawi argues in his paper (Zenawi 2012). He defines the "developmental state" as the single-minded pursuit of accelerated development with the strong superiority of the public sector over the private sector. Along with this policy direction, the government led by Prime Minister Meles Zenawi and his successor Prime Minister Hailemariam Desalegn undertook 14 capacity-building programs to accelerate industrial development including Technical and Vocational Education and Training (TVET), Engineering Capacity Building Program (ECBP), Textile and Garments Capacity Building Program (TG-CBP), Private Sector Development Program (PSDP) and Information Communication Technology Development Program (ICT-DP).

Outcomes of the capacity-building programs included the establishment of eight institutes, such as the Textile Industry Development Institute (TIDI), Leather Industry Development Institute (LIDI), and Metal Industry Development Institute (MIDI). These institutes provide support for the development of specific technical skills, which is technical capacity, for private companies in priority subindustries. Furthermore, the government has been simultaneously investing heavily in the development of key infrastructures such as transportation, power supply and industrial parks, and applying different industrial development tools to attract foreign direct investment as Oqubay (2015) describes.

Since 1991, the economy of Ethiopia had fluctuated, attributing to the character of a rain-fed agrarian economy. However, from 2004 the economy has been in a high growth trajectory and performed double-digit growth for more than a decade.[2] This growth was sustained by a balanced growth of agriculture, industry and services[3] until 2013. From 2014, growth of the industry has become higher than that of other sectors, which has triggered economic transformation.[4] On the other hand, growth of the manufacturing industry is not significantly high and its share in GDP remains at 4.3 percent as of 2016, which is not higher than its average between 2003 and 2016 (4.7 percent). Therefore, the country does not yet reach a stage wherein growth of the manufacturing industry leads to the country's economic growth. It means that the impact of *Kaizen* at the macro level in the manufacturing industry is not yet visible. In addition, causality between *Kaizen* and economic growth in the macro level is always difficult to analyze due to the complex multifactorial influences affecting both.

2.2 **Kaizen** ***Promotion by the Government***

The introduction of the Japanese *Kaizen* approach into Ethiopia was initiated by then Prime Minister Meles Zenawi in 2008, who directly requested assistance related to *Kaizen* from the Japanese government. Zenawi referred to a book chapter written by Kikuchi (2008) about a quality and productivity improvement project in Tunisia supported by the Japan International Cooperation Agency (JICA), and explained to the mission members[5] sent by JICA headquarters that he wanted to develop a *Kaizen* approach, as JICA had done in Tunisia, among other tools to promote industrial development. He promised the mission that the government would assign five to ten staff members to form a new unit that will work with Japanese experts on *Kaizen*.

His intentions regarding technology transfer are clearly detailed in his article on the developmental state (Zenawi 2012). He argues that the investment in human resources development to create continuous upgrading of standards is more effective in mastering existing technologies during the catch-up process for developing countries than investment in research infrastructure for innovation. Meles deliberately chose the Japanese *Kaizen* as a relatively low-cost approach for investing in human resources. In fact, *Kaizen* promotes the gradual and continuous improvement of existing technologies by utilizing the know-how of floor workers without the need for large-scale capital investment. Strong guidance by Meles was one of the reasons why the government has maintained a firm commitment to *Kaizen*.

In 2009 *Kaizen* was introduced to the Ethiopian manufacturing sector through the first project titled the "Study on Quality and Productivity Improvement (KAIZEN) in the Federal Democratic Republic of Ethiopia"[6] to test its applicability in the Ethiopian context. After verifying its effectiveness, the *Kaizen* unit with ten staff was expanded to become the Ethiopia Kaizen Institute (EKI) in 2011, an independent organization with a technical staff of 60 people who were trained to be consultants. This rapid scale-up of the implementing body of *Kaizen* created the capacity in the government to apply *Kaizen* across a wider range of targets. Several sector-specific development institutes, such as TIDI, LIDI and MIDI, were put in place to facilitate human resources development for industrialization. EKI is communicating closely with these sector-specific institutes and trying to mainstream *Kaizen* training for future industrial extension agents.

In mid-2014, the government formed the National *Kaizen* Council chaired by then Prime Minister Hailemariam Desalegn. The Council is the highest decision-making body for the national *Kaizen* movement and meets quarterly to deliberate on plans and endorse new directions. During the first extraordinary meeting that the Council had in September 2014, the Council set the month of September (the first month *Meskerem* in the Ethiopian calendar, commencing on September 11 or 12, depending on the leap year) as *Kaizen* month in order to promote the concept as a national movement. The government also started creating regional *Kaizen* institutes in the major regional states to further strengthen the dissemination of *Kaizen* across the country.

EKI, the main promoter of *Kaizen* activities in Ethiopia, provided training to 68,954 trainees and established 9658 *Kaizen* Promotion Teams (KPTs; a customized version of the Quality Control Circle (QCC)[7] in Ethiopia) in 473 target institutes from 2012/2013 to 2016/2017 (Mekonen 2018). It provides training and consultations to large and medium enterprises directly and training to micro and small enterprises through Technical and Vocational Education and Training (TVET) as Suzuki and Sakamaki report in Chap. 7 of this book. EKI received its recurrent and capital budget from the government, which amounted to 119.3 million birrs[8] since its establishment in 2011 until 2016/17.[9] EKI estimated that the benefits of *Kaizen* implementation between 2011 and 2016 reached 2169.5 million birrs, equivalent to US$105 million (Mekonen 2018). Mekonen vividly illustrates the details about the strategy, activities and challenges of EKI regarding *Kaizen* promotion.

One remarkable point is that while EKI implemented the *Kaizen* training within a framework of the project agreement between JICA and the government, EKI also started providing basic *Kaizen* consultations—soon after mastering basic skills—to the large-scale parastatal companies located outside Addis Ababa, who were not targets of the project. Such activities of EKI initially created tension between EKI members and JICA experts because the JICA team complained about the potential negative effects on the quality of *Kaizen* training implemented only by EKI staff, as well as delays in their project activities.

However, as a symbolic episode, it shows the strong ownership of and expectations by the Ethiopian participants related to *Kaizen* promotion in the country—a point that is now highly appreciated by JICA.[10] The management of EKI also became more strategic and capable of handling requests from high-level government officials regarding the application of *Kaizen* to parastatal factories, while at the same time working to maintain project activities supported by JICA.

Based on these achievements, the government of Ethiopia incorporated a proposal for *Kaizen* mainstreaming into its five-year national development plan, the Growth and Transformation Plan II (GTP II), in order to scale up *Kaizen* promotion across the country (NPC 2016).

On the other hand, in 2015 the government changed the supervising ministry of EKI from the Ministry of Industry to the Ministry of Public Service and Human Resource Development, which represents its policy expansion to applying *Kaizen*, not only to the development of industry but also to the public sector and broader human resources development. Local *Kaizen* institutes were also established in Addis Ababa and Dire Dawa municipalities and the Oromia Regional Government promoted *Kaizen* in local institutes and companies.

From 2013, EKI started sharing its experiences of *Kaizen* promotion with neighboring countries, receiving study missions from Sudan, the Democratic Republic of Congo, Tanzania and Zambia (JICA et al. 2018b). NEPAD also sent a mission in 2017 to learn about the Ethiopian model of *Kaizen* promotion in order to prepare a position paper on the Africa Kaizen Initiative, which aims to accelerate industrialization, economic transformation and creation of decent work in Africa between 2017 and 2026. Therefore, other countries and organizations in Africa are expecting to learn something from the case of Ethiopia.

3 *Kaizen* Practices and Outcomes in Companies/Organizations

Regarding the outcomes of *Kaizen*, there are several cases studied. Desta (2014) reported on the case of the *Kaizen* approach in the Methara Sugar Factory, which is located 200 km southeast of Addis Ababa. He cites data from the sugar company, indicating that the outputs of the sugarcane plantation and sugar production increased by 35 percent and 37 percent, respectively, as a result of *Kaizen* techniques introduced in 2013. These improvements came after a serious decline in sugar output from 120,000 tons to 80,000 tons in the four years between 2009 and 2012.

Desta and Gebrehana (2015) further analyze the case of the Wonji Sugar Factory and conclude that the achievements of the factory thus far can be considered quite laudable, particularly those made by the factory workers and sugarcane producers, while the achievements by the employees in service and administrative work lagged behind.

3.1 *Outline of the Survey*

In order to articulate how the practitioners in the companies understand the outcomes of *Kaizen* techniques, a questionnaire survey and interviews were conducted. The target group of the survey is 60 companies/organizations with accessible contact e-mail addresses[11] that EKI had provided to the author out of 631 companies trained as of July 2017. As multiple respondents[12] from one company were accepted, the 38 responses were collected from 33 companies/organizations.

Out of 33, 19 are large-scale companies/organizations, 9 are medium-scale ones, 1 is a small company and 4 are unknown ones. Regarding industry, eight are in textile, four are in construction, four are in metal, three are in food/beverage, three are in leather, five are in other manufacturing sector and six are in the service sector. In terms of location, 18 are in Addis Ababa and its suburb. Six are in Mekele, eight are in other rural towns and one's location is unknown.

These companies evaluated their *Kaizen* activities quite positively. Therefore, in order to avoid selection bias, the chapter doesn't judge if *Kaizen* is well accepted or not in Ethiopia. It can be said that the survey represents the opinions of a sample that is sympathetic to *Kaizen*, and who can provide an explanation of why *Kaizen* has been accepted by them. However, for the judgment on acceptance of *Kaizen* in Ethiopia, it needs to observe further proliferation of *Kaizen* in the country.

3.2 *Outcomes of* Kaizen *in Companies/Organizations*

Figure 5.1, composed of two bar graphs, compares two interlinked features—one is tools applied by *Kaizen* activities on the left side and another is changes created in the workplace as results of *Kaizen* activities on the right side.

Figure 5.1 (1) shows the percentage of the respondents who answer the question on what kinds of *Kaizen* tools are applied in the respondents' own workplace (multiple-choice). As *Kaizen* consists of many different

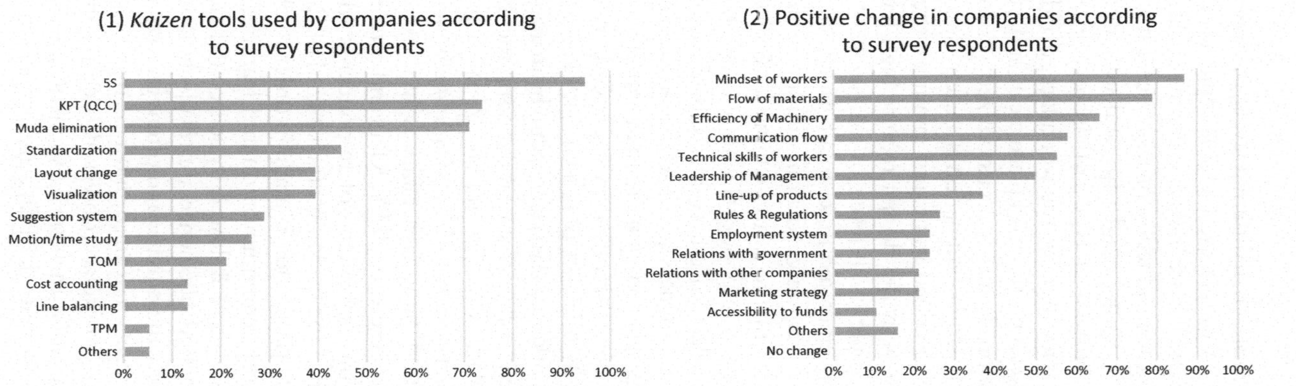

Fig. 5.1 *Kaizen* tools and positive changes. (Source: Author)

tools and methods categorized in different levels, the replies vary. However, in more than half of the workplaces, the tools applied are 5S, KPT (QCC), and *muda* elimination, which are basic and common *Kaizen* tools that can target several issues in the production process (see Table 5.2).

5S (sort, set in order, shine, standardize and sustain) is a housekeeping tool to implement the bottom-up type participatory process of sorting out and disposing unnecessary items at the workplace, deciding where to put necessary items, and keeping the workplace clean and in good condition. KPT (*Kaizen* Promotion Team) is a customized version of the Quality Control Circle (QCC). *Muda* elimination is an activity to identify any step which does not produce added value and minimize them from the production process. These activities do not require high-level technical skills but participation of people in all levels of management, supervisors and workers to apply simple rules and make small efforts.

Figure 5.1 (2) shows responses to a question on what kinds of positive change have resulted from the introduction of *Kaizen*. The bar graph indicates the percentage of respondents who select each choice (multiple-choice) although the selection criterion is subjective based on working experiences of each respondent who is a leader of *Kaizen* activities in each workplace. The change selected by more than half of respondents, ranked in order according to the most often chosen, are (1) mindset of workers, (2) flow of materials, (3) efficiency of machinery, (4) communication flow, (5) technical skills of workers and (6) leadership by management. "Mindset of workers" was chosen by 87 percent of the respondents as a feature that changed in the workplace. Changes in flow of materials and efficiency of machinery can be direct results of 5S and *muda* elimination. Changes in mindset, communication flow, leadership as well as technical skills of workers can be indirect results of all 5S, KPTs and *muda* elimination.

Figure 5.2 shows the percentage of respondents who select choices (multiple-choice) against the question of what kind of changes in mindset have been observed. This question is made in order to clarify what mindset change is. Teamwork, communication and learning attitudes are the most commonly chosen three followed by self-confidence and proactiveness, while punctuality and obedience are relatively low. Although these changes are not precisely measurable and often ignored in many quantitative studies on the impact of *Kaizen*, most of respondents as leaders of *Kaizen* activities in the workplace observed such features as changes in mindset of workers based on their own experience. They are categorized as core capacity in the framework of capacity assessment.

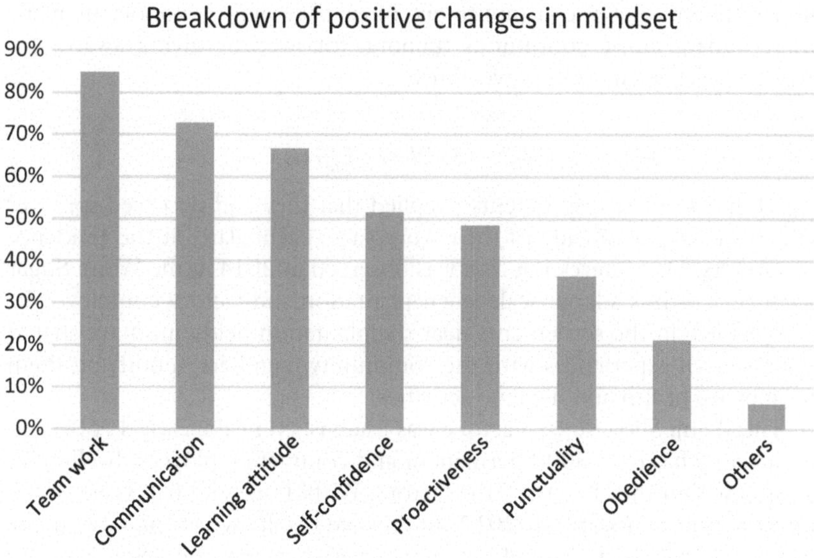

Fig. 5.2 Mindset changes. (Source: Author)

Regarding the responses to a question on profits created by the introduction of *Kaizen*, half of the respondents[13] selected that profits have increased a lot, while the other half chose that profits have increased only a little. The impacts on profit do not appear to depend on the length of *Kaizen* practice among this limited number of the sample. For the next step, all of them want to participate in higher level *Kaizen* training and a half of them are willing to participate even if they have to pay a training fee (current *Kaizen* training is provided by EKI free of charge).

Other results obtained from the survey indicate that, out of a total of 38 responses, only one respondent says that there has been a negative impact resulting from the introduction of *Kaizen*, referring to the time lost due to weekly meetings. For the other 36 respondents (excluding one non-answer), there has been no negative impacts caused by the implementation of *Kaizen* in their workplace.

Regarding challenges to sustainability, from the multiple-choice answers, the low participation of workers was chosen by one-third of respondents, with turnover of staff and limited training opportunities also selected by one-third of the respondents. For countermeasures, more than four-fifths say that the commitment of management is important while three-fourths chose continuous training, followed by giving awards for *Kaizen* practice chosen by two-thirds.

3.3 Spillover Effects

Three-fifths of the respondents[14] replied that they had observed spillover effects of *Kaizen* outside of their workplace, particularly at the residence of workers. One interesting case was observed in 2014 at the Wonji Sugar Factory, which is a large-scale sugar plantation and factory complex. The workers live in the settlements near the plantation fields and have shared their *Kaizen* experiences with the community members, modifying them to improve health and hygiene activities.

The Wonji Shoa Sugar Factory was established in the early 1960s, and it currently has over 3000 permanent and contract employees dwelling in a camp within the vicinity of the factory. Within one and half years of the introduction of *Kaizen* in 2012, impressive results were obtained at the health facilities that were also targets of *Kaizen* activities. Some of the rapid achievements observed include (1) an increase in customer satisfaction, (2) a decrease in the rate of malingerers visiting the health post, (3) a decrease in the incidence of health leave and referral system abuse, (4) improved resource management, (5) changes in the attitude of the physicians in that they started to perceive themselves as an integral part of the sugar production process and (6) removal of two top killer diseases—malaria and bilharzia (schistosomiasis)—which were among the top-ten health risks affecting the workforce.

Gradually, the frontline workers utilizing 5S who were impressed by the participatory nature of *Kaizen* started to take *Kaizen* practices with themselves from the factory floor to their homes and implemented it themselves, without management support. Recognizing the positive actions that individual workers had shown, the management was very encouraged and showed its willingness to support further implementation of *Kaizen* practices within workers' families in their settlements. Workers' family members and neighboring sugarcane growers outside of the plantations have been organized into women's and men's "development armies" and their activities are integrated into health extension services. These groups gather for weekly meetings every Friday, discuss their problems and search for robust solutions. Moreover, they perform weekly cleaning in their respective villages, drain swamp areas, burn dry waste, and tackle local crime through community policing.

These activities in the communities are a spillover effect of the introduction of *Kaizen* into factories and health facilities, especially through the development of the core capacity of the people, as discussed later. And they are similar to community development activities in the post-war reconstruction period in Japan called livelihood improvement or *Seikatsu-Kaizen* (JICA 2011).

However, business at the Wonji Shoa Sugar Factory has been stagnating during the last several years because of financial constraints, logistic issues and security conditions caused by political instability in the country.[15] Although the workshop of the factory has been maintained in good condition due to 5S practices and the hospital workers are continuing KPT activities as of early 2018, the sustainability of *Kaizen* has become a critical issue. The turnover of staff who have been trained as *Kaizen* leaders and the lack of upgraded information and training programs have affected the motivation of workers, although the company keeps providing basic training programs for newly recruited staff. Some workers have started feeling that KPT is creating additional work for them, and the momentum within the groups has not been as high as before.

4 Discussion

4.1 The Role of the Government

As the past actions of the government of Ethiopia described in Sect. 2 show, promotion of *Kaizen* in the country was initiated and guided by the government, particularly by former Prime Ministers, Meles Zenawi and Hailemariam Desalegn. The government established EKI, a promotion organization, and allocated the necessary resources. The management of EKI was capable and strategic in effectively utilizing resources mobilized from Japan, a fact that was also highly appreciated by the JICA staff. EKI and high-ranking government officials organized a big campaign to raise public awareness. The *Kaizen* promotion system has been further strengthened by the establishment of regional *Kaizen* institutes. These actions resulted in the change of mindset of workers in addition to improving the flow of materials and efficiency of machinery described in Sect. 3.

This pattern of *Kaizen* promotion is similar to the one introduced to Singapore, led by then Prime Minister Lee Kuan Yew and supported by JICA, in the 1980s (NPB and JICA 1990). The case is a typical example of government-led *Kaizen* dissemination argued by Homma in Chap. 6 of this book. And an important point of the case in Ethiopia is that the approach taken by the government is neither top-down enforcement nor uniform application of *Kaizen* activities to companies/organizations. It creates good practices first by applying *Kaizen* to selected companies to be a model for other wider target groups and encourages them to adopt similar practices.

Even prior to the *Kaizen* promotion, the government of Ethiopia was undertaking a series of efforts to improve the capacity of the public sector starting from the mid-1990s. This was followed by efforts to support the private sector from the mid-2000s, backed up by a deliberate policy study on the developmental state by Zenawi. Therefore, it is obvious that the proactive role of the government as a promoter of *Kaizen* is one of the key factors to create the results.

The institutional setting of EKI is summarized in Table 5.3 (1) as capacity development of a *Kaizen* promotion organization, which is a supply side system in Ethiopia. As a promoter of *Kaizen*, EKI has introduced incentive systems, a better salary system than other public organizations and the opportunity of a master's degree education to promising staff, as important organizational capacity (Mekonen 2018). EKI keeps providing training to its staff through classroom training and in-company training, which develop the technical skills of *Kaizen* as well as the mindset of staff as individual capacity.

4.2 *Responses by the People in the Workplace*

Although monetary benefit is important, there are other benefits that are not in monetary terms but appreciated by the practitioners. It is because half of the survey respondents have selected that monetary benefit is only a little but show willingness to learn more about *Kaizen*. The practitioners appreciated changes created by *Kaizen*.

Out of six major positive changes created by *Kaizen*, flow of materials, efficiency of machinery, and technical skills of workers are categorized as technical aspects of capacity. Mindset of workers, communication flow and leadership of management are understood as human aspects of the capacity under the framework of capacity assessment (see Table 5.3 (2)).

Table 5.3 Issues improved by creation of EKI and introduction of *Kaizen* in companies

	(1) Institutional setting of EKI		(2) Positive change in companies	
	Kaizen Promoters		*Kaizen* Practitioners	
	Technical Aspects	Human Aspects	Technical Aspects	Human Aspects
Enabling Environment	Developmental state policy and public sector reforms by the government		Economic growth and atmosphere of social change	
Organizational Capacity	Establishment of EKI, allocation of budget, and preparation of work plan with quantitative targets	Strategic leadership, better salary and education system as incentives for the staff	Better flow of materials and efficiency of machinery (by 5S and *muda* elimination)	Better communication and leadership in the company (by implementation of 5S, *muda* elimination and KPT activities)
Individual Capacity	Technical knowledge and methodologies to be *Kaizen* consultants	Development of *Kaizen* mindset among staffs as consultants	Improved technical skills of workers	Changed mindset of workers and managements (in terms of team work, communication and learning attitude)

Source: Kimiaki Jin

Changes in flow of materials and efficiency of machinery are typical outputs of *Kaizen* activities and technical skills of workers may be developed in connection with them.

4.2.1 Development of Core Capacities Through Kaizen

It can be said that observed change of mindset of workers (teamwork, communication, learning attitude) and leadership of management are results of collective activities of 5S, QCC and *muda* elimination.

As explained in Sect. 3, 5S involves bottom-up-type participatory activities of housekeeping, which can foster capacity of people to work in a group with good communication and to keep rules and regulations that they have set. Although it is a simple and basic tool, it provides foundation for application of advanced tools of *Kaizen* like Total Quality Management (TQM), Toyota Production System (TPS) and Total Productive Maintenance (TPM) (Sugimoto 2018). There are JICA cooperation projects for improvement of hospital management that introduce 5S-CQI (continuous quality improvement)-TQM in Sri Lanka, Bangladesh,

Tanzania and other African countries (Take et al. 2015; Kanamori et al. 2016).

QCC involves small group activities in which workers are encouraged to contribute to improvement of daily work. QCC creates opportunity to utilize knowledge of frontline workers who are conversant with the conditions of the workplace. Through the efforts of improving their own work, workers can also develop better learning attitudes so that they can positively accept and manage various changes in workplace.

The Ethiopian government recognized the broad applicability of *Kaizen* to other sectors. Therefore, the government changed the supervising ministry of EKI from the Ministry of Industry to the Ministry of Public Service and Human Resource Development in 2015 and then to the Civil Service Commission under the Prime Minister's Office in 2018.

The capacities that provide foundation for utilizing other technical methodologies and influence on attitude and leadership as crosscutting competencies are the one we call core capacity. Mindset change of people through *Kaizen* application can be said to be a process of core capacity development. This core capacity, once developed, is referred to as a *Kaizen* mindset and is an important part of the development of society beyond traditional systems. And the development of core capacity is appreciated by people in Ethiopian context.

As the spillover effects observed among practitioners of *Kaizen* demonstrate, capacities developed by *Kaizen* have broad applicability. And the *Kaizen* mindset of people strengthened by better communication, teamwork and learning processes in the workplace may create stronger coherence of the workforce in the company, hence higher collective productivity. That is one of the reasons why *Kaizen* is accepted by many practitioners even if monetary profits are not necessarily high.

4.2.2 Job Security of Workers

Another minor but important aspect to be noted is that no one is really affected negatively by *Kaizen*. People do not want to be treated like a disposable workforce by employers through a reform process. This point has critical importance in societies with limited dynamism in labor markets, such as Ethiopia, because it is difficult to find new job opportunities once people are dismissed. Workers don't appreciate any reform activities that affect their job security negatively, which is the other side of the coin of productivity improvement.

It can be learned from the case of BPR that aims to reorganize existing systems effectively and dismantle the non-value-adding activities and processes. However, workers did not support BPR because of its technical and engineering approach and inadequate attention to human aspects (Debela 2009; Kebede and Abetwe 2017). *Kaizen* attracts more support from workers and creates a mindset to participate in change because it takes a balanced and human-centered approach between the technical and human aspects shown in Table 5.3.

A JICA report on the *Kaizen* project phase I in Ethiopia (JICA and GDMC 2011) briefly discusses two domains of dissemination of *Kaizen* activities in its conclusion chapter—namely institutionalization and human factors. For the human factors, the report states as follows:

> It is the men and women in the organization who actually work and execute what the organizations are supposed to deliver. An organization should manage its human resources in alignment with the organization activity goals and, in so doing, should strive to create a motivated workforce. Workplace *Kaizen*, in part, helps to improve employee motivation.

Sugimoto (2018) explains how *Kaizen* management responds once surplus manpower is generated through labor-saving activities. He says that it is the worst case if management makes the surplus workers redundant in order of their inferior work-related competence. A better way of labor saving is to pick out excellent workers from the production floor and to assign them to more creative jobs. This is one of the essences of *Kaizen*.

4.2.3 Sustainability of Kaizen *Activities*

Sustainability is another issue that requires careful examination. Most of the respondents selected one or more challenges related to sustainability, such as the limited participation of workers, limited training opportunities and high turnover of staff. Wonji Sugar Factory was once a good performer of *Kaizen*, but its officers in charge are now reporting challenges and remarking on the importance of continuous support from EKI for advanced training to maintain momentum. As countermeasures, the commitment of management and continuous training for workers are selected by the respondents.

These results imply that *Kaizen* is easy to start—even with limited investments—because of its significant focus on human aspects such as mindset change. However, in order to sustain the activities, continuous stimulation of the workers and tangible commitment from the management are essential.

In other words, *Kaizen* may be more sustainable if the *Kaizen* mindset is incorporated into corporate culture shared among the management and labor. In this context, the JICA *Kaizen Handbook* (2018a) states that the core value of *Kaizen* is placed in creating the attitude shared among all members of an organization who consistently pursue advanced levels of quality and productivity. Shared value among a certain size of a group of people has strong influence on the mindset of its members.

5 Concluding Remarks

Strong ownership and proactive actions—including the establishment of promotion organizations, resource allocation and public campaigns—are measures that the government can work on. However, these efforts may depend on how seriously the government believes in the effectiveness of *Kaizen* among other policy options. In the case of Ethiopia, the government has a clear vision that *Kaizen* needs to be promoted by the public sector instead of leaving it to the market mechanism.

If government doesn't have such developmental policy, the requirement of strong ownership may create a chicken-and-egg argument because the realization of tangible success in a short period requires a strong commitment from the government and strong commitment requires tangible evidence for success. However, visionary leaders (in terms of economic growth of a nation),[16] such as Lee Kuan Yew and Meles Zenawi, had their own confidence and guided their respective national movements.

Kaizen is effective in changing the mindset of people, particularly in strengthening motivation toward teamwork, communication and learning attitudes, which are categorized as core capacity. Hence, *Kaizen* can be one of the answers to the question on how to enhance core capacity effectively pointed out by Hosono et al. (2011). And, it may contribute to the development of socio-behavioral skills of workers that are increasingly important in the changing nature of work according to the World Bank (2019).

In many African countries, there may be a large potential to improve quality and productivity through the development of core capacity as observed in Ethiopia. These changes don't require high technical skills and large capital investment but do require collective efforts among people who can think and act by themselves with their own intrinsic motivation. We have to encourage and capacitate people by using *Kaizen* because, at the end of the day, all development we seek is for people.

Appendix

Table 5.4 Results of selected questions in the questionnaire survey

No.	*Question*	*Choices*	*Result*
C-20	When did your company introduce *Kaizen*?[a]	Before 2013	7
		2013/14	10
		2014/15	5
		2015/16	3
		2016/17 and after	13
		No introduction	1
C-21	What kind of *Kaizen* tools did you apply (multiple)?	5S	36
		Muda elimination	27
		Standardization	17
		Visualization	15
		Suggestion system	11
		KPT	28
		Line balancing	5
		Layout change	15
		Motion/time study	10
		Cost accounting	5
		TQM	8
		TPM	2
		Others	2
C-22	What kind of positive changes, if any, have been created by *Kaizen* activity (multiple)?	No change	0
		Efficiency of machineries	25
		Material flow	30
		Line-up of products	14
		Accessibility to funds	4
		Marketing strategy	8
		Relation with government	9
		Relation with other companies	8
		Rules and regulations	10
		Employment system	9
		Leadership of management	19
		Communication flow	22
		Technical skill	21
		Mindset of workers	33
		Others	6

(*continued*)

Table 5.4 (continued)

No.	*Question*	*Choices*	*Result*
C-23	If you chose "mindset of workers" in the above question, what kind of changes have been observed (multiple)?	Proactiveness[b]	17
		Self-confidence	18
		Learning attitude[b]	23
		Punctuality	13
		Obedience	8
		Communication	25
		Team work	29
		Others	2
C-24	Is there any negative change induced by *Kaizen*?	No negative change	36
		Yes	1
C-25	Do these changes bring better profit in monetary terms to the company?	No	0
		Yes, but only a little	16
		Yes, a lot	18
		Don't know	1
C-31	What are key challenges in sustaining *Kaizen* activities in your company (multiple) ?	None	3
		Participation of workers	14
		Difficulty of method	5
		Finance	5
		Training opportunity	12
		Business environment	4
		Turnover of staff	12
		Low commitment by management	9
		Security	0
		Others	4
C-32	What kind of measures are effective in sustaining *Kaizen* activities (multiple)?	Nothing	0
		KPT	23
		Awarding	25
		Commitment by management	33
		Continuous training	29
		Government campaign	3
		Economic growth	5
		Combination with other business support	7
		Others	4

(*continued*)

Table 5.4 (continued)

No.	*Question*	*Choices*	*Result*
C-34	Are you willing to participate in a higher level of *Kaizen* training?	No	0
		Yes, if free	21
		Yes, even charged	21
C-35	Do you know any spillover effect of *Kaizen* activities outside of your company?	No	14
		Yes	21
		Business partner	9
		Neighboring community	9
		Staff residence	14
		Others	2
C-37	Have you created or experienced any innovations in your company?	No	12
		Yes	24
C-38	If yes, did *Kaizen* contribute to the innovation?	No	5
		Yes	19

[a]The total number of responses to C-20 is 39 because one respondent selected two choices. The author interpreted that the company introduced *Kaizen* twice

[b]Regarding mindset, motivation and creativity are reworded to proactiveness and learning attitude, respectively, since others find it difficult to recognize motivation and creativity

Notes

1. For example, see https://www.bbc.com/news/business-26542963, https://www.bbc.com/news/av/business-31551228/ethiopian-businesses-adopt-japanese-kaizen-philosophy and https://allafrica.com/stories/201609261329.html.
2. The average GDP growth rate between 2004 and 2016 was 10.6 percent according to calculation based on the World Development Indicators. GDP per capita in constant 2010 US$ was 511 dollars in 2016 (WB 2018).
3. Between 2004 and 2014, both agriculture and service sectors maintained more than 40 percent of GDP share, respectively, while share of the industry sector was lower than 15 percent (WB 2018).
4. Share of industry in GDP grew from 11.9 percent in 2013 to 20.3 percent in 2016 (WB 2018).
5. Members of the mission who met Prime Minister Zenawi in December 2008 were Prof. K. Ohno, Prof. I. Ohno, Prof. Hosono, Mr. Kikuchi and the author.

6. The project was implemented from 2009 to 2011 as phase I, and included pilot activities of *Kaizen* in 30 companies, verified effectiveness of *Kaizen* and produced a set of manuals.
7. QCC is a small group at the workplace who discusses about and improves work at the production floor.
8. Equivalent to around US$5.8 million. The budget covered the whole cost for implementation of JICA project phase II during 2011–2014 (Project on Capacity Building for Dissemination of Quality and Productivity Improvement (KAIZEN)) and a part of the project phase III during 2015–2020 (Project on Capacity Development for KAIZEN Implementation for Quality and Productivity Improvement and Competitiveness Enhancement) as well as EKI's own promotion activities of *Kaizen*.
9. Project cost borne by JICA from JFY2011 to JFY2016 is 870.3 million yen (equivalent to US$9.42 million based on OECD Stat exchange rate).
10. JICA President awarded EKI in 2015 for its outstanding performance as a project counterpart.
11. EKI selected companies who have e-mail addresses and can smoothly communicate in English with a good response.
12. *Kaizen* officers in different departments in a large company were encouraged to respond to the questionnaire. Responses from the same company vary depending on departments due to different timing of *Kaizen* introduction and the character of independent small group activities in parallel. Hence the response obtained from each department is treated equally as other responses.
13. The respondents exclude three public organizations that don't earn any profit.
14. See C-35 in the Appendix.
15. A series of demonstrations, road blocks and burning down of public offices called Oromo protest that happened during 2015–2018 was one of the political and security problems of the country.
16. There may be different arguments on leaders in terms of democracy and human rights.

References

Chanie, P. 2001. The Challenges of the Civil Service Reform in Ethiopia: Initial Observation. *East African Social Science Research Review* 17 (1): 79–102.

Debela, T. 2009. Business Process Reengineering in Ethiopian Public Organizations: The Relationship Between Theory and Practice. *Journal of Business and Administrative Studies* 1 (2): 20–59.

Desta, A. 2014. The Art of the Kaizen Approach for Sugar Production in Ethiopia: Lessons from the Methara Sugar Factory. *International Journal of Operations and Logistics Management* 3 (3): 212–221.

Desta, A., and A.A.G. Gebrehana. 2015. Kaizen Management Issues at the Wonji Sugar Factory in Ethiopia: A Comparative Analysis. *European Journal of Management* 15 (2): 7–26.

Gebrehiwot, B.A. 2010. Comparative Analysis of Some Western versus Japanese Management Techniques in the Context of Ethiopia. http://www.grips.ac.jp/forum/af-growth/support_ethiopia/document/Berihu_Kaizen&BPR.pdf.

Hosono, A., S. Honda, M. Sato, and M. Ono. 2011. Inside the Black Box of Capacity Development. In *Catalyzing Development, A New Vision for Aid*, ed. H. Kharas, K. Makino, and W. Jung. Washington, DC: Brookings Institution Press.

Japan International Cooperation Agency (JICA). 2008. *Capacity Assessment Handbook: Project Management for Realizing Capacity Development*. Tokyo: JICA Research Institute.

JICA. 2011. *Wisdom of the Livelihood Improvement (KAIZEN) in Post-War Japan: Lessons Learnt from the First Developing Country*. Tokyo: JICA. http://open_jicareport.jica.go.jp/810/810/810_000_12066163.html.

JICA, and Global Development & Management Consultants (GDMC). 2011. The Study on Quality and Productivity Improvement (KAIZEN) in the Federal Democratic Republic of Ethiopia, Final Report. Tokyo: JICA. http://open_jicareport.jica.go.jp/810/810/810_000_12066163.html

JICA, UNICO International, and Japan Productivity Centre (JPC). 2018a. *Kaizen Handbook*. Tokyo: JICA. https://www.jica.go.jp/english/news/field/2018/180625_01.html.

———. 2018b. *Project Kenkyu Africa Kaizen Shien-ni-kakaru, Hyojun Approach Sakutei Chosa* [Study on Standardizing *Kaizen* Approaches for Further Dissemination and Deployment in Africa]. Tokyo: JICA.

Jin, K. 2018. Role of Kaizen in Japan's Overseas Development Cooperation. In *Applying the Kaizen in Africa: A New Avenue for Industrial Development*, ed. K. Otsuka, K. Jin, and T. Sonobe. Cham: Palgrave Macmillan.

Joshi, H. 2014. Non-cognitive' Skills: What are They and How Can They Be Measured in the British Cohort Studies? *CLS Working Paper 2014/6*. Institute of Education, University of London, London.

Kanamori, S., M. Castro, S. Sow, R. Matsuno, A. Cissokho, and M. Jimba. 2016. Impact of the Japanese 5S Management Method on Patients' and Caretakers' Satisfaction: A Quasi-experimental Study in Senegal. *Global Health Action* 9: 32852.

Kebede, A., and D. Abetwe. 2017. Implementation of BPR at a Public University in Ethiopia: A Fashion or a Solution? In *Management Challenges in Different Types of African Firms*, ed. L. Achtenhagen and E. Brundin. Singapore: Springer.

Kikuchi, T. 2008. The Quality and Productivity Improvement Project in Tunisia: A Comparison of Japanese and EU Approaches. In *Diversity and Complementarity in Development Aid—East Asian Lessons for African Growth*, ed. GRIPS Development Forum. Tokyo: GRIPS.

Mekonen, G.T. 2018. Kaizen as Policy Instrument: The Case of Ethiopia. In *Applying the Kaizen in Africa: A New Avenue for Industrial Development*, ed. K. Otsuka, K. Jin, and T. Sonobe. Cham: Palgrave Macmillan.

Ministry of Civil Service (MoCS). 2013. *In Brief: The Civil Service Reform Program in Ethiopia*. Addis Ababa: Ministry of Civil Service.

National Planning Commission (NPC). 2016. *Federal Democratic Republic of Ethiopia: Growth and Transformation Plan II (GTP II) (2015/16–2019/20). Vol. I: Main Text.* Addis Ababa: NPC.

National Productivity Board (NPB) and Japan International Cooperation Agency (JICA). 1990. *Further Fields to Conquer… A PDP Commemorative Publication.* Singapore and Tokyo: National Productivity Board and JICA.

Oqubay, A. 2015. *Made in Africa, Industrial Policy in Ethiopia*. Oxford: Oxford University Press.

Setegn, D., M. Ensernu, and P.K. Moorthy. 2013. Assessing the Effect of Business Process Reengineering on Organizational Performance: A Case Study of Bureau of Finance and Economic Development (BoFED), Oromia Regional State, Ethiopia. *Researchers World* 4 (1): 115–123.

Sugimoto, S. 2018. Kaizen in Practice. In *Applying the Kaizen in Africa: A New Avenue for Industrial Development*, ed. K. Otsuka, K. Jin, and T. Sonobe. Cham: Palgrave Macmillan.

Take, N., S. Byakika, H. Tasei, and T. Yoshikawa. 2015. The Effect of 5S-Continuous Quality Improvement-Total Quality Management Approach on Staff Motivation, Patients' Waiting Time and Patient Satisfaction with Services at Hospitals in Uganda. *Journal of Public Health in Africa* 6: 486.

United Nations Development Programme (UNDP). 2008. *Capacity Assessment Practice Note*. New York: UNDP.

World Bank (WB). 2018. World Development Indicators. https://data.worldbank.org/products/wdi.

World Bank. 2019. *World Development Report 2019: The Changing Nature of Work*. Washington, DC: World Bank.

World Bank Group. 2013. Implementation Completion Report (ICR) Review—Public Sector Capacity Building Program Support Project (PSCAP). Independent Evaluation Group (IEG). http://lnweb90.worldbank.org/oed/

oeddoclib.nsf/DocUNIDViewForJavaSearch/8525682E0068603785257B96007187CD?opendocument.

Zenawi, M. 2012. States and Markets: Neoliberal Limitations and the Case for a Developmental State. In *Good Growth and Governance in Africa, Rethinking Development Strategies*, ed. Akbar Noman, Kwesi Botchwey, Howard Stein, and Joseph E. Stiglitz, 140–174. Oxford: Oxford University Press.

CHAPTER 6

Kaizen Dissemination Through the Government and Private Sector in Southeast Asia: A Comparative Study of Malaysia, Indonesia, and Myanmar

Toru Homma

1 Introduction

Kaizen is an integral part of Japanese-style management (Imai 1986). Dissemination of *Kaizen* has accelerated in East Asia as Japanese companies moved abroad under the 1985 Plaza Accord (Ohno et al. 2009). In Southeast Asia, the approach to improving quality and productivity that underpins the operations of Japanese manufacturing industries has been introduced as part of long-term development. Japanese Foreign Direct Investment (FDI) and Official Development Assistance (ODA) contributed to this trend (JICA and JBIC 2008). *Kaizen* training has a positive effect on production management skills (Higuchi et al. 2015).

However, the methods by which *Kaizen* has been introduced, disseminated, and transformed in manufacturing industries in the context of specific Southeast Asian countries have not been thoroughly analyzed. Specifically, it is not yet known how the government and the private sector within each country have contributed to the dissemination process. It is

T. Homma (✉)
Senior Advisor, Japan International Cooperation Agency (JICA), Tokyo, Japan
e-mail: Homma.Toru@jica.go.jp

A. Hosono et al. (eds.), *Workers, Managers, Productivity*,
https://doi.org/10.1007/978-981-15-0364-1_6

essential to know how the government and the private sector can share the role of disseminating *Kaizen* in manufacturing industries so that government and donor community can consider how to intervene in *Kaizen* dissemination.

The patterns of *Kaizen* dissemination in Southeast Asian countries differ depending on their circumstances but can be categorized into government led and private sector led. Under the strong leadership of the government, the government-led pattern aims to improve productivity/quality, such as by introducing *Kaizen* systematically and often with the establishment of an exclusive public organization on productivity improvement. Singapore[1] and Malaysia are typical examples of this. In the private sector-led pattern, active investment by Japanese manufacturing companies and the establishment of factories in host countries, coupled with the formation of a supply chain involving local supporting industries, have brought about close business ties with local suppliers. Under such relationships, Japanese manufacturers, especially those in the automobile and electronics industries, actively introduce *Kaizen* to improve the quality and productivity of the local suppliers of parts and components. Thailand[2] and Indonesia are examples of this, although the former also has a strong government initiative in place.

This chapter compares the experiences of Malaysia and Indonesia, considered to represent the variations in these two patterns. The chapter examines the patterns in the introduction, diffusion, customization, and evolution of *Kaizen* in each country, focusing on the roles of government and the private sector.

In addition to Malaysia and Indonesia, Myanmar, which just opened up its economy in 2011, is another case study. In Myanmar, there is neither a strong government initiative nor a significant private sector movement in the manufacturing supply chain. However, there have been sporadic attempts by individual companies and organizations to introduce *Kaizen*.

As *Kaizen* is an integral part of Japanese-style management, some Japanese organizations[3] actively disseminate *Kaizen* in Southeast Asia for the mutual benefit of Southeast Asian countries and Japan.

2 Research Methodology

The research for this chapter is based on semi-structured interviews carried out in Malaysia, Indonesia, Myanmar, and Japan. In Malaysia, a series of semi-structured interviews were conducted in January 2018 with 11 Malaysia Productivity Corporation (MPC) officials (9 former management officials since the 1960s and 2 current ones), and 8 Malaysian-based companies mainly in the manufacturing industry. Similar interviews were conducted in Indonesia in January 2018, in Myanmar in February 2018, and in Japan sporadically from December 2017 to March 2018.

In addition to these interviews, Japan International Cooperation Agency (JICA) conducted a field enterprise micro-data survey in Indonesia from August to November 2017 to provide for an empirical analysis of supply chains and production networks under an industrial study project. The field survey was conducted by a contracted research team in the Institute for Economics and Social Research, Faculty of Economics, University of Indonesia (LPEM-FEUI[4]). This JICA-LPEM survey itself was composed of two parts: (a) a national-level survey in major cities with 262 interviewees and (b) a metalworking small and medium enterprise (SME) cluster in the Tegal Regency of the Central Java Province with 500 interviewees. This survey was not necessarily designed for this chapter but partially covered *Kaizen*-related questions and is utilized for this chapter's study (JICA and NRI 2019).

Based on the research methodology presented in this section, the following three (3) sections describe the dissemination of *Kaizen* in Malaysia, Indonesia, and Myanmar. The three sections are followed by aggregated findings from the research and then conclusions and implications.

3 *Kaizen* Dissemination in Malaysia

3.1 *The Malaysia Productivity Corporation (MPC) as the Key Driver for* Kaizen *Dissemination*

Malaysia has 31.6 million people (estimated in 2017)[5] with a GDP of US$ 296 billion (current US$ in 2015). Its GDP per capita is close to US$ 10,000 (current US$ 9768 in 2015). Its industry sector contributes to its economy and accounts for 39.6 percent (estimated in 2017) of gross value added (GVA). The electric and electronics, automobile, and other manufacturing industries emerged during the rapid industrialization process that began in the 1970s. Malaysia also has a strong government initiative toward industrialization, in particular during Prime Minister Mahathir's first term since the 1980s to early 2000s. Malaysia conducts a unique national car program such as Proton and Perodua, which aggregately have been overwhelming foreign car manufacturers including Japanese, although national car shares have been declining recently (JICA and IDCJ 2017).

Under the leadership of the Malaysian government, the Malaysia Productivity Corporation (MPC) has played a significant leading role in productivity/quality improvement since the setup of its predecessor the National Productivity Centre (NPC) in 1962 as a joint project between the United Nations (UN) and the International Labour Organization (ILO). The NPC became a statutory body in 1966, was transformed into the National Productivity Corporation (NPC) in 1991, and was finally renamed the Malaysia Productivity Corporation (MPC) in 2008. MPC itself has been evolving overtime. Its main focus has shifted from human resource development to productivity awareness, research and development, and competitiveness and innovation. MPC has approximately 200 staff members and it provides training programs, corporate consultation services, research and development, information, publications, system development, and other services (MPC 2018 and NPC 2006).

Kaizen and associated Japanese methodologies were introduced into Malaysia through the Malaysia Productivity Corporation (MPC), particularly through the Look East Policy, a Malaysian government initiative to learn from the nation-building experiences of Japan (and Korea) in 1983. Thousands of Malaysian people from the government, NPC, private sector, and academia were dispatched to Japan as trainees and students to learn from Japan including *Kaizen*. Once *Kaizen* was introduced into NPC/MPC, the *Kaizen* tools were customized to suit the Malaysian way of doing things and MPC's comprehensive approach. Typical examples are "5S" and the "Quality Control Circle (QCC)," which were customized as "Quality Environment (QE)" and the "Innovation and Competitiveness Circle (ICC)" (MPC 2013).

JICA and IDCJ (2018) suggest that the government-created NPC (now Malaysia Productivity Corporation (MPC)) was given a pioneering role in productivity and quality improvement and produced human resources for industries, together with the following training programs under the Look East Policy. The Association for Overseas Technical Cooperation and Sustainable Partnerships (AOTS) and the Asian Productivity Organization (APO) also provided training programs for industries. These formed the basis for Malaysian industry and multinational companies (MNCs), including Japanese automobile and electronic industries, to introduce their productivity improvement approaches including *Kaizen*. MNCs also contributed to the dissemination of *Kaizen* in Malaysia through their supply chain. Maarof and Mahmud (2015) suggested continuous improvement by *Kaizen* is necessary for Malaysian SMEs for improving their performance.

In Malaysia, *Kaizen* has been understood in various ways but has generally been integrated as a part of a comprehensive productivity improvement system, together with Total Quality Management (TQM), Lean Management, and Six Sigma, rather than the prevailing *Kaizen* umbrella concept. That being said, its core concept is well recognized as "continuous improvement" and it is considered as an effective tool to motivate *gemba* (the factory floor), according to the series of interviews.

3.2 Results from Semi-structured Interviews

This subsection discusses the value of Malaysia Productivity Corporation (MPC) as a contributor to *Kaizen* dissemination in the Malaysian manufacturing sector. The series of semi-structured interviews[6] carried out in Malaysia reveals that MPC interviewees strongly agreed—at a 4.82 average on a scale[7] of 0–5—that the MPC has contributed to productivity and quality improvement in the Malaysian manufacturing sector. Likewise, the MPC interviewees strongly agreed—at a 4.55 average on the same scale—that the MPC has been contributing to dissemination of *Kaizen*. Meanwhile they agreed at a slightly lower level of 3.27 point on the same scale that productivity/quality improvement approaches have been well disseminated in the Malaysian manufacturing sector because dissemination at SME level has not been fully achieved. Interviewed companies noted at a level of 4.75 that productivity/quality improvement approaches such as *Kaizen* are useful for their operations. These data are shown in Fig. 6.1.

This result represents a limited number of views and is biased because it is Malaysia Productivity Corporation (MPC's) self-evaluation and interviews on *Kaizen* by Japanese interviewers. However, it is significant that it shows relatively strong recognition by ex-MPC high-level officers and interviewed companies of the MPC's contribution to productivity and quality improvement in the manufacturing sector in Malaysia, as well as that of *Kaizen*. At the same time, the usefulness of productivity/quality improvement approaches such as *Kaizen* is also well recognized.

From a series of interviews, Malaysia Productivity Corporation (MPC's) strengths can be summarized as follows: (a) strong mandate to lead productivity improvement in Malaysia, (b) appropriate and timely adaptation/shift of MPC's function along with necessities, (c) customization of foreign practices such as *Kaizen* to the Malaysian culture, and (d) a wide variety of services to deliver such services efficiently.

In summary, Malaysia Productivity Corporation (MPC) has played a significant role in *Kaizen* dissemination in Malaysia's manufacturing sector reflecting strong government initiative in productivity improvement and it has triggered the private sector's own contributions to *Kaizen* dissemination in Malaysia.

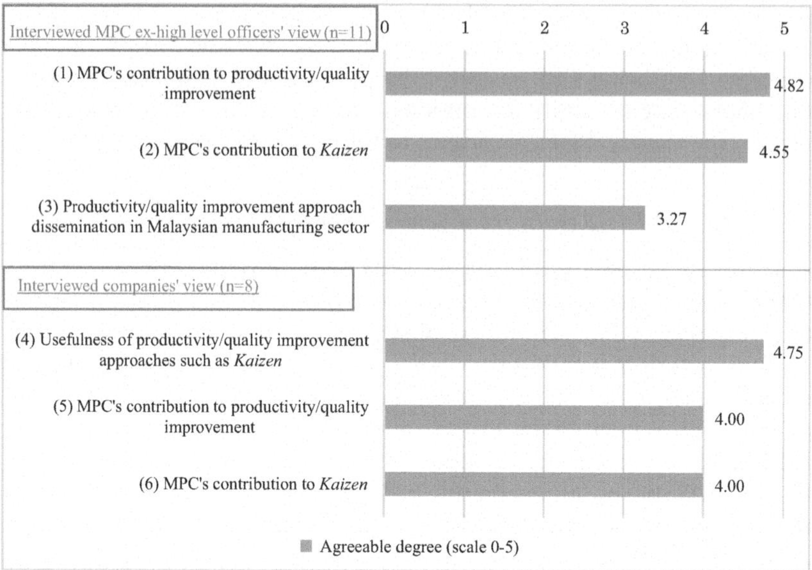

Fig. 6.1 Subjective recognition on dissemination of productivity/quality improvement approach such as *Kaizen* in the manufacturing industry in Malaysia. (Source: Author)

4 *Kaizen* Dissemination in Indonesia

4.1 Kaizen *Dissemination Through Supply Chain Transaction*

Indonesia has the largest population in Southeast Asia and the fourth largest in the world, at 264.0 million (estimated in 2017)[8] with a GDP of US$861 billion (current US$ in 2015). Hence its domestic market potential is huge. Indonesia's GDP per capita is US$3347 (current US$ in 2015), which is just above the commonly considered threshold (US$3000 per capita) to begin rapid motorization. Its industry sector counts at 41.3 percent (estimated in 2017) of GVA. Indonesia is the second largest automobile producer and has the largest market in Southeast Asia at around 1.2 million per year. After the 1970s, almost all major Japanese automobile assemblers settled their factories under joint venture with local capital and they count much more than 90 percent of automobile domestic production share[9] in Indonesia. They have established firm supply chain networks involving several hundreds of local suppliers from tier-1 (those that produce parts and components and supply them directly to the assemblers) and tier-2 (those that produce parts and components and supply them to tier-1 companies), and further subcontracting local smaller parts and component manufacturers.

In Indonesia, the private sector played a significant role in introducing *Kaizen*, in particular, the factory operations of Japanese manufacturers and their supply chain transactions with local suppliers. They act as the vehicles for disseminating *Kaizen* in Indonesia. For example, an automobile manufacturing company identifies several local suppliers every year and provides an intensive program for them to acquire practical quality and productivity improvement methodologies including *Kaizen*. Compared to Malaysia's, Indonesia's private sector played a more significant role in disseminating *Kaizen* in its manufacturing sector.

Figure 6.2 shows that the JICA-LPEM survey[10] reveals that 77.5 percent of the surveyed companies (n = 262) conduct *Kaizen*[11] and 84.4 percent of them do 5S.[12] The surveyed companies obtain information/services/support from around 40 percent of their customer companies,[13] while they also receive information/services/support from 25 to 30 percent of their suppliers.[14] With an average of 207.7 employees, the surveyed companies are relatively large-scale companies,[15] capable[16] enough to systematically learn and implement *Kaizen*.

While many surveyed companies rely on *Kaizen*-related information/services/support from their customer companies and suppliers, fewer surveyed companies also obtain such information/services/support from other companies (domestic/foreign/SOE[17]) within their supply chain (customers/suppliers), government, or NGO/CSO[18] as shown in Fig. 6.2(b). This implies[19] that some surveyed companies obtain *Kaizen*-related information/services/support from multiple sources, including non-supply chain companies, governments, and others, but less frequently than from their supply chain companies (customers/suppliers).

4.2 The Effectiveness of Kaizen *in Indonesia*

The JICA-LPEM Survey provides some clues on the effectiveness of *Kaizen* at least among the surveyed companies (n = 262) in major cities[20] in Indonesia, disseminated mainly through their supply chain relationship. The *Kaizen* Engagement Index (KEI), created in this chapter and calculated using Eq. (6.1) below, is designed to show whether *Kaizen* and 5S are implemented in a surveyed company and whether information/

services/support for *Kaizen*/5S are provided by its customer companies. KEI's score is calculated on a 0–10 scale.

$$\textit{Kaizen}\ \text{Engagement Index}\left(\text{KEI}\right) = \left(ck + cf + \Sigma_{i=1}^{5} kc_i / 5 + \Sigma_{i=1}^{5} fc_i / 5\right) / 2.5 \quad (6.1)$$

where *ck* is a yes/no variable showing whether a surveyed company conducts *Kaizen* for its production process improvement and *cf* is a yes/no variable showing whether the surveyed company conducts 5S. The vari-

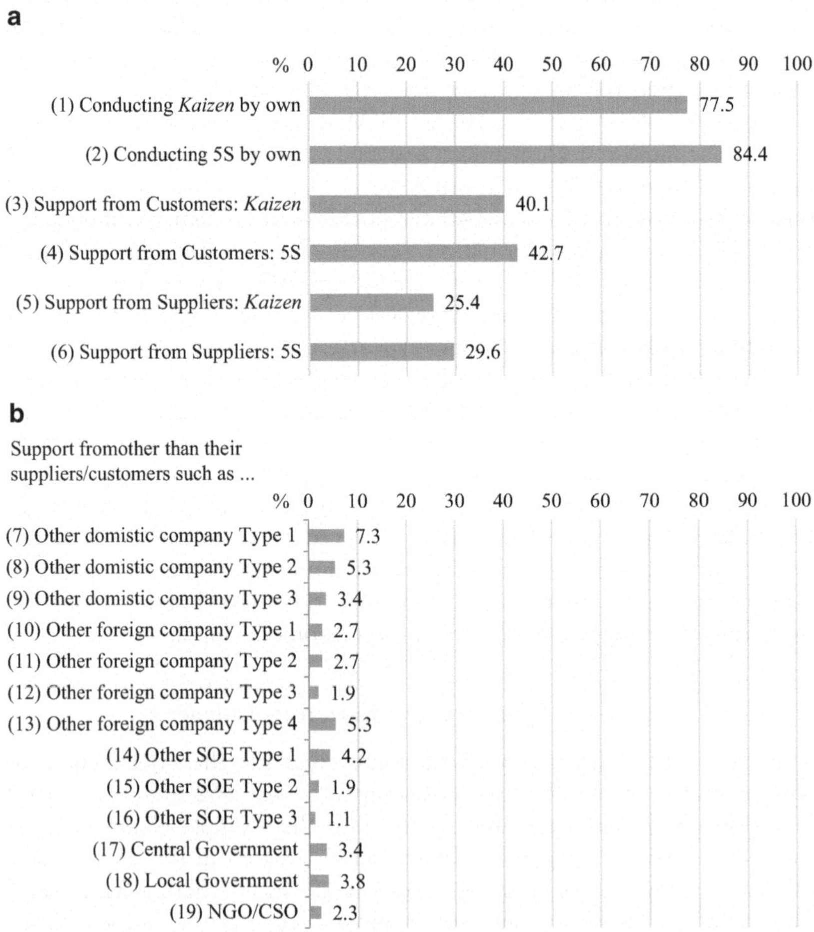

able kc_i is the variable that shows whether the top-five customers provide information/services/support for *Kaizen* to the surveyed company, and fc_i shows whether the top-five customers provide information/services/supports for 5S. As the maximum value of the KEI should be 25, it is divided by 2.5 to be on a 0–10 scale.

In other words, the *Kaizen* Engagement Index (KEI) values how a company is engaged in *Kaizen*/5S activities from the following two (2) aspects, which is also presented in Fig. 6.2(a):

1. *Kaizen*/5S implementation: How far a company implements *Kaizen*/5S by themselves.

Fig. 6.2 Indonesian companies' involvement in *Kaizen* and 5S implementation and information/services/supports from outside: (a) *Kaizen*/5S implementation by own and *Kaizen*/5S information/services/supports from their customers and suppliers ($n = 262$), (b) (for reference) Information/services/supports on *Kaizen*, 5S, QC (Quality Control), and others from other type of companies or institutions (other than their customers and suppliers). *Note 1*: "Support" in this figure means information/services/support gained from someone outside their companies, such as their customers (such as the companies that order the surveyed companies to make products/components), their suppliers (such as the companies that supply material/parts for the surveyed company's production), and others listed in the (b) above. *Note 2*: The sample size was 262 except for the following: 922 for (3) and (4) and 786 for (5) and (6), because the 262 respondents were asked to list their multiple major customers/suppliers at maximum five (5). *Note 3*: In the items from (7) to (16), Type 1 refers to a company within the same province with the surveyed company; Type 2 means a company in a different province but within the same island with the surveyed company; Type 3 means a company on a different island as the surveyed company but within Indonesia; Type 4 means a company outside Indonesia; SOE means State-owned enterprise; and NGO/CSO means nongovernmental organization/civil society organization. *Note 4*: 5S is a working environment improvement methodology including *Seiri* (Sort/orderliness), *Seiton* (Set in order/tidiness), *Seisou* (Shine/cleaning up), *Seiketsu* (Standardize/cleanliness), and *Shitsuke* (Sustain/discipline) (Shimada et al. 2013). *Note 5*: This JICA-LPEM Survey inquires about *Kaizen* and 5S separately in some parts (such as the data used for Fig. 6.2(a)) and aggregately on *Kaizen* and 5S, and furthermore includes other types of management activities such as QC, ISO, and others in other part (such as the data used for Fig. 6.2(b)). This is because this survey was not necessarily designed for this chapter but for other purposes. However, the survey is still useful for discussions on *Kaizen* dissemination in Indonesia in this chapter. (Source: Processed by Author, data derived from JICA-LPEM Survey)

Fig. 6.3 Relationship between *Kaizen* engagement and labor productivity ($n = 262$). Note: IDR means Indonesian rupiah (Indonesian currency). (Source: Processed by Author, data derived from JICA-LPEM Survey)

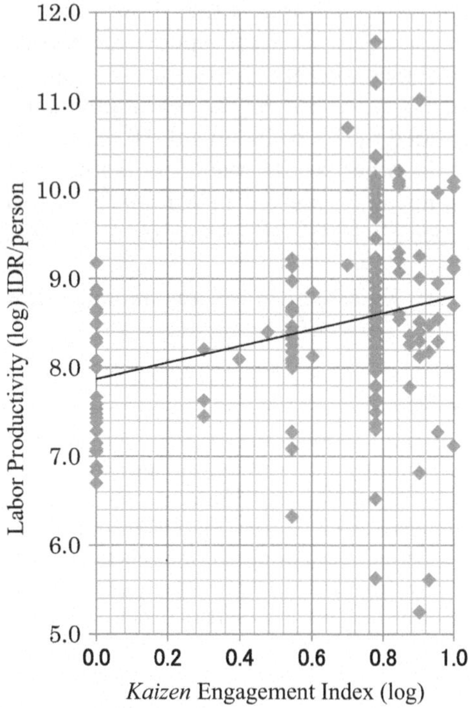

2. Access to information/service/support for *Kaizen*/5S via its customers.

Figure 6.3 shows a mild correlation between the *Kaizen* Engagement Index (KEI) and labor productivity for the surveyed companies ($n = 179$, where labor productivity value is available) in Indonesia (t value = 3.912, $p < 0.05$, Pearson's correlation coefficient: $r = 0.28211$). This implies the possibility that companies engaged in *Kaizen*/5S by themselves and/or support from their customers through their supply chain may achieve higher labor productivity, or in other words, *Kaizen*/5S by themselves and their customers' support may contribute to improved productivity.

The Indonesian field survey also reveals a mild correlation between *Kaizen* implementation and process innovation implementation (t value = 3.564, $p < 0.05$, Pearson's correlation coefficient: $r = 0.21585$, $n = 262$). This implies that engagement in *Kaizen* in the supply chain may enhance process innovation.[21]

4.3 *The Role of Private and Public Organizations*

Apart from the survey results in the previous Subsects. 4.1 and 4.2, there are some more missing *Kaizen* players.[22] Among them are various private sector organizations that have contributed to this process in Indonesia. There are two (2) major types. One works as a facilitator, including private associations dealing with QC Circle conventions on a large scale, such as the Indonesian Quality Management Association (IQMA) and the Indonesian Quality and Productivity Management Association (IQPMA). Both IQMA and IQPMA actively and separately organize annual QC Circle conventions involving several hundreds to thousands of participants mainly from private manufacturing companies, including domestic and foreign companies. The associations provide these companies with opportunities to improve their productivity and quality through *Kaizen*, 5S, and other quality control or productivity improvement approaches. At the same time, their annual conventions contribute to strengthening networks and disseminating *Kaizen* in Indonesian manufacturing industries. IQMA and IQPMA are also gateways to the international quality and productivity community; IQMA is a member of the International Convention on Quality Control Circles (ICQCC) and participates in annual conventions[23] held in 13 member countries with some private companies. IQMA also hosted two ICQCC annual conventions in the past. IQPMA is a member of Asia Pacific Quality Organization (APQO).

Practical training institutes are another type of private sector organization. An automobile industry conglomerate's foundation that provides several training programs for SMEs, including *Kaizen*, is a typical case. This foundation utilizes Indonesian engineers in the group of automobile companies as trainers, and frequently delivers various training programs including *Kaizen*/5S among group companies as well as for SMEs outside the group as a part of the industry conglomerate's corporate social responsibility (CSR) activities.

In summary, the private sector has actively disseminated *Kaizen* mainly through two channels: (a) Japanese manufacturers and their local supply chains involving local suppliers through their supply chain management systems (Subsects. 4.1 and 4.2 in this chapter) and (b) private sector organizations to organize productivity/quality-related programs including conventions and training (Subsect. 4.3 in this chapter).

Meanwhile, the Directorate General of Training and Productivity Development under the Ministry of Manpower and Transmigration acts as

Indonesia's National Productivity Organization against APO. Indonesia became a member of the APO in 1968 and the Ministry's approach for productivity improvement started at that time. The Ministry classifies past experiences with productivity improvement since then into three phases: (a) the awareness phase, (b) the improvement phase, and (c) the maintenance phase. It has accumulated experience and provides a kind of standard approach for productivity improvement in Indonesia.

4.4 *Conclusion on* Kaizen *Dissemination in Indonesia*

As discussed throughout Sect. 4, the private sector supply chain flow (customer companies and supplier relationships) in Indonesia effectively disseminates *Kaizen* through the provision of information/services/support, rather than other sources (Subsect. 4.1). Analysis of the *Kaizen* Engagement Index (KEI) implies that a company's engagement in *Kaizen* either on its own or with information/services/support from its customers through its supply improves labor productivity (Subsect. 4.2). The organization of productivity/quality-related programs, including conventions and training, is another means by which the private sector disseminates *Kaizen* in Indonesia (Subsect. 4.3). On the whole, the private sector seems to have a more central role to disseminate *Kaizen* in Indonesia.

5 *Kaizen* Dissemination in Myanmar

5.1 Kaizen-*Disseminating Organizations*

Myanmar is considered the last promising investment destination in Southeast Asia, thanks to its rapid open-up reform since 2011 under the transition period toward democratization. Its untapped domestic market of 53.4 million people (estimated in 2017)[24] attracts investors to this emerging market. Its GDP is US$ 62.6 billion (current US$ in 2015) and its GDP per capita is rapidly growing from US$ 239 in 2005 to US$ 1162 in 2015 (current US$). The industry sector's share in Myanmar's economy amounts to only 14.6 percent (estimated in 2017) of GVA. Its economy including the manufacturing sector is growing rapidly, but the sector is concentrated in the labor-intensive garment sector and it is still in its infancy, without a firm industrial structure with established supply chain, such as the manufacturing of automobiles and their parts and components. Some companies have introduced *Kaizen* by chance on their own with limited external support. There may be room to learn from the Malaysian and Indonesian experiences.

The Myanmar Productivity Center (MPC) was created in 2016 as a small unit within the Union of Myanmar Federation of Chambers of Commerce and Industry (UMFCCI) with the support of the Japan Productivity Center (JPC). In the two years of activities since then, three MPC *Kaizen* consultants were certified and another three were nominated as candidate MPC *Kaizen* consultants. MPC identified nine Myanmar manufacturing companies as model companies in the last two years and JPC provided each of them with three consultations at their factories. The establishment of the MPC was endorsed in the Industrial Policy issued in 2016 by the Ministry of Industry of Myanmar.

As another Japanese collaboration with the UMFCCI, the Myanmar-Japan Center for Human Resource Development (MJC) is supported by the Japan International Cooperation Agency (JICA) as its technical cooperation project with the Ministry of Commerce of Myanmar. Approximately 400 training courses and seminars have been provided for close to 15,000 participants in total, mainly from Myanmar SMEs, in the five years since its establishment in 2013. Around 20 percent of these were in relation to Japanese-style management and continuous improvement (*Kaizen*), according to the MJC. JICA also assisted the Ministry of Industry to conduct 5S seminars in Myanmar in 2018 through a technical cooperation project.

The Association for Overseas Technical Cooperation and Sustainable Partnerships (AOTS) of Japan also provides training for industrial human resource development. Since 1959, some of around 2000 trainees have been dispatched from Myanmar to Japan for training programs, while around 6000 trainees have been trained in Myanmar in the same period. A major part of these training programs in Japan and Myanmar are management training programs that focus on *Kaizen* and 5S. Other training courses have many flavors of the basics of Japanese-style management approaches.

5.2 A Case Study in the Private Sector

One of the leading electric and electronic manufacturing companies in Myanmar (Company A, located in Yangon, with approximately 300 employees) provides good practice in Myanmar. Its long journey on productivity improvement started in 1997 when the current owner participated in a Malaysian Training Cooperation Program organized by the Malaysia Productivity Corporation (MPC) in Malaysia. Immediately after he came back from this training, he introduced a series of *Kaizen* approaches, starting with 5S in his factory. He produced a 5S pocket handbook in the Myanmar language and set up 5S Day. Second, he introduced QC Circle in his factory. He also participated in a training course organized by AOTS and held in Yokohama in 2003. He continuously followed what he learnt from the training and through his own process. He then introduced Total Productive Maintenance (TPM) and finally reached ISO 9001, and Company A was certified in 2004 within only eight months. He has not just introduced *Kaizen* as he learned, but always considered the importance of "adopt, adapt, and adjust" according to the actual situation. For example, he skipped Total Quality Management (TQM) as he thought it was too early to introduce it into his factory.

His effort has been gradually disseminated outside his factory as an interesting approach. Company A was awarded by the Yangon City Mayor for his effort and invited to introduce the 5S concept to the Yangon township administration. He then became a Joint Secretary General of the UMFCCI, in charge of the establishment of the Myanmar Productivity Center (MPC). He is now one of the most influential business people. Still he continuously learns *Kaizen* and implements "continuous improvement" day by day, which is the most essential meaning of "*Kaizen*." In 2016, his company was accepted as a model company of the MPC training course and received consultations from Japanese experts dispatched by JPC.

Thus far *Kaizen* dissemination in Myanmar is still limited, but voluntary sporadic initiatives have been popping up, especially in the private sector. It is expected that such initiatives will be streamlined along with rapid economic growth and industrial development.

6 Major Findings and the *Kaizen* Dissemination Model

This research has examined how *Kaizen* has been disseminated in Southeast Asia, focusing on three countries as typical cases: Malaysia, Indonesia, and Myanmar. The process is complicated, although the major findings can be summarized as follows.

6.1 *Stakeholders' Roles and Relations in* Kaizen *Dissemination (Possible Standard Model)*

First, there are various stakeholders, organizations, and institutions disseminating *Kaizen* in Southeast Asia, both in the government (such as ministries in charge and public productivity organizations like Malaysia Productivity Corporation (MPC) in Malaysia) and in the private sector (local suppliers and assemblers). There are also some active private or semi-private organizations such as quality control organizations and training institutes that provide services on a fee basis. Some of them are relatively common across the countries, while there are some country-specific private entities engaged in *Kaizen* dissemination, for example, Indonesia's IQMA and IPQMA. Contributions from various Japanese and Japan-based organizations to each stakeholder can be seen in the three countries, developing managerial and technical capability, training programs, expert dispatch programs, model consultation programs, policy/planning support, and financial assistance. They mainly support *Kaizen* dissemination through their counterpart organizations in the recipient countries. In general, standard stakeholders for *Kaizen* dissemination in Southeast Asia (at least in the three countries studied in this chapter) can be summarized as indicated in Fig. 6.4. The figure illustrates the supply chain network (in the shaded and rounded rectangular shape) that mobilizes *Kaizen* dissemination toward local manufacturers as local suppliers, while there are various public and private organizations that provide *Kaizen* services directly to local manufacturers and thereby contribute to *Kaizen* dissemination in the local industries.

6.2 *Government- or Private Sector-Led* Kaizen *Dissemination*

Second, however, as set out in the hypothesis at the beginning of this chapter, the Malaysian government (or more precisely Malaysia Productivity Corporation (MPC) as the public organization in Fig. 6.4) took the initiative disseminating *Kaizen* in Malaysia. On the other hand, *Kaizen* dissemination in Indonesia has been led by the private sector, particularly through supply chain mechanism and contributions by private organizations, as shown in a series of interviews and some results from the field survey.

What is the cause for this difference between the two countries? Are there any factors determining whether the process is led by the government or the private sector?

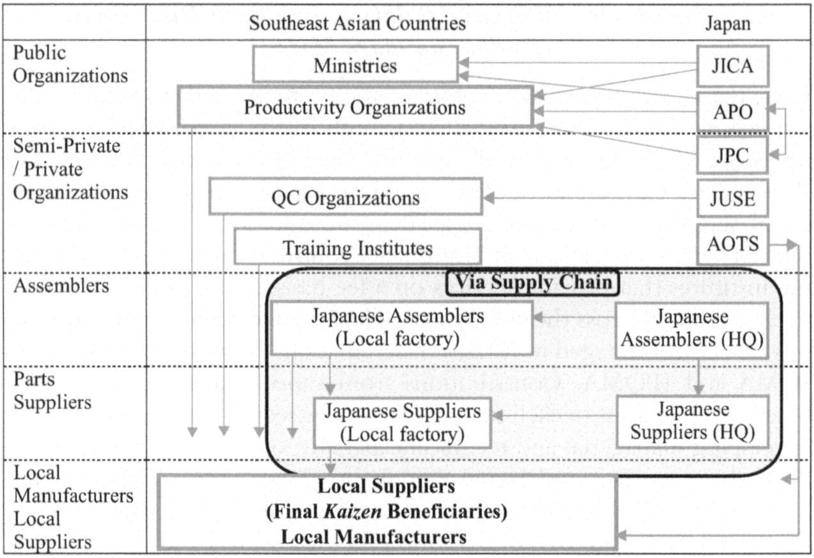

Fig. 6.4 Stakeholders' roles and relations in *Kaizen* dissemination (possible standard model). (Source: Author)

The first factor is how firmly established the supply chain within the country led by Japanese assemblers is. As mentioned in Sect. 4, Indonesia is the second largest automobile producer in Southeast Asia and after the 1970s, almost all major Japanese automobile assemblers settled their factories under joint venture with local capitals contributing more than 99 percent of its domestic production share. It is this deep, long-lasting supply chain structure in Indonesia that nurtures *Kaizen* dissemination through the private sector supply chain path. Meanwhile, although Japanese car manufacturers also contributed a lot to *Kaizen* dissemination in Malaysia, their presence there is not as strong as that in Indonesia partially due to the national car program. Myanmar's car manufacturing industry is still too premature to build up automobile production supply chain.

The second factor is the government's strength and willingness to disseminate productivity improvement such as *Kaizen*. Malaysia has already established an exclusive and professional governmental body Malaysia Productivity Corporation (MPC) to disseminate productivity improvement more than half century ago and has been acting as a leading organization.

Finally, comparing the first and second factors determines the tendency for either the government or the private sector to lead. The private sector is stronger in Indonesia, while in Malaysia the government is. Thus, *Kaizen* dissemination in Malaysia is considered to be government-led while in Indonesia it is private sector-led. It is still too early to determine whether Myanmar is government or private sector led, although the private sector—some of which are supported by Japanese organizations—seems to be slightly more active.

6.3 Kaizen *Dissemination Path Model: Five-Stage Paths of* Kaizen *Dissemination*

Third, there are stages or phases of *Kaizen* dissemination. As we can see from the cases of each country presented in this chapter and others, *Kaizen* cannot be disseminated overnight. At the beginning, an introduction is necessary for those unfamiliar with *Kaizen*. Then it will be diffused through certain channels with practical activities. During this introduction and diffusion, some may notice the need to customize the approach to *Kaizen* according to their ecosystem. These movements finally produce the need for standardization within a country, as illustrated in Fig. 6.5(a): the "*Kaizen* Dissemination Path Model."

The five stages in the *Kaizen* Dissemination Path Model above can be described as follows:

1. *Introduction*: *Kaizen* is introduced as basic knowledge through translation, publication, seminars, lectures, training, pilot implementation, and other methods based on the experiences of Japan and other experienced countries. The core purposes of this stage are raising awareness and introducing potential benefits.
2. *Diffusion*: After the introduction stage, those who experience *Kaizen* and find it useful involve others in *Kaizen* practice and multiply *Kaizen* practitioners. At this stage, measures and activities related to *Kaizen* become more practical and systematic, for example, the training of trainers (TOT), technical consultations within companies, in-company training, and others.
3. *Customization*: Based on the experience at the introduction and the diffusion stages, related people and organizations accumulate knowledge and experience and identify areas to be modified according to their own custom and culture. Examples include the Malaysian

a

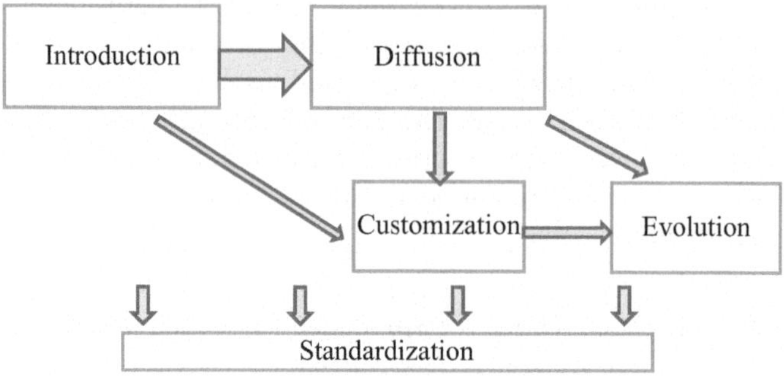

b

	Government / Public organization	Private sector	
		Private organization	Private company
Dissemination Stage			
Introduction	Yes (For General / SMEs)	Yes (For willing companies)	Yes (For own supply chain)
Diffusion	Yes (Public awareness)	Yes (Public awareness)	Yes (Within own supply chain)
Customization	Yes (Country context)	Yes (Country context)	Yes (Group/company context)
Evolution	Yes (Developing country methodology)	Yes (Developing own methodology)	Yes (Developing own methodology)
Standardization	Yes (Most fit to government role)	Partially Yes	Can contribute
Country Context			
Malaysia	Strong	Fair	Relatively Strong
Indonesia	Fair	Strong	Very strong
Myanmar	Still weak	Fair	Weak (partially Fair)

Fig. 6.5 *Kaizen* dissemination path model: Paths of *Kaizen* dissemination in a country: (a) dissemination stage outline and (b) dissemination stages and stakeholders' major roles (Source: Author)

Malaysia Productivity Corporation (MPC's) transformation of 5S into Quality Environment and the case of the company in Myanmar.

4. *Evolution*: In some cases, customization may advance beyond modification, for example, MPC's Innovation and Competitiveness Circle (ICC). ICC has evolved from the original version of Quality Control Circle (QCC) with more emphasis on innovation. Some forms of evolution may be considered "reverse innovation," meaning an innovation born in developing countries that moves to developed countries as a new approach.
5. *Standardization*: All the effort conducted in any of the four stages above may need to be summarized and documented as the standard procedure, methodology, or approach for the purpose of replicating such efforts by others. This contributes to *Kaizen* becoming firmly rooted in a country.

6.4 *Stakeholders' Major Roles in* Kaizen *Dissemination*

Fourth, each government/public organization, private organization, and private company have their roles and all of them may contribute to the dissemination of *Kaizen*. Although these roles may differ somewhat by country, Fig. 6.5(b) summarizes each party's possible major roles along with the dissemination stage designated in Fig. 6.5(a). It shows that each party (government/public organization, private organization, and private company) can contribute to each stage. However, their targets and directions often differ as indicated in brackets in each cell in Fig. 6.5(b). In this sense, close collaborations to complement each other in terms of mandates, capacity, financial resource, geographical coverage, access/reach, and so on may work. The bottom of Fig. 6.5(b) illustrates the relative strength of each party in each country.

6.5 *Proactive Role of Government and Public Organizations*

Fifth, government and public organizations can work proactively to disseminate *Kaizen*. Malaysia shows strong government/Malaysia Productivity Corporation (MPC) leadership and has already discussed proactive roles for *Kaizen* dissemination. Indonesia's case shows strong contributions from the private companies' supply chain management and various private organizations, but the government also raises awareness, standardizes the *Kaizen* methodology/philosophy, and acts as the country window for APO. In Myanmar government dissemination of *Kaizen* seems so far to be weak, but there may be room to support the private organization's initiative and private sector's sporadic movements.

7 Conclusions

This chapter has discussed the roles of stakeholders, particularly the government (including public organizations) and the private sector (private organizations and private companies) in three countries: Malaysia, Indonesia, and Myanmar. Each country shows a different path toward the dissemination of *Kaizen*, with a clear contrast between the government-led Malaysian case and the private sector-led Indonesian case. However, all the stakeholders have their own roles in each of the three country cases and complement each other.

On the other hand, the dissemination of *Kaizen* can be summarized in the five-stage *Kaizen* Dissemination Path Model comprising Introduction, Diffusion, Customization, Evolution, and Standardization.

Finally, this research needs further comparative analysis among more Southeast Asian countries than just the three piloted countries to provide further numerical evidence to contribute to the emerging countries in Southeast Asia and other regions for them to disseminate *Kaizen* accordingly in each country.

Notes

1. Singapore has initiated a productivity movement under the strong leadership of then Prime Minister late Lee Kuan Yew. He requested that Japan conduct technical cooperation and Japan International Cooperation Agency (JICA) started the Productivity Development Project (PDP) in 1983 with Singapore's National Productivity Board (NPB) as the counterpart agency. It was the very first technical cooperation by JICA on productivity improvement or *Kaizen* in the world. Since then technical cooperation on *Kaizen* has been implemented all over the world, spread from Asia, Eastern Europe, Latin America, and Africa (Jin 2018).
2. The Thai government requested the Japanese government to provide technical cooperation to promote a national-level productivity movement and the Thailand Productivity Development Project from 1994 to 2001. Its implementing agency was Thailand Management Development and Productivity Center (TMDPC) established by the Thai government in

1962 at the beginning of the Project and then followed by the new Thailand Productivity Institute (FTPI). From the private sector, *Kaizen* was already introduced into Thai companies especially from Japan in the 1990s (Jin 2018).

3. In the area of productivity improvement, the Japan Productivity Center (JPC) has been actively engaged in *Kaizen* by receiving trainees from Southeast Asia and dispatching experts. JPC is the national productivity organization for the Asian Productivity Organization (APO), whose lead donor is Japan and whose headquarters is located in Tokyo (JPC 1985). APO has been funding various programs on productivity through JPC and others. The Union of Japanese Scientists and Engineers (JUSE) has contributed to quality improvement through the International Convention on Quality Control Circles (ICQCC) and others. The Association for Overseas Technical Cooperation and Sustainable Partnerships (AOTS) has also received a great number of trainees in this area. Under its ODA program, the Japan International Cooperation Agency (JICA) has implemented a pioneering technical cooperation project on productivity in Singapore and Thailand (Hosono 2016), as well as other forms of cooperation such as training programs on *Kaizen* in Japan for other Southeast Asian countries. There have also been a number of JICA's technical cooperation projects on metal processing technology such as casting and mold/die in Indonesia, Malaysia, Thailand, and Philippines. These technical cooperation projects contained production control and quality control components, which naturally featured *Kaizen* (Homma 2009 and JICA 2004).
4. Lembaga Penyelidikan Ekonomi dan Masyarakat, Fakultas Ekonomi Universitas Indonesia.
5. The statistical data in this paragraph come from United Nations (2018) unless otherwise noted.
6. See the previous section on research methodology for further details of the interview.
7. The scale represents the level of agreement to each question. Scale 5 corresponds to "Strongly yes," Scale 4 "Yes," Scale 3 "Partially yes," Scale 2 "Neither yes nor no," Scale 1 "No," and Scale 0 "Strongly no."
8. The statistical data in this paragraph are from United Nations (2018) unless otherwise noted.
9. According to the Association of Indonesia Automotive Industries (GAIKINDO), Japanese brand car production share reaches 99.59 percent in 2016 out of Indonesia's annual production amount 1,177,797 vehicles.
10. See the previous Research Methodology section for further details.
11. In the field survey questionnaire, *Kaizen* is defined as any systematic activity in which workers discuss problems in the workshop and try to solve them and does not need to be called "*Kaizen*."

12. In the field survey questionnaire, 5S is defined as any systematic activity to clean the workshop and put products and materials together in an orderly way.
13. For example, in the case of tier-1 car part and component manufacturer/supplier, car assemblers that purchase tier-1 companies' products (parts and components) are tier-1 companies' customers.
14. For example, in the case of tier-1 car part and component manufacturer/supplier, tier-2 companies that supply subparts and subcomponents for the tier-1 companies' production.
15. According to the definition of the Indonesia's national statistical agency *Badan Pusat Statistik* (BPS), a company with 100 or more employees is defined as a large company.
16. Their average year of operation is shown as 25.1, meaning that these companies on average survived the Asian Monetary Crisis, which hit Indonesia around 1998.
17. State-owned enterprise.
18. Nongovernmental organization/civil society organization.
19. Although the questionnaire in Fig. 6.2(a) on customers/suppliers (supply chain) and Fig. 6.2(b) on non-supply chain sources is slightly different (see Notes of Fig. 6.2 for further details), the tendency for supply chain companies to be the preferred source can be seen.
20. Jakarta (Special Capital Region) and major cities in the provinces of Banten, West Java, Central Java, East Java, and Riau Islands.
21. It may be interesting to study how far conducting *Kaizen* can contribute to process innovation, for example, by increasing firm capability, in particular, managerial capability, which is the initial step to future innovation (Cirera and Maloney 2017).
22. This is due to the survey design and limitations. As previously mentioned, the survey is not necessarily exclusively designed for this chapter.
23. The ICQCC annual convention started in 1976. Since then, 42 annual conventions have already been held in 13 member countries in turn.
24. The statistical data in this paragraph are from United Nations (2018), unless otherwise noted.

References

Cirera, Xavier, and William F. Maloney. 2017. *The Innovation Paradox: Developing-Country Capabilities and the Unrealized Promise of Technological Catch-Up*. Washington, DC: The World Bank Group.

Higuchi, Y., V.H. Nam, and T. Sonobe. 2015. Sustained Impacts of *Kaizen* Training. *Journal of Economic Behavior and Organization* 120: 189–206.

Homma, Toru. 2009. Quality and Productivity Improvement: Experience of JICA's Project in Indonesia. Presentation prepared for the First Ethiopia-Japan High Level Forum on Industrial Development in Ethiopia, Addis Ababa.

Hosono, Akio. 2016. Industrial Strategies: Toward a Learning Society for Quality Growth. In *Efficiency, Finance, and Varieties of Industrial Policy*, ed. A. Noman and J.E. Stiglitz, 306–352. New York: Columbia University Press.

Imai, Masaaki. 1986. *Kaizen: The Key to Japan's Success*. New York: McGraw-Hill.

Japan International Cooperation Agency (JICA). 2004. *Final Report on the Project on Supporting Industries Development for Casting Technology*. Tokyo: JICA.

Japan International Cooperation Agency (JICA) and International Development Center of Japan (IDCJ). 2017. *The Study on Achievements and Roles by Japanese Official Development Assistance for Social and Economic Development in Malaysia: Final Report*. Tokyo: JICA.

———. 2018. *The Study on Applying Development Experience A on Third Country Training Programme in Malaysia: Final Report*. Tokyo: JICA.

Japan International Cooperation Agency (JICA) and Japan Bank for International Cooperation (JBIC). 2008. *Report of the Stocktaking Work on the Economic Development in Africa and the Asian Growth Experience*. Tokyo: JICA.

Japan International Cooperation Agency (JICA) and Nomura Research Institute (NRI). 2019. *Data Collection Survey on Promotion for Globally Competitive Industry: Final Report*. Tokyo: JICA.

Jin, Kimiaki. 2018. Role of *Kaizen* in Japan's Overseas Development Cooperation. In *Applying the Kaizen in Africa: A New Avenue for Industrial Development*, ed. K. Otsuka, K. Jin, and T. Sonobe, 31–68. Cham: Palgrave Macmillan.

Maarof, Mohd Ghazali, and Fatimah Mahmud. 2015. *A Review of Contributing Factors and Challenges in Implementing Kaizen in Small and Medium Enterprises*. New York: Elsevier B. V.

Malaysia Productivity Corporation (MPC). 2013. *Quality Environment: Step-by-step Implementation*. Petaling Jaya, Malaysia: MPC.

———. 2018. *Malaysia Productivity Corporation (MPC)*. Petaling Jaya, Malaysia: MPC.

National Productivity Corporation (NPC). 2006. *40 years NPC 1966–2006—Productivity & Quality for Competitiveness*. Petaling Jaya, Malaysia: NPC.

Nihon Seisannsei Hombu (in Japanese, Japan Productivity Center: JPC). 1985. *Seisansei Undo 30 Nenshi* [Productivity Movement over 30 Years]. Tokyo: JPC.

Ohno, I., K. Ohno, and S. Uesu. 2009. Introduction. In *Introducing Kaizen in Africa*, ed. the GRIPS Development Forum, 1–12. Tokyo: GRIPS.

Shimada, G., T. Homma, and H. Murakami. 2013. Industrial Development of Africa. In *For Inclusive and Dynamic Development in Sub-Saharan Africa*, ed. JICA, 173–194. Tokyo: JICA Research Institute.

United Nations. 2018. UN Data. Accessed June 2018. http://data.un.org.

CHAPTER 7

Opportunities for *Kaizen* in Africa: Developing the Core Employability Skills of African Youth Through *Kaizen*

Momoko Suzuki and Eriko Sakamaki

1 Introduction

Kaizen seems to be expanding its reach across Africa. While it was originally introduced as an approach to improve organizational management by enhancing quality and productivity in the workplace, several African countries have noticed the favorable impact of *Kaizen* on core employability skills' development and have started to introduce it into their education sectors—in particular through technical and vocational education and training (TVETs) and universities.

In Ethiopia, TVETs are providing *Kaizen* training to enhance student attitudes toward work. This is a common course for all TVET students. In South Africa, universities of technology have introduced *Kaizen* training and are offering it in all departments. In these two countries, *Kaizen* is

M. Suzuki (✉)
Industrial Development and Public Policy Department, Japan International Cooperation Agency, Tokyo, Japan
e-mail: Suzuki.Momoko@jica.go.jp

E. Sakamaki
Japan Overseas Cooperation Volunteers, Japan International Cooperation Agency, Tokyo, Japan

A. Hosono et al. (eds.), *Workers, Managers, Productivity*,
https://doi.org/10.1007/978-981-15-0364-1_7

seen as an approach to enhance core employability skills. Other countries such as the Democratic Republic of Congo and Senegal are also introducing *Kaizen* in TVETs.

While the scale and progress of introducing *Kaizen* into the educational sector differ between countries, the objective is common—to enhance students' capacity in preparation for joining the workforce. The United Nations has projected that the African continent's population will double by 2050 (UN DESA 2019). Considering the small size of the private sector, absorbing the increasing working age population within the currently restricted labor market will be almost impossible. Furthermore, many CEOs feel that new graduates do not have the basic skills needed in the workplace (Aring 2012). Creating job opportunities as well as developing the skills that meet the needs of the labor market is crucial for Africa's sustainable development.

This chapter explores how *Kaizen* has been integrated into education systems in African nations and how it creates opportunities to enhance the core employability skills of graduates. We first discuss the definition of employability and core employability skills, followed by an examination of the relationship between the *Kaizen* approach and the enhancement of core employability skills. In later sections, we look at two countries where *Kaizen* has been introduced, Ethiopia and South Africa. The former has introduced *Kaizen* into TVETs and the latter into universities. These cases demonstrate how *Kaizen* has been introduced along with the impacts and lessons learned so far.

2 Defining and Categorizing Core Employability Skills

2.1 Definition of Employability

The concept of employability, as promulgated in the late 1990s (see ILO 2000; UN 2001), was driven by the awareness of a shift in the world toward knowledge and skill-based economies and societies. The International Labour Organization (ILO) report (2000) examined how globalization, technological advancement, and new organizational management have impacted on the labor market, leading to shifts in the skills required, and resulting in unstable and insecure employment. The literature regarding employability argues that current education and training systems remain largely unrelated to labor market needs and, therefore, the "skills gap" between graduates of education systems and the labor market is widening. However, there seems to be a variation in the definition of employability and the elements that constitute it.

Hillage and Pollard (1998) define "employability" as having the capacity in terms of knowledge (what they know), skills (what they do with the knowledge), and attitudes (how they do it) to gain initial employment, maintain employment, and obtain new employment if required. The ILO's definition puts more emphasis on the changing world of work and characterizes employability as "portable competencies and qualifications that enhance an individual's capacity to make use of the education and training opportunities available in order to secure and retain decent work, to progress within the enterprise and between jobs, and to cope with changing technology and labor market conditions" (ILO 2004, Recommendation 195). Yorke (2006, 3) sees employability as a set of achievements that impacts not only oneself but also society. He defines "employability" as "a set of achievements—skills, understandings and personal qualities—that makes individuals more likely to gain employment and be successful in their occupations, which benefits themselves, the workforce, the community and the economy." He deliberately uses the words "understandings" and "personal qualities" instead of "knowledge" and "attitude" to signal the importance of a rich appreciation of the relevant fields.

From the definition above, it seems fair to say that employability is an individual's capacity (or competencies, or a set of achievements) that enables them to gain a job and progress in their career and successful life. Employability should be transferrable across sectors and malleable to changing technologies. Yorke (2006) also points out the significance of metacognition in employability. Metacognition encompasses self-awareness and the capacity to reflect on one's learning. It is especially important if individuals seek to progress their career in the modern world where technology and the environment surrounding the labor market rapidly change.

Furthermore, the three definitions indicate that individuals are most employable when they have appropriate knowledge (understanding), skills, and attitudes (personal qualities). In this chapter, we call these three competencies—knowledge, skills, and attitudes—the competencies for employability.

Yorke (2006) argues that employers are more or less satisfied with subject-specific knowledge, skills, and attitudes as a consequence of broad-based education, but they are less content with generic skills like communication, teamwork, and time management. While Yorke's argument is based on the labor situation in the United Kingdom, other literature regarding employability suggests that similar skill gaps exist in other areas of the world (METI 2006, 2007; Brewer 2013; British Council 2014). In this chapter, where this gap is identified, we refer to these generic skills as "core employability skills."

2.2 Core Employability Skills

Core employability skills are built upon and strengthen those developed through basic education, such as reading and writing (knowledge), technical skills needed to perform specific duties (skills), and personal qualities such as honesty, reliability, and time management (attitudes) (Brewer 2013). They overlap with other competencies (knowledge, skills, and attitudes) and develop through a spiraling process by interacting with one another through an individual's various experiences (METI 2006).

While much attention has been given to core employability skills by the labor market, government policy has long overlooked their importance. These skills are often not certified nor formally recognized (Brewer 2013).

Yorke and Knight (2006) attempt to identify and categorize aspects of core employability skills in order to embed them into school curriculums. They divide aspects of core employability skills into three categories: core skills (relating to knowledge and understanding), process skills (relating to skills), and personal qualities (relating to attitudes). A total of 39 aspects are listed. Twelve aspects are listed under core skills such as reading and writing, numeracy, information retrieval as well as self-management, creativity, and critical analysis. Seventeen aspects are identified as process skills, including problem-solving, teamwork, negotiation, and planning. Ten aspects are listed under personal qualities, such as self-awareness, self-confidence, and willingness to learn, as well as emotional intelligence, adaptability, stress tolerance, and reflectiveness. Yorke and Knight's listing contributes to the understanding that, even within core employability skills, there are multiple aspects, thus making it difficult to grasp what the core employability skills are.

Brewer (2013) pools skills and abilities that consistently appear in employer surveys and various documents and categorizes them into four broad skill categories: learning to learn, communication, teamwork, and problem-solving. While the list is not exhaustive, it points out the skills that are valued across sectors and nations.

Learning to learn refers to the ability to pursue and persist in learning and to be able to organize one's learning, including effective management of time and information, both individually and in groups. Skills such as self-awareness, self-management, and willingness to learn are all related to learning to learn.

Communication skills means being able to articulate one's thoughts using written, verbal, and non-verbal communication methods. One also needs to be able to listen and read, understand the context, interpret the world, and relate to others.

3 Core Employability Skills in Africa

While the skills gap has been one of the main development challenges in Africa for some time, the importance of core employability skills has not been fully acknowledged by policymakers. More interest has been focused on enhancing the quality of basic education and improving enrollment rates in secondary and tertiary education.

Studies show that 80% of Malian third graders and more than 70% of Ugandan third graders are illiterate (Cloutier et al. 2011). Only 26% of students in South Africa meet the Program for International Students Assessment (PISA) standard (World Bank 2019). Furthermore, the gross enrolment ratio in higher education is only 8.17% in sub-Saharan Africa (the global average is 32.88%), so it is not difficult to understand why this remains the highest priority.

However, this does not mean that core employability skills are not important in the labor markets of Africa. Although there are widespread concerns regarding the work readiness of graduates, there are very few studies that have investigated the specific skills that employers see as the gaps. One study conducted by the South Africa Graduate Recruiters Association (SAGRA) in 2013 demonstrated that core employability skills do actually matter (Fig. 7.1). The study shows that employers consider willingness to learn, teamwork, communication, and problem-solving to be some of the most important skills that graduates should have, and yet employers are not satisfied with employee abilities in these areas. Employers also feel that interpersonal skills, commitment, and proactivity are some key areas where there is a skills gap.

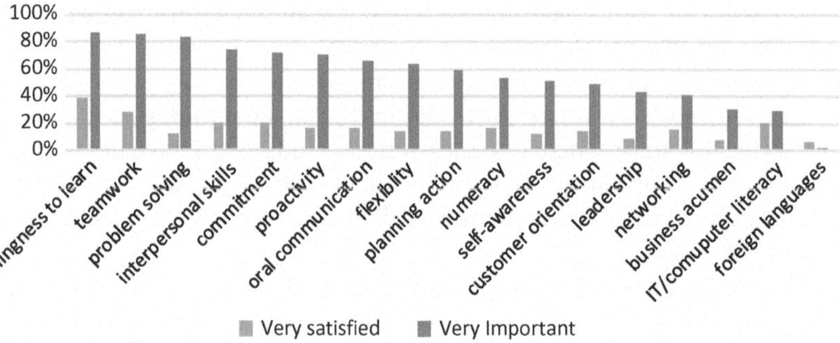

Fig. 7.1 The importance of core employability skills in South Africa. (Source: SAGRA Survey 2013, adapted from British Council 2014)

While employers feel that there is a skills gap between what is expected and the actual performance of the graduates, core employability skills are rarely taught in formal education across the world. Many universities and TVETs are still dominated by knowledge-based teaching through one-way lecturing and Africa is not an exception. Few opportunities exist for students to engage in discussion, to critique and to apply the ideas conveyed, and experience learning by doing (McCowan et al. 2016). Furthermore, these skills are expected to develop within society or in workplaces through learning by doing. However, in Africa, most enterprises are micro and small enterprises (MSEs) and do not have sufficient capacity to train their workers. Society may not have a modern work mentality, and it may be difficult to gain skills that are needed in formal waged jobs. This is why there is a growing demand for the education sector to take greater responsibility.

4 Core Employability Skills and *Kaizen*

The development of core employability skills is actually what many company managers expect from workers when implementing *Kaizen* activities. Although *Kaizen* is known as a management tool for quality and productivity enhancement, it is also an approach used by many Japanese companies to develop their workers' capacities. For example, Shimada and Sonobe's (2017) study in Central America and the Caribbean found that *Kaizen* improved employee attitudes toward work.

Kaizen activities are a continuous cycle of (1) problem identification, (2) analysis of root causes, (3) taking measures, (4) verifying the hypothesis, and (5) improving skills. The activities are usually practiced in groups and, most importantly, all of the workforce is involved. Improvement suggestions from operational staff are welcomed. Through practicing the *Kaizen* approach, workers accumulate skills such as problem identification/solving, teamwork, and self-sustainability. Thus, *Kaizen* is expected to have an impact—especially toward personal qualities (learning to learn) and process skills (teamwork and problem-solving)—as depicted in Table 7.1.

Table 7.1 Four main core employability skills

Personal qualities	Learning to learn	• Willingness to learn • Self-awareness • Self-confidence • Self-management • Independence • Adaptability • Emotional intelligence
Core skills	Communication	• Competence in reading and writing • Articulating ideas and thoughts • Negotiation • Active listening • Emotional intelligence • Logical thinking • Use numeracy effectively
Process skills	Teamwork	• Ability to work cross-culturally • Interact with coworkers • Work toward group consensus in decision-making • Leadership (lead effectively, lead when appropriate) • Conflict management
	Problem-solving	• Problem identification • Applying subject understanding • Analyzing data and information • Creative thinking • Critical/logical thinking • Project planning/implementation/management • Prioritizing • Planning and time management

Source: Yorke and Knight (2006) and Brewer (2013), modified by the authors

Jin (2018) argues that *Kaizen* activities in their basic stages can promote the formation of core capacities through learning by doing 5S (Sort, Set in order, Shine, Standardize, and Sustain). He also states that these capacities are related to people's mindsets on punctuality and self-regulation and have more far-reaching impacts than the operation and maintenance of machinery, infrastructure, and performance in service delivery. The development of these core capacities is crucial for the further development of knowledge, skills, and personal qualities.

For this reason, *Kaizen* is highly acclaimed by many government officials in Africa. In response to their requests, projects to disseminate *Kaizen* have been implemented by Japan International Cooperation Agency (JICA) in eight countries: Cameroon, Ethiopia, Ghana, Kenya, South Africa, Tanzania, Tunisia, and Zambia. These projects aim to disseminate *Kaizen* within the private sector, as well as to enhance quality, productivity, and competitiveness.

However, what we are seeing in Africa today is something other than this. *Kaizen* is being introduced in universities and TVETs to enhance the employability and core skills of the students. The following sections show how *Kaizen* is taught in this new form.

In Sects. 5 and 6 of this chapter, the authors attempt to explore the *Kaizen* trainings designed to enhance core employability skills that are carried out in TVETs in Ethiopia and technical universities in South Africa. The Ethiopian case uses Yorke and Knight's (2006) categorization of core employability skills for assessment, while the South African case uses the core employability skills that are recognized by technical universities in South Africa.

5 The Case of Ethiopia

5.1 Introduction

5.1.1 Ethiopian Context

In Ethiopia, promotion of the manufacturing industry is regarded as a crucial strategy for accelerating economic growth in the five-year national development plan (Growth and Transformation Plan (GTP) II). The government has a vision for the country to become a light manufacturing hub in Africa during the next ten years. Multiple measures are being undertaken to achieve this, including human resource development through

TVET. The main objective of TVET is thus "to produce lower and middle level, competent, motivated, adaptable and innovative workforces, which can contribute to poverty reduction and social and economic development through facilitating demand-driven, quality vocational education and the transfer of technology" (Federal Ministry of Education 2015). GTP II also introduced *Kaizen* as an approach able to bring about sustained and continuous improvements in productivity, quality, and competitiveness, as well as to minimize cost, ensure good working environments and worker safety, and promote attitudinal change.

5.1.2 TVET Reform in Ethiopia

TVET systems around the world have faced several criticisms. One of the best-known critiques was that by Psacharopoulos (1986, 1994), who demonstrated that both the private rate of return and the social rate of return are low in TVET compared with the general education. Likewise, TVET systems in developing countries, especially in sub-Saharan Africa, have been criticized for not responding to the needs of the labor market (AfDB/OECD 2008).

While these criticisms are still valid, the importance of TVET to national development policies is gradually being reconsidered. In a counterargument to Psacharopoulos, Bennell (1996) asserted that the social rate of return is high in TVET when considering the difference of the economic situation between students of general education and TVET in developing countries. Ogawa and Tansel (2005) also found that the employment rate of TVET graduates is higher than for those in general education in Turkey. More countries are recognizing TVET as essential for developing the human resources needed for achieving economic transformation.

In Ethiopia, TVET reformation has been implemented to meet international standards and the needs of the labor market. Competency-based training and an outcome-based system have been introduced. The Ethiopian TVET recognizes skills, knowledge, and attitudes as aspects of occupational competencies, which is a similar term to competencies for employability, as described in Sect. 2.1 (Centre of Excellence for Engineering 2015). In 2012, *Kaizen* courses were introduced into the Ethiopian TVET curriculum to foster good working attitudes. This means that Ethiopia believes that teaching *Kaizen* to TVET students will foster core employability skills that are especially related to attitudes.

This section aims to discover how *Kaizen* is utilized in TVETs in Ethiopia to enhance attitudes among the competencies for employability as well as core employability skills. This case study first focuses on the features of *Kaizen* courses in TVET, it then examines the awareness of occupational competencies (competencies for employability) among TVET graduates, and, last, it explores whether core employability skills have been fostered through TVET *Kaizen* courses.

5.2 *Methods*

The survey was conducted in Addis Ababa from December 2017 to February 2018. Data were collected through questionnaires, interviews, and observations. Questionnaires were distributed randomly to a total of 200 workers engaged in micro, small, and medium enterprises (MSMEs) in the manufacturing sector and in industries such as textiles and garment, leather, automobile, metal, woodwork, and plastics. Two enumerators collected the data from industrial clusters and from SMEs in Addis Ababa. The questionnaire included questions on competencies for employability and core employability skills, as well as basic information.

This case study analyzes core employability skills using Yorke and Knight's framework (see Table 7.2). The case study focuses on core employability skills relating to the personal qualities and process skills—presented in Table 7.1—in areas where *Kaizen* is believed to have had the greatest impact. To compare the differences between the graduates who had taken the *Kaizen* courses and those who had not, the questionnaire was distributed to 100 TVET graduates and 100 non-TVET graduates. Since the purpose of this study is to analyze *Kaizen* learning in TVET and/or the workplace and to compare the results with workers who have no previous *Kaizen* experience, we excluded the 25 respondents who had experienced *Kaizen* at school (not in TVET) or home or had received information about it from friends.

The respondents have been categorized into four groups according to their *Kaizen* experiences as follows:

- Group 1 (both TVET and at workplace): 46 respondents who took the *Kaizen* courses in TVET and are practicing *Kaizen* activities at their workplace;
- Group 2 (only in TVET): 21 respondents who took the *Kaizen* courses in TVET but are not practicing *Kaizen* at their workplace;

Table 7.2 Comparison of perceptions on core employability skills

		1. Both TVET & at workplace (%)	*2. Only in TVET (%)*	*3. Only at workplace (%)*	*4. No* Kaizen *(%)*
Personal qualities	Self-awareness	23	22	16	18
	Self-confidence	18	27	27	25
	Willingness to learn	15	14	16	10
	Independence	14	16	20	17
	Adaptability	11	10	9	10
	Initiative	8	6	5	4
	Stress tolerance	7	1	5	11
	Reflectiveness	4	4	3	5
	TOTAL	100	100	100	100
Process skills	Teamwork	35	38	33	30
	Planning	16	11	12	11
	Negotiating	8	6	8	15
	Problem-solving	6	5	8	9
	Arguing for and/or justifying a point of view or a course of action	6	2	6	5
	Prioritizing	5	1	5	4
	Decision-making	5	6	5	4
	Applying subject understanding	4	9	6	5
	Resolving conflict	4	6	6	5
	Acting morally	4	2	1	4
	Ethical sensitivity	3	13	7	3
	Commercial awareness	3	2	3	4
	Total	100	100	100	100

Source: The authors

Note: Scores for priority were calculated by adding points for each level of priority: 3 points to the first priority, 2 points to the second priority, and 1 point to the third priority

- Group 3 (only at workplace): 80 respondents who are practicing *Kaizen* at their workplace but did not learn about *Kaizen* in TVET or in any other form of education; and
- Group 4 (no *Kaizen*): 28 respondents who do not have *Kaizen* experience in TVET nor were practicing it in the workplace.

Semi-structured interviews were conducted with key actors, such as the Director General of the Ethiopia Kaizen Institute (EKI), the Deputy Director of the Federal TVET Agency, the staff of the TVET institutes, including the instructors and *Kaizen* focal persons, and the staff of individual enterprises. Information on the *Kaizen* courses was collected from TVET-related personnel. Core employability skills required from new recruits were discussed with recruitment staff at the enterprises.

In addition, participant observations were carried out to observe the actual situation at six TVET institutes in Addis Ababa: General Winget TVET Institute, Lideta TVET Institute, Nifas Silk TVET Institute, Misrak Polytechnic College, Tegbareid TVET College, and Yeka TVET Institute.

The survey had some limitations: firstly, interviews with enterprises were conducted only with three companies and, secondly, the questionnaire was based on an opinion poll and subjective answers might be included.

5.3 *The Features of* Kaizen *Courses in TVET*

The curriculum of the *Kaizen* courses includes the *Kaizen* philosophy and tools that are taught in the classroom (Federal Ministry of Education 2014). These tools include 5S (Sort, Set in order, Shine, Standardize, and Sustain), 3MU (Mura, Muri, and Muda), 4P (Policy, Procedure, People, and Plant), 4M (Material, Method, Man, and Machine), and PDCA (Plan, Do, Check, Act). The students learn *Kaizen* through theory and practice. The curriculum was designed by EKI, the Federal TVET Agency, and Misrak Polytechnic TVET College (one of the TVET institutes in Addis Ababa).

Kaizen training progresses through five levels, from 1 to 5, along TVET grades. Level 1 teaches the overall concepts of *Kaizen*, applying the first 3S (Sort, Set in order, Shine), and organizing Junior *Kaizen* Promotion Teams (KPT). Level 2 teaches work safety and applying 2S (Standardize and Sustain) for the first 3S. Level 3 includes eliminating and preventing waste (MUDA); Level 4 involves applying problem-solving techniques and tools; and Level 5 teaches management of the continuous improvement process (*Kaizen*).

Kaizen activities such as 5S are integrated into the technical skills class and practiced by the students. Students also practice *Kaizen* while being placed in the workplace as part of cooperative training. TVET students are required to spend 70% of their time in the workplace to acquire practical skills. Furthermore, TVETs put extra effort into fostering a *Kaizen* culture within TVET. "Safety first" and "5S" signboards are seen everywhere. "*Kaizen* boards" to share information on problems, improvement points, and solutions are placed at the entrance of technical training classrooms. The Ethiopian TVET emphasizes practice or, in other words, learning by doing.

In support of this, training of the trainers (ToT) also seems to be contributing to fostering a *Kaizen* culture. TVET instructors from around Addis Ababa gather in one place to participate in ToT. During the training, TVET instructors learn how to practice 5S and PDCA cycles. The author observed groups of instructors discussing current problems of 5S implementation in TVET and proposing countermeasures to improve the situation and, thus, they were practicing problem identification and analysis with each other. This provides a better understanding of *Kaizen* when they teach their own students.

5.4 Findings from the Questionnaire and Interviews

5.4.1 Perceptions Toward the Competencies for Employability

Figure 7.2 compares the answers of those who graduated (valid responses = 79) before 2012 (N = 15) and after 2012 (N = 64) to the question on what were the most useful competencies for their current job among skills, knowledge, and attitudes learned in the TVET institute/polytechnic colleges. The results show that perceptions concerning the importance of attitudes increased from 0% to 16% after 2012 when the *Kaizen* courses were introduced within TVET. The responses reflect the Ethiopian government's policy toward enhancing the work readiness of TVET graduates and improving their focus on attitudes, which relates to

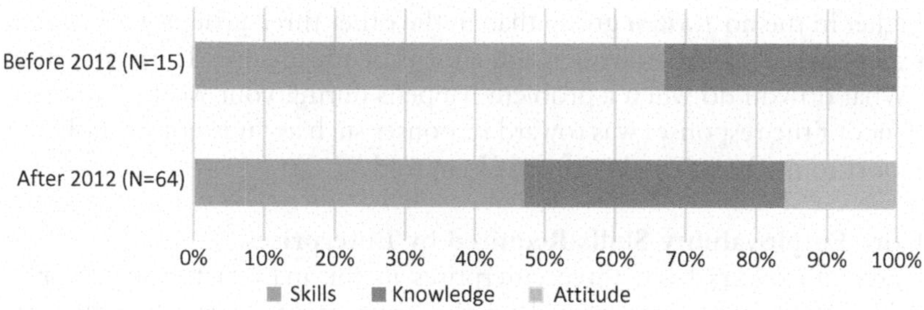

Fig. 7.2 Changes in perceptions of competencies for employability (skills, knowledge, and attitude). (Source: The authors)

core employability skills. More graduates feel that skills relating to attitudes are also important in their jobs.

5.4.2 *Perceptions of the Core Employability Skills*

In this section, we pay attention to the core employability skills related to personal qualities and process skills explained in Table 7.1, points where *Kaizen* is expected to have the greatest impact.

Core Employability Skills

Table 7.2 indicates the perceptions of core employability skills from the 175 respondents. The table compares the results among the four respondent groups. They were each asked to choose the top three sub-skills needed for work from personal qualities and process skills.

Among personal qualities, sub-skills such as self-awareness, self-confidence, willingness to learn, and independence seem to be highly regarded by all groups. Groups 1 and 2, who had taken the *Kaizen* courses in TVET, seem to have a greater appreciation of self-awareness than those who did not learn *Kaizen* in TVET. Compared to Group 4, willingness to learn is higher in Groups 1, 2, and 3, all of whom have experience of *Kaizen* in either TVET or/and the workplace. Compared to Group 4, the scores for willingness to learn are 5% higher for Group 1, 4% higher for Group 2, and 6% higher for Group 3. On the other hand, stress tolerance is higher for the no-*Kaizen* group than for the *Kaizen* groups.

Among process skills, all four groups seem to perceive teamwork as an important core employability skill. The score is particularly high compared to other sub-skills. Scores for planning are also relatively high among the process skills. The score is higher for *Kaizen* in TVET and at the workplace group than the other groups. On the other hand, negotiating is higher in the no *Kaizen* group than in the other three groups with *Kaizen* experience. Problem-solving is not a focus of any groups. To the question "What do you do when a problem happens during your work?," the tendency of the responses was toward responses such as "it is not my task," "I report to my boss," and "do what I am told."

Core Employability Skills Required by Enterprises

Three employers from three enterprises in the manufacturing sector in Addis Ababa were interviewed on the core employability skills that are important in their workplace. They chose willingness to learn, initiative, self-confidence, problem-solving, teamwork, and applying subject understanding. All three responded that willingness to learn and problem-solving are essential when recruiting new employees. One respondent revealed that, when hiring new graduates, willingness to learn is more important than having technical skills. They perceive that technical skills can be better acquired through work rather than in TVET, especially when there is no technical course that teaches skills relating to new materials or new machinery that enterprises are handling. The respondent also stated that no one has any technical skills at the beginning; therefore, an ambitious and positive attitude toward learning is more important.

Core Employability Skills Learned in the *Kaizen* Courses
A question on core employability skills was also asked to TVET graduates. There were 63 valid responses from the 67 TVET graduates who had taken the *Kaizen* courses, of which 57 students belonged to Levels 1–3. Each respondent chose the top three sub-skills learned in the *Kaizen* courses from personal qualities and process skills, such as self-confidence (43 votes), self-awareness (36 votes), willingness to learn (29 votes), independence (29 votes), and process skills such as teamwork (49 votes). Participants perceive that these personal qualities are fostered mainly through *Kaizen*.

5.5 *Analysis*

The results regarding core employability skills show that the *Kaizen* courses have fostered self-confidence, self-awareness, willingness to learn, independence, and teamwork in graduates. Furthermore, the results from Table 7.2 also demonstrate that the respondents feel these four skills are important in the workplace. This section endeavors to explore the findings in detail.

The percentage of those selecting self-confidence as an important core employability skill was high for all four groups (18%, 27%, 27%, and 25%, respectively). However, within the four groups, the percentage for Group 1 is lower than that for other groups. This shows that, while all workers feel that self-confidence is important for work, Group 1 (both TVET and at the workplace) indicates that other skills have relatively more importance—in particular, self-awareness. Self-awareness also has a relatively high percentage in all four groups but, for Groups 1 and 2, the percentage is significantly higher compared with Groups 3 and 4 (23%, 22%, 16%, and 18%, respectively).

It seems that for those who implemented *Kaizen* in both TVET and workplace, self-awareness is more important than self-confidence. This means that the longer the *Kaizen* experience, the more the importance of self-awareness grows. The *Cambridge English Dictionary* (2019) defines "self-awareness" as good knowledge and judgment about yourself. Self-awareness involves objective self-examination in order to notice one's strengths and weaknesses using absorbed knowledge. It is understandable that *Kaizen* activities of plan-do-check-action (PDCA) enhance self-awareness because they force employees to check their activities. However, 57 out of 63 valid responses belonged to *Kaizen* Levels 1–3, in which most respondents have only studied 5S and eliminating waste. This suggests that it is not the knowledge itself, but the culture that TVET is creating through implementing the *Kaizen* courses and emphasizing learning by doing—it is this change in culture that encourages students to self-reflect.

The perception toward the willingness to learn and independence is also relatively high in all four groups. However, for those who have experience of *Kaizen* in TVET or/and workplace (Groups 1, 2, and 3), there is a higher appreciation of the willingness to learn than among those who have no *Kaizen* experience (Group 4) (15%, 14%, 16%, and 10%, respectively). On the other hand, independence has a relatively high importance for Group 3 compared with the other groups (14%, 16%, 20%, and 17%, respectively). This may suggest some differences between *Kaizen* experience in TVET and the workplace. Perhaps, *Kaizen* in the workplace places greater emphasis on the independence of the workers.

All four skills fall under the category of learning to learn in Table 7.1. This means that all four groups perceive learning to learn as an important skill for work, and that, for those who had training in *Kaizen* in TVET see that the training courses have fostered their skills regarding learning to learn.

Among the process skills, the percentage of those perceiving teamwork to be an important skill was significantly higher compared to other skills in all groups (35%, 38%, 33%, and 30%). It seems that those who practice *Kaizen* have slightly higher levels of appreciation for teamwork. Teamwork also gained the highest votes among process skills for the skills learned in TVET.

On the other hand, the importance of problem-solving received a low percentage across all groups. This skill was also not selected as skills fostered in TVET training. This outcome was rather surprising, since *Kaizen* is actually a process of problem-solving.

However, understanding the *Kaizen* levels of the respondents clarifies the responses to the question. Many of the respondents belonged to Levels 1–3 in TVET, which provides the curriculum for basic *Kaizen* and does not expressly include fostering problem-solving in the contents. Problem-solving skills are developed through training in Levels 4 and 5 at PDCA. Furthermore, TVET graduates may not be placed in positions where problem-solving is needed. Perhaps they might feel that problem-solving is for managers and not for them. However, in the real world, problems exist at every level of employment and all workers are required to have some level of problem-solving skills.

In conclusion, the results show that the *Kaizen* courses in TVET foster learning to learn and teamwork but not problem-solving (communication was outside the scope of this study). In particular, the study confirmed that several skills related to learning to learn had been fostered through the *Kaizen* courses and that the graduates' appreciation of these skills is also high. This is a positive sign since learning to learn may be one of the most important skills among the core employability skills. As mentioned in Sect. 2, learning to learn is the key to self-development and life-long job security. Within a lifetime, many employees will experience different jobs in different sectors. All the aspects of learning to learn, such as self-awareness, self-confidence, and willingness to learn, will help workers transition between roles throughout their working lives. Positive outcomes arising in several layers of learning to learn indicate that the graduates' skills and perceptions of learning to learn have surely risen.

The findings of the study confirm that the Ethiopian government's policy of enhancing graduates' attitudes toward work is producing results. Enterprises also require graduates to have skills related to willingness to learn when entering the company. The three interviewees identified willingness to learn and self-confidence as skills to be required from graduates. On the other hand, since problem-solving skills are required not only in every layer of work but also in everyday life, there may be room to place greater emphasis on problem-solving skills at earlier levels.

6 The Case of South Africa

6.1 Context and Policy

South Africa's youth unemployment is exceptionally high and was reported to be 53.3% in 2017 (OECD 2018). One of the reasons is the relatively high wages compared to acquired skills. The National Treasury of South Africa stated in its 2011 discussion paper that "The gap between real wages and productivity is particularly high for young and lower-skilled workers, due to poor education, low skills and lack of work experience, and contributes to the problem of youth unemployment, as companies are reluctant to increase hiring when they cannot adequately assess potential" (2011, 6, National Treasury of South Africa). A study conducted by British Council in Kenya, Nigeria, Ghana, and South Africa confirms that while employers are generally satisfied with the academic skills of students, they are unsatisfied with their soft/cognitive skills (British Council 2014). Figure 7.1 shows the employers' views on the importance attached to different skills by university graduates (orange bar) and their level of satisfaction (blue).

The largest gap exists around problem-solving, teamwork, interpersonal skills, proactivity, and commitment. To address this gap, the Department of Higher Education and Training (DHET) published a White Paper for Post School Education and Training in 2013, indicating that workplace training and work-integrated learning (WIL) must be a central part of South Africa's training system. In 2014, 6–12 months of WIL became mandatory for diploma students studying at universities of technology. For TVET college students, an 18-month workplace program became mandatory. Even so, there seems to be a lack of discussion regarding workplace skills and personal qualities. To offset this, JICA's Employability Improvement Project (EIP) started to implement two days of training for third-year students of universities of technology before they enter the 6–12 months of the WIL program.

6.2 Employability Improvement Training

Employability Improvement Training is a two to three-day training program offered in seven universities in South Africa to prepare students for the WIL program. The training is positioned at an introductory stage of the WIL program, and funding assistance for activities is provided by the National Skills Fund (NSF). So far, 4164 students and 45 lecturers have participated in this training. The curriculum was developed by an expert team dispatched from JICA to implement the Employability Improvement Project (EIP). The training is aimed at developing seven skills that the project has identified as core employability skills: self-management, communication, teamwork, leadership, problem identification/solving, creativity, and critical/logical thinking. Training in the skills is provided through half-day lectures and a day and a half of hands-on practice.

The project identified these skills through an enterprise survey. Note that while some skills—such as communication, teamwork, and problem-solving—are listed as core employability skills in Table 7.1, other skills are also highlighted, including self-management, leadership, creativity, and critical/logical thinking. In South Africa, the market requires skills other than the four broad-based skills but, if you look at Table 7.1 carefully, you will notice that these skills also relate to the four broad-based skills. For example, self-management contributes to learning to learn, leadership to teamwork and creativity, and critical/logical thinking to problem-solving skills.

The curriculum is divided into four modules based on 3i (implementation, improvement, and innovation). The program was initially designed to be disseminated over five days but is currently delivered in two to three days due to constraints on the availability of students and lecturers.

The most distinctive feature of employability improvement training is that students experience assembling toy-trucks three times while practicing *Kaizen* and all the seven skills that they learned in the half-day of lectures. In their first round, the students are instructed to assemble the trucks by themselves or in a group of two. They are handed out a manual that indicates the quantity of each of the necessary parts and the exact specifications of the truck. It usually takes them around 1.5 hours to assemble the truck, in their first attempt. Many would have to do this a couple of times because they failed the quality checks.

In the second round, the students are put together in groups of eight to ten. Each team decides who will play the role of a supervisor, the parts shop staff, and the assembly line staff. This time, they are instructed to assemble 10 trucks within 40 minutes. In the third round, the students are encouraged to be more creative and see whether they can improve their productivity and defect rate. Before each round starts, the students are given planning time. During this time, they review the previous round and discuss how they can improve productivity and quality in the next round.

The Nissan Motor Corporation originally developed this as a hands-on learning program for schoolchildren to experience the joy of *Monozukuri*[1] and *Kaizen* as one of their Corporate Social Responsibility (CSR) activities (Nissan Motor Corporation 2018). The Employability Improvement Project got permission to use their models and modified the program to make it suitable for university students as a learning kit.

6.3 Methods

The author visited Tshwane University of Technology and Durban University of Technology in February 2018 and observed training conducted with lecturers and students. The author conducted interviews with two Japanese experts, two EIP coordinators/trainers, seven lecturers, and five students in their fourth year of the Bachelor of Technology (B Tech). The interviews were conducted in a semi-structured way. Another four students responded via e-mail questionnaire. Additionally, participant observation was conducted with the EIP training done at both universities.

Section 6.4 will discuss the findings from participant observation of EIP, while Sect. 6.5 will discuss the findings and analysis from the survey.

6.4 Participant Observation of EIP Training

6.4.1 Observations from the First Round

It is amazing to see student expressions change during the training. Students who seemed to be overly confident during the lecture, boasting that they will be the first to finish, become suddenly serious while assembling the truck. Their first attempt in assembling the "toy truck" is not going so well. Somehow, the parts being used do not allow them to assemble the truck as the instructions specify. They need to change the parts to the right ones.

One lecturer who took the course as per the instruction from the school management discussed this experience "I am teaching engineering to students so I thought that it (assembling a truck) would be easy. Once I started assembling one, it was not easy. I found out that I needed to read the instructions more carefully and that the details are important. It was a learning experience for me too." The instructions are written in a way that, unless the trainees read them carefully, they miss out on key information, so they struggle during the assembly process. The Japanese experts explained that the first round is designed to create just such a problem: it is a simulation of real life. Miscommunication and misunderstandings derived from incomplete key information occur every day—the important question is what you do about it.

6.4.2 Observations from the Second Round

In the second round, assembly time improved dramatically, and most teams had fewer defects. In this round the trainees were working in teams.

Before the assembly starts, they share their previous experiences, analyze the problems that occurred, and discuss how they can avoid them. Groups that emphasize teamwork achieve the best results. Some "supervisors" are able to react to the struggles the "operators" are facing and help them out. Others just run about not knowing what to do. Some "operators" help others when their work finishes early. This is all a working experience to shorten the delivery time and to produce a high-quality truck.

In the interviews, several students said that they had never had an opportunity to work in teams like this before. They wished that they had more opportunity like this in regular classes. Furthermore, working in teams seems to help the students realize what their strengths and weaknesses are. One lecturer commented that students often lack confidence because they have not appreciated whether or not they are good at a task.

A student's comment verified this lecturer's comments: "The training helped me realize the importance of listening to others. Sometimes, I am stubborn. Working as a team helped me look at things more objectively. I learned to be patient with other people. Taking a leadership role is not hard for me—being supportive is. I feel that I really want to change and improve. Teamwork has everything to do with it."

6.4.3 Observations from the Third Round

The third round is an attempt to enhance productivity, teamwork, and creativity. Rie Shinozaki from JICA said that "While doing the assembly work two or three times, the students gradually began to develop their own ideas and started to make more finished products with higher efficiency. This includes cleaning up the desk that serves as their work area and creating an assembly line system for the parts" (JICA 2018). The experience of thinking for themselves rather than just doing things according to the instructions—like when the students implemented countermeasures after finding traps in the manual—changes the behavior of young people in the places where they work.

6.5 Findings from the Survey

6.5.1 Results of the Survey

Nine students responded to the survey on how EIP training impacts the development of the seven core employability skills (Table 7.3).

Table 7.3 Impact of EIP training in seven core employability skills

	Change in daily action	*Took action couple of times after the training*	*Adapted the way of thinking but have not acted upon it*	*Acknowledged the concept*	*No change at all*
Learning to learn					
Self-management	5	1	3	0	0
Communication	5	2	0	2	0
Teamwork	3	4	2	0	0
Leadership	1	3	4	1	0
Problem identifying/solving	5	1	2	1	0
Critical/logical thinking	7	2	0	0	0
Creativity	2	1	1	5	0

Source: The authors

Six out of nine students indicated that they had experienced changes in self-management, seven in communication, another seven in teamwork, four in leadership, six in problem-solving, nine in critical/logical thinking, and three in creativity. The results of the survey show that more students felt the training had fostered their critical/logical thinking. Substantial numbers of students also felt that the training had an impact on self-management, communication, and teamwork. The results varied with regard to leadership and creativity.

6.5.2 *Analysis*

With the limitations of the respondents, it is hard to determine whether or not the students acquired the intended skills. Furthermore, skills are usually acquired over time. Students may need more practice to be able to deploy them in an effective way. However, it might be concluded that the training had some impact on the awareness of the skills, especially self-management, communication, teamwork, problem identification/solving, and critical/logical thinking. It would have been interesting to explore results related to self-awareness; however, this was not included in the survey items. The comments of students in the participant observations provide some indication that the training might have had some impacts on self-awareness.

Furthermore, the survey results also demonstrate that there are some skills that students have had more opportunities to exhibit than others. For instance, students may have greater opportunities to utilize skills such as teamwork, communication, and logical thinking, rather than leadership and creativity. All respondents are four-year B Tech students who have experienced internships. Employers may not expect interns to display their leadership or creativity.

7 Conclusions

While *Kaizen* is often implemented to enhance worker's core employability skills, both the Ethiopian and South African cases demonstrate how *Kaizen* training can be applied in the education sector. The Ethiopian government has been emphasizing the need to change the attitudes of its people and incorporates *Kaizen* in the TVET curriculum to aid this. In South Africa, employability improvement training is being implemented to enhance seven core employability skills and preparedness to work.

In both cases, the practice of *Kaizen*—or in other words learning by doing—is emphasized. TVET in Ethiopia has made great efforts into creating a *Kaizen* culture within TVET. In the case of South Africa, *Kaizen* is practiced through assembling toy-trucks. These are, in some ways, simulations of the workplace. The South African case shows that *Kaizen* activities are a combination of learning to learn, communication, teamwork, and problem-solving experiences.

Through continuous improvement activities and self-assessment observed in the three rounds of truck assembly in EIP training, students do become aware of their faults as well as their strengths (self-awareness). They question themselves about ways that they can improve. This question is itself a way of learning to learn. The students discuss with others their theories on how to improve (communication and teamwork). They implement their theories and assess the results (problem-solving).

Furthermore, in the case of Ethiopia, the survey results confirmed that the *Kaizen* courses foster learning to learn (self-confidence, self-awareness, and willingness to learn) and teamwork. To see whether the courses impacted problem-solving, we need more respondents from levels 4 to 5, where problem-solving is taught. The survey also shows that *Kaizen* courses have had an impact on the mindsets of students. Awareness toward learning to learn, especially self-awareness and willingness to learn, is higher for those who had *Kaizen* trainings in TVET.

While recognition of core employability skills is slowly increasing in Africa, penetration is still minimal. Many skills development projects are targeted more toward subject-specific knowledge and skills. The fact that there is no unified understanding of what core employability skills are and the lack of established curricula to enhance core employability skills may also contribute to low penetration. Workplace-based programs that focus on non-cognitive skills are known to be effective in promoting work-related skills. This chapter proposes that *Kaizen* should include activities in the school/TVET curriculum as one option to enhance the core employability skills of students.

These experiences may be much more precious in developing countries compared to more advanced economies where many other options exist. Students in advanced countries can prepare for work through internships, extracurricular activities, and volunteer work. These experiences are undoubtedly valuable for developing core employability skills. However, in many cases in Africa, getting an internship is itself a challenge.

Finally, additional studies are needed to confirm whether *Kaizen* training in TVET and technical universities has really enhanced core employability skills among graduates and whether there has been any increase in satisfaction from the employers. Further studies are also needed to understand the best way to incorporate the development of core employability skills into school curriculums in Africa.

Note

1. Monozukuri literally means "production" in Japanese. The broader term encompasses Japanese spirit towards production.

References

AfDB/OECD. 2008. *African Economic Outlook. African Development Bank Centre of the Organisation for Economic Co-operation and Development.* France: OECD Publication.

Aring, Monika. 2012. Skills Gaps Throughout the World: An Analysis for UNESCO Global Monitoring Report 2012. Paper Commissioned for the EFA Global Monitoring Report 2012.

Bennell, P. 1996. Using and Abusing Rates of Return: A Critique of the World Bank's 1995 Education Sector Review. *International Journal of Educational Development* 16 (3): 235–248.

Brewer, L. 2013. *Enhancing Youth Employability: What? Why? and How? Guide to Core Work Skills*. Geneva: International Labour Office, Skills and Employability Department, ILO.

British Council. 2014. Can Higher Education Solve Africa's Job Crisis? Understanding Graduate Employability in Sub-Saharan Africa, Going Global 2014. https://www.britishcouncil.org/sites/default/files/graduate_employability_in_ssa_final-web.pdf

Cambridge Dictionary. 2019. Self-awareness. Accessed May 9, 2019. https://dictionary.cambridge.org/dictionary/english/self-awareness

Centre of Excellence for Engineering. 2015. *Module Apply 3S Level I. Based on Occupational Standard (OS)*. Addis Ababa: Ethiopian TVET-System.

Cloutier, Marie-Helene, C. Reinstadtler, and Isabel Beltran. 2011. Making the Grade: Assessing Literacy and Numeracy in African Countries. DIME Brief. Washington, DC: World Bank

Federal Ministry of Education. 2014. Occupational Standard NTQF Level. Addis Ababa: Federal Democratic Republic of Ethiopia.

———. 2015. Education Sector Development Programme V (ESDP V). Addis Ababa: Federal Democratic Republic of Ethiopia.

Hillage, Jim, and E. Pollard. 1998. Employability: Developing a Framework for Policy Analysis. *Labour Market Trends* 107: 83–84.

International Labour Organisation (ILO). 2000. *Training for Employment: Social Inclusion, Productivity Report V*. Geneva: ILO.

———. 2004. R195 Human Resources Development Recommendation, Geneva, 92nd ILC session. https://www.ilo.org/dyn/normlex/en/f?p=NORMLEXPUB:12100:0::NO::P12100_ILO_CODE:R195

JICA. 2018. South Africa-Rainbow of Promise: Looking Ahead to the Future. *JICA's World*, July. https://www.jica.go.jp/english/publications/j-world/1807_01.html.

Jin, K. 2018. Role of Kaizen in Japan's Overseas Development Cooperation. In *Applying the Kaizen in Africa: A New Avenue for Industrial Development*, ed. K. Otsuka, Chap. 2. New York: Palgrave Macmillan.

McCowan, Tristan, Melanie Walker, Sam Fongwa, Ibrahim Oanda, Daniel Sifuna, Segun Adedeji, Stephen Oyebade, Eric Daniel Ananga, Vincent Adzahlie-Mensah, and Emmanuel Tamanja. 2016. *Universities, Employability and Inclusive Development Project (2013–2016)*. London: British Council.

Ministry of Economy, Trade, and Industry of Japan (METI). 2006. *Shakaijinkisoryoku ni kansuru kenkyukai 'chukan torimatome* [Interim Report of Study of Core Employability Skills]. Tokyo: METI.

———. 2007. *Shakaijinkisoryoku' ikusei no susume. shakaijinkisoryokuikusei puroguramu no fukyu wo mezashite* [Recommendations on Fostering Core Employability Skills. Towards Promoting Program on Core Employability Skills]. Tokyo: METI.

National Treasury of South Africa. 2011. Confronting Youth Unemployment: Policy Options for South Africa. Discussion Paper for Public Comment. http://www.treasury.gov.za/documents/national%20budget/2011/Confronting%20youth%20unemploymen%20-%20Policy%20options.pdf

Nissan Motor Cooperation. 2018. https://www.nissan-global.com/JP/CITIZENSHIP/MONOZUKURI/program.html

Ogawa, K., and A. Tansel. 2005. Transition from Education to Labor Market in Turkey. *Journal of International Cooperation Studies* 12 (3): 113–143.

Organization for Economic Cooperation and Development (OECD). 2018. *Unemployment Rate* (indicator). https://doi.org/10.1787/997c8750-en.

Psacharopoulos, G. 1986. Curriculum Diversification, Cognitive Achievement and Economic Performance: Evidence from Colombia and Tanzania. Paper Presented at the Conference on Vocationalizing General Education, Institute of Education, University of London, May 7–8.

———. 1994. Returns to Investment in Education: A Global Update. *World Development* 22 (9): 1325–1343.

Shimada, G, and T. Sonobe. 2017. Impacts of Kaizen Management on Workers: Evidence from the Central America and Caribbean Region. Paris: OECD.

United Nations (UN). 2001. *Recommendations of the High-Level Panel of the Youth Employment Network.* New York: United Nations General Assembly, September 28.

United Nations, Department of Economic and Social Affairs, Population Division. 2019. World Population Prospects 2019, Volume I: Comprehensive Tables (ST/ESA/SER_A/426).

World Bank. 2019. The Changing Nature of Work. World Development Report Working Draft. May 14, 2018. New York: World Bank. http://documents.worldbank.org/curated/en/816281518818814423/pdf/2019-WDR-Report.pdf

Yorke, M. 2006. *Employability in Higher Education: What it Is-What it is Not*, Learning and Employability Series One. York: The Higher Education Academy.

Yorke, M., and P. Knight. 2006. *Embedding Employability into the Curriculum*, Learning and Employability Series One. York: The Higher Education Academy.

PART II

The Effectiveness of *Kaizen* in Large Companies

CHAPTER 8

The Role of *Kaizen* in Participation in the Global Value Chain: The Case of the Mexican Automotive Industry

Keiji Katai

1 Introduction

The Global Value Chain (GVC) is providing new opportunities for developing countries to promote their industrialization. Taglioni and Winkler (2016) describe a value chain as "the sequence of productive (value-added) activities that capital and labor (or firms and workers) perform to bring a good or service from its conception to end use and beyond." From a business organization perspective the GVC can be described as a value chain that goes beyond country borders. However, rather than having to develop the whole chain themselves and compete in the consumer market with multi-national enterprises (MNEs), developing countries can now participate in those segments of the GVC where they may have a comparative advantage.

The GVC provides several benefits to firms in developing countries, such as access to larger markets, access to quality inputs, and access to knowledge. Benefits at the company level can also have a positive impact

K. Katai (✉)
Private Sector Development Group, Industrial Development and Public Policy Department, Japan International Cooperation Agency, Tokyo, Japan
e-mail: Katai.Keiji@jica.go.jp

A. Hosono et al. (eds.), *Workers, Managers, Productivity*,
https://doi.org/10.1007/978-981-15-0364-1_8

at the country level. Kummritz (2016) shows that an increase in GVC participation causes a rise in domestic value added and in productivity. The issue then is: how can domestic firms join the GVC and under what kind of policy?

Taglioni and Winkler (2016) present a strategic framework for lower and middle-income countries (LMICs) that will maximize their gains from participation. Acknowledging the wide variety of issues identified, this chapter focuses on the capabilities of firms, especially production management capabilities, and analyzes whether *Kaizen*, a production management system developed in Japan for improving the quality and productivity of manufacturing, can assist domestic firms participation in the GVC.

A leading company in GVC requires a variety of suppliers to produce final goods, and it is important that all deliver inputs/parts of the required quality and quantity at competitive prices without any failures. If one company does not supply the required parts and if it is difficult to otherwise source them, the leading company might need to stop sales of final goods. Considering the above, the reliability of firms backed by effective production management systems is a critical factor in the GVC.

This chapter reports on the Mexican automotive industry. The performance of 17 domestic firms that received training in *Kaizen* is analyzed. Mexico has attracted major car makers and their direct suppliers (Tier-1) that use the country as a strategic base for export to the US market. In 2016, Mexico produced 3,465,615 cars and was ranked number seven in the world. Also, major global Tier-1 firms are located in Mexico and provide opportunities for domestic firms to participate in the automotive GVC, if they meet the criteria set by the buyers (Tier-1s).

Taglioni and Winkler (2016) provide policy options for GVC participation and point out the importance of the absorptive capacity of domestic firms in relation to this. However, to the best of the author's knowledge, no study has explained changes in position in the GVC in relation to the capabilities of firms, especially their production management capabilities.

The structure of this chapter is as follows: Sect. 2 presents a review of the literature on GVC participation and the effect of foreign direct investment (FDI) on productivity improvement. Section 3 provides an overview of the automotive industry and a comparison with Thailand and Indonesia, other major developing countries engaged in automotive production. Section 4 provides the hypothesis, and Sect. 5 explains the data from the study. Analyses of these data are undertaken in Sect. 6, and policy implications and conclusions are presented in Sect. 7.

2 Literature Review

2.1 How to Participate in the GVC?

The goal of this study was to promote the participation of domestic firms in the GVC. Kummritz et al. (2017) show that favorable infrastructure, connectivity, openness of investment policy, business climate and institutions, financial and labor markets, education and skills, innovation and product standards, labor standards, social standards, and environmental standards can magnify the gains from GVC for domestic added.

Taglioni and Winkler (2016) present a strategic policy framework for LMICs to maximize their gains from the GVC. They suggest attracting FDI by providing an excellent business environment with international connectivity, guaranteeing investor protection, and so on. Once FDI is attracted, LMICs can promote participation in the GVC by backward and forward linkages, strengthening absorptive capacity, and creating an excellent workforce.

2.2 Value Chain Disaggregation and the Automotive Value Chain

Value addition and value chain disaggregation are widely used in analyzing GVCs. Mudambi (2008) shows this in the case of the iPhone (Fig. 8.1). Both ends of the value chain show high-value addition and the "smile curve." That paper used the Japan International Cooperation Agency (JICA) framework (JICA forthcoming) to analyze the automotive value chain in the Philippines (Fig. 8.2). Currently, this industry is going through a drastic transformation to cope with ride sharing, automated driving technology, electric vehicles, and so on. However, its hierarchical characteristics are still strong. The main value chain is the automaker original equipment manufacturer (OEM) from product planning to aftersales and service. The value chain of the Tier-1 (system/module parts producers) is closely related to OEM and the value chain of the Tier-2 is closely related to Tier-1.

We depict the supply chain for automobile production by connecting the midstream of these three layers (Fig. 8.2). The focus of this chapter is

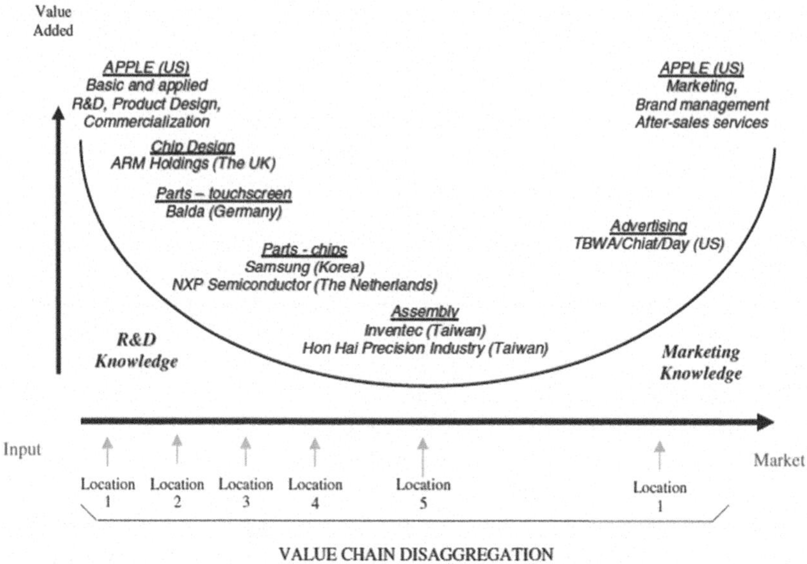

Fig. 8.1 Value creation for the iPhone. (Source: Mudambi 2008)

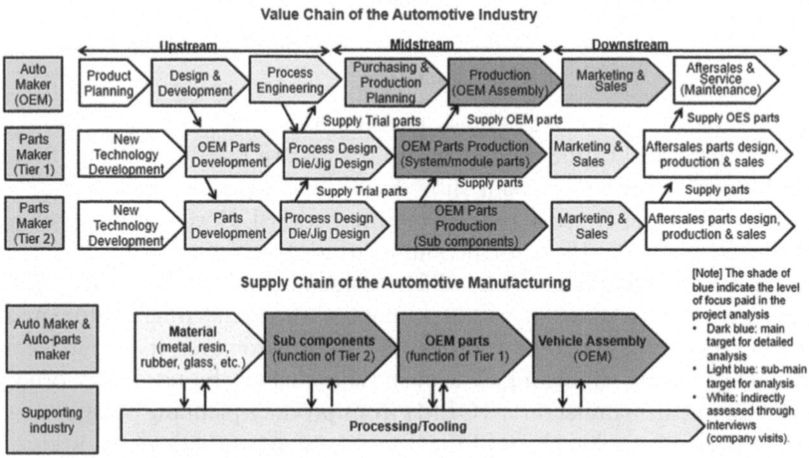

Fig. 8.2 Value chain and supply chain of the automotive industry. (Source: JICA forthcoming)

on Tier-2, but it is necessary to analyze the Tier 2/Tier 1 relationship as they sometimes collaborate in developing new parts.

2.3 GVC Stages in the Automotive Industry and the Individual Firm's Position

Even among parts makers (Tier-2), there are differences in buyer relationships. Cirera and Maloney (2017) divide the firms in the GVC from the viewpoint of capability and describe the stages of engagement as (1) the proto-connecting stage, (2) the connected stage, (3) the upgrading stage, and (4) the mature stage. They show that their characteristics are as follows: (1) at this stage firms have a minimum scale of transactions, but participation in the GVC is yet to be achieved; (2) the connected stage is an initial stage of GVC participation where the relationship is unstable and is affected by the market, but firms have basic capabilities in production and management, and can leverage these competencies to meet client demand; (3) at the upgrading stage, firms have high standards of quality and delivery and a deep relationship with other players in the chain; and (4) at the mature stage, firms have a direct relationship with the lead firm and can collaboratively conduct innovative activities.

Considering these definitions, this chapter defines the stages as follows: Stage 1 is the audit or non-supplier stage where buyers implement audits in terms of production management systems; Stage 2 is a back-up/periodic supplier; Stage 3 is a regular supplier; Stage 4 is a major supplier; Stage 5 is a partner supplier; and Stage 6 is a global partner supplier. Stages 3–5 are a breakdown of the upgrading stage as shown in Fig. 8.3.

At Stage 1, buyers use documentation, factory visits, quotations, and sample production, to examine the capacity of the potential supplier. At Stage 2, buyers order relatively small amounts of product to check whether they can use the supplier. Buyers order from these suppliers if demand increases or if there is a problem with existing suppliers. At Stage 3, buyers use several regular suppliers to diversify risk. If a supplier creates serious problems in quality or delivery, they can be downgraded to a back-up supplier. At Stage 4, the supplier has the full trust of the buyer. If the buyer has a new project, these suppliers will be the first to be asked to provide a quote. At Stage 5, the buyer develops new products in collaboration with a supplier. At Stage 6, the supplier will supply and develop products not only to domestic buyers but also to global buyers.

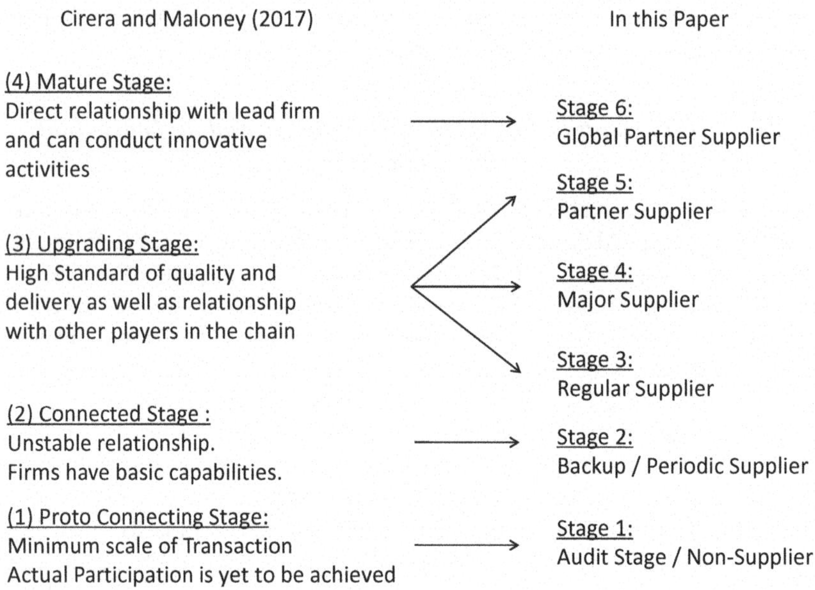

Fig. 8.3 The concept of GVC stages. (Source: Author)

This chapter looks at whether the introduction of the *Kaizen* production management system can have positive impact on firms' position in the Mexican automotive GVC using these analytical stages.

2.4 *The Driving Force for Improving Positioning in the GVC: Evaluation Based on QCD*

For Tier-2 companies to move position in the GVC, they need to satisfy their clients (Tier-1s), and in the automotive sector suppliers are selected based on quality, cost, and delivery (QCD). Individual car makers or Tier-1 companies have their own evaluation criteria of new suppliers covering many items. Recently, sustainability has been emphasized in purchasing policy, but QCD is always included. Renault-Nissan uses the evaluation criteria of QCDDM (Quality, Cost, Delivery, Development, and Management).[1] Honda uses QCDD (Quality, Cost, Delivery, and Development),[2] and while Toyota does not mention QCD, it requires quality items at a low price and in a timely manner, which is equal to

QCD.[3] It is thus critical for Tier-2 firms to improve Tier-1 company evaluations from the viewpoint of QCD.

2.5 *Productivity Improvement,* Kaizen, *and Firm Capabilities*

How can Tier-2 companies improve their capabilities related to QCD? They can improve capacity either through obtaining additional internal resources or through using external resources such as backward/forward linkages with FDI and direct technical support. The concept of productivity spillover from FDI has been widely explored in earlier studies of the causal relationship between FDI and productivity improvement in forward/backward linkages. However, these produced mixed results (Görg and Greenaway 2004). While a statistically significant spillover effect on forward linkages was not observed, empirical studies have shown a causal relationship in backward linkages (see Gorodnichenko et al. 2014; Blalock and Gertler 2008; Javorick 2004).

Guzman-Anaya (2013) analyzed inter-industry productivity spillovers from Japanese and US FDI in the Mexican manufacturing sector. Their study showed that Japanese FDI increases productivity in backward-linked industries but the productivity gains accrue to foreign rather than domestic suppliers. This study targets the automotive industry in Mexico and it is possible that, in this sector, we might see positive spillover effects on domestic industries. However, productivity spillovers from FDI to domestic industry do not always happen. Cusolito et al. (2016) note that the impact of local MNEs on SMEs and other firms in low-income countries is difficult to predict. According to them it is important to look at the quality and standards that are emphasized by MNEs when upgrading domestic firms and they suggest providing direct technical assistance to firms, given that demand effects alone have a limited impact on spillover and support from MNEs tends to cover more general matters.

One possible way to implement direct technical assistance is to introduce *Kaizen*. As described in the introductory chapter, *Kaizen* is an inclusive and participatory approach to the continuous improvement of quality and productivity, resting on its distinctive philosophy and tools/methods, and is the base of management systems, including Total Quality Management (TQM) and Toyota Production System (TPS), developed in Japan and adapted to other countries. The virtue of *Kaizen* is its characteristic of self-sustainability. Once a company acquires capacity to implement *Kaizen*, it can continue to improve productivity and quality without relying on outside experts and it can enhance its absorptive capacity to learn from FDI.

3 The Mexican Automotive Industry

Since Mexico concluded the North American Free Trade Agreement (NAFTA) in 1994, it has developed the automotive industry as a base for exports to the United States. In 2016, the country exported 2,768,000 cars, ranking number three in the world. Mexico is thus a major hub for car manufacturing. However, the major players in the industry are FDI car makers and suppliers, and the presence of domestic firms in the industry is low. Also, the aggregate size of Tier-2 and Tier-3 parts makers in comparison with Tier-1 parts makers is much smaller than that in Thailand. Table 8.1 shows that the ratio of Tier-2 and Tier-3 firms to Tier-1 firms in Thailand is more than 4 times that of Mexico. Also, the local procurement ratio by Japanese car manufacturers and suppliers is 34.6 percent and this is considerably lower than that in Indonesia (43.3 percent) and Thailand (63.1 percent) (JETRO 2018).

In 2017, 92 firms of the top-100 global Tier-1s were in Mexico. Global players increased investment recently and such trend can be seen in the changes in the countries' trade specialization index. This index is derived as (Export – Import)/(Export + Import) and it shows the dependence on imports of individual products. If a country depends on products from abroad, the index becomes negative. If the country expands local capacity reducing dependence on imports, the index comes closer to zero and when it expands further and exports more than it imports, the number becomes positive. Table 8.2 shows that the auto parts trade specialization index in Mexico has improved recently and some parts have turned positive, compared with Indonesia where most parts are still negative. At the

Table 8.1 The structure of the automotive industry

	Indonesia	*Thailand*	*Mexico*
(a) Production of vehicles in 2016 (000)	1177	1944	3597
(b) Number of Tier-1 firms	550	635	383
(c) Number of Tier-2 and Tier-3 firms	1000	1700	233
(d) Tier-2 and Tier-3 ratio (= (c) / (b))	1.8	2.7	0.6

Source: Production Data from JETRO (2017). The tier structures of Indonesia and Thailand are based on Mizuho Financial Group (2017). The tier structure of Mexico is based on Hoshino (2015)

Table 8.2 Trade specialization index of Indonesia, Thailand, and Mexico

HS code	*Year*	*Indonesia 2016*	*Thailand 2016*	*Mexico 2012*	*Mexico 2016*	*Mexico Change*
8703	Motor cars and other mother vehicles designed to transport of persons	0.37	0.85	0.58	0.52	−0.07
8708	Parts & access for motor vehicles	−0.13	0.08	−0.04	0.07	0.11
870810	Bumpers	−0.43	0.43	−0.21	−0.10	0.11
870821	Safety seat belts	−0.09	0.88	0.76	0.83	0.08
870829	Vehicles, parts and accessories of bodies, other than safety seat belts	−0.05	0.22	−0.02	0.08	0.10
870830	Brakes and servo-brakes	−0.45	0.21	−0.08	0.09	0.18
870840	Gear boxes	0.14	−0.50	−0.45	−0.23	0.22
870850	Drive-axels with differential	−0.39	−0.07	0.11	0.31	0.20
870870	Road wheels	0.64	0.27	0.00	0.20	0.20
870880	Suspension systems	−0.39	0.18	−0.17	0.03	0.20
870891	Radiators	0.34	0.32	−0.10	−0.00	0.10
870892	Mufflers and exhaust pipes	−0.57	0.10	−0.42	−0.30	0.12
870893	Clutches	−0.08	0.07	−0.50	−0.44	0.06
870894	Steering wheels, steering columns, and steering boxes	−0.81	0.33	0.03	0.10	0.07
870895	Safety airbags with inflater system	−0.76	0.32	0.24	0.28	0.04
39	Plastics and articles	−0.51	0.17	−0.45	−0.45	−0.00
40	Rubber and articles	0.54	0.69	−0.45	−0.42	0.03
73	Iron or steel articles	−0.27	−0.23	−0.23	−0.24	−0.01
76	Aluminum and articles	−0.56	−0.37	−0.62	−0.44	0.18

Source: Author created the table using the United Nations Commodity Trade Statistics Database (UN Comtrade)

Note: Trade specialization index is derived as (Export − Import) / (Export + Import)

same time, the Mexican trade specialization index for raw materials such as plastics, rubber, iron, and aluminum remains negative.

Thus, we can assume that Mexico has become a hub for vehicle production and automotive parts from the number of car makers and, Tier-1 suppliers located there; however, the presence of domestic Tier-2 firms is still small and a large percentage of parts are supplied from abroad. Using the framework of Taglioni and Winkler (2016), Mexico has already achieved the first step of attracting foreign investors in the automotive sector and this can be the starting point for expanding and strengthening GVC participation.

4 Hypothesis and Methodologies

4.1 Hypothesis

In this study, the following hypothesis is tested: *Kaizen* has a positive impact on Tier-2 firms for upgrading in the GVC stages and then on business expansion. In this chapter, we define *Kaizen* as including not only 5S but also several tools from the Toyota Production System (TPS) such as Just in Time and Single Minutes Exchange of Die (SMED), which focus on eliminating any kind of inefficiency in production.

The theory of change in the hypothesis is illustrated in Fig. 8.4. First, if properly implemented (STEP 1), *Kaizen* can bring about benefits for Tier-2s in terms of quality and productivity (STEP 2). For example, if abnormal conditions in the production space are visualized through 5S, the production of defective products may be avoided. If mold changing time is reduced, operators can improve productivity. Second, improvement in quality and productivity of Tier-2 suppliers can trigger improvement in their QCD evaluations by Tier-1 buyers (STEP 3). For example, if the defect/product ratio is reduced by Tier-2 suppliers, Tier-1 buyers may improve their evaluations related to quality. Also, if the production of defective products is reduced in-factory, this can lower production costs. This may be reflected in price quotations and may have positive impact on cost evaluations by Tier-1 firms. Also, if the changing time for mold is reduced, this will enable firms to produce products with minimum stoppage times of machines. This flexibility may improve delivery times to Tier-1 buyers. All changes in quality and productivity can thus have positive impacts on the evaluation of QCD by Tier-1 firms.

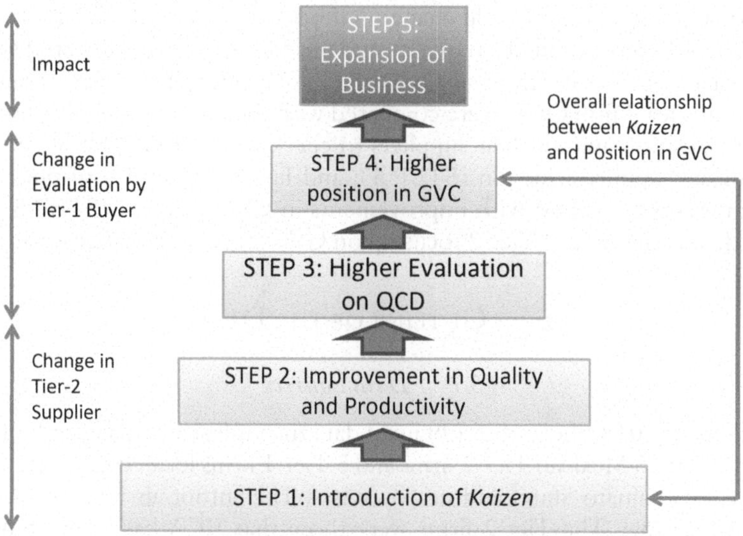

Fig. 8.4 The impact from *Kaizen* on GVC position and business. (Source: Author)

Third, if Tier-1 buyers can improve their evaluation of Tier-2 suppliers using QCD, they may feel more comfortable about relying on the supply of parts by Tier-2 suppliers and this can improve their evaluation of Tier-2 suppliers in the GVC (STEP 4). Fourth, if Tier-1 firms recognize a Tier-2 supplier as more important and if their position in the GVC is higher, business between them may be expanded. This may also have positive impacts on other Tier-1 buyers when sourcing parts within the automotive industry (STEP 5).

4.2 *Methodology*

This study analyzed flows of impact (Fig. 8.4) using information from both Tier-2 firms and Tier-1 firms. Changes in Tier-1 firm evaluations of GVC position before and after *Kaizen* were used to identify the overall relationship between intervention using *Kaizen* and position in the GVC (STEPS 1 and 4).

The analysis of step-by-step impact was carried out as follows: first, improvements in quality and productivity as measured by defective product ratios and reductions in mold changing times were analyzed (STEPS 1 and 2); second, improvements in quality and productivity were compared with the Tier-1 firm evaluations of QCD (STEP 3); third, Tier-1 firm evaluations of Tier-2 firm QCD were compared with their evaluation of the same firm's position among their suppliers to check whether QCD evaluations influence supplier selection (STEP 4); and finally, expansion of business volume was compared with improvements in GVC position (STEP 5) to check the relevance of Tier-2 focusing on GVC stages to enhance business.

5 Outline of the Data

5.1 Data Sources

In January 2018, the author obtained data through semi-structured interviews with 15 Mexican Tier-2 firms and 5 Tier-1 firms located in Queretaro State, Guanajuato State, and nearby states. The author also visited factories if possible. The Tier-2 firms were those that JICA has supported in their capacity building efforts and in the introduction of *Kaizen*. Tier-1 firms are the Japanese FDI firms that buy the products of the Tier-2 firms (partner Tier-1s). However, as the Tier-1 firms were Japanese FDI only, there is the possibility of selection bias in the results.

Tier-2 firms provided information relating to total sales volume, sales volume for the automotive business, sales volume for major clients, defective product ratios in-factory as well as at-customer, time required for changing molds, and so on. Tier-1s provided an evaluation of their suppliers (Tier-2s) on quality, cost, delivery, overall QCD, and position in the GVC.

5.2 Outline and Intention of the JICA-Supported Project

Based on a request from the Government of Mexico, JICA supported a project for automotive supply chain development from 2012 to 2015. Under this project, JICA collaborated with the state governments of Guanajuato, Queretaro, and Nuevo Leon, as well as with ProMéxico, which is a government agency for promoting trade and investment, in strengthening the supply chains between Japanese Tier-1 firms and domestic Tier-2 firms.

One of the major components of that project was the capacity development of Tier-2 firms in the field of *Kaizen*. JICA supported 27 Tier-2 firms in collaboration with 7 Tier-1 firms by assigning *Kaizen* experts with experience in the automotive industry, conducting diagnoses of each firm, setting improvement targets in collaboration with buyer Tier-1s, and supporting the implementation of activities for one year. Typical topics were 5S, reduction of defective product ratios, improvements in job throughput per hour, reduction in mold changing times, reductions in down time, and reduction in inventory.

6 Findings and Analysis

In this study, the relationships between *Kaizen* and improvement in quality and productivity and positioning in GVC were analyzed. Due to the constraint of survey time, this study covered only Tier-2 firms in the states of Guanajuato and Queretaro.

6.1 *The Overall Relationship Between* Kaizen *and Position in the GVC*

Under this project, *Kaizen* activities in the field of productivity and quality by Tier-2 firms were carried out, along with setting goals in collaboration with Tier-1. The results of the evaluation for each Tier-2 firm before and after intervention are shown in Fig. 8.5. Of 17 Tier-2 firms that received feedback from their buyers (Tier-1), 8 (47 percent) improved their position (above the line), 5 (29 percent) maintained their position (on the line), and 4 (24 percent) dropped position (below the line). Regarding those firms that dropped position, two had stopped being a supplier due to their high costs and their partner Tier-1 firm's policy of reducing supplier numbers. One stopped being a partner supplier to major suppliers due to trouble with internal management. The remaining firm was evaluated as a major supplier, received higher orders, and constructed a new factory, but their partner Tier-1 degraded evaluations temporarily while settling down the factory. The medium rating before *Kaizen* was regular supplier (Stage 3) and the medium rating after *Kaizen* was major supplier (Stage 4). However, the information received was only for the treated group and information on changes in positioning in the GVC of the control group or the overall Mexican automotive parts industry could not be obtained. The absence of a control group also affects our ability to infer causality. According to the Tier-1 firms, the number of Tier-2 suppliers supported under the project remained unchanged or was reduced. This

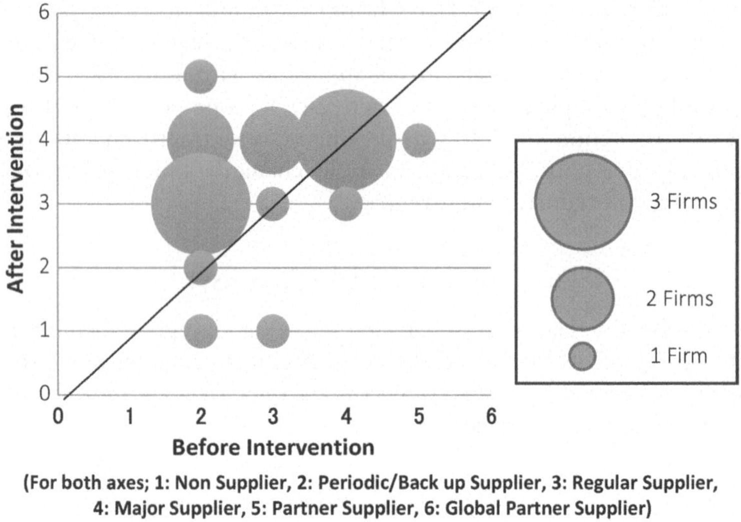

Fig. 8.5 Changes in position in the GVC before and after *Kaizen*. (Source: Author)

suggests that the relative position of Tier-2 suppliers who improved position in the GVC outperformed other Tier-2 suppliers. To conclude, among those firms that implemented *Kaizen* during the study period, 76 percent improved or maintained their position in the GVC in comparison to the other Tier-2 suppliers to the same Tier-1 buyer.

6.2 STEPS 1 and 2: Impact of Kaizen *on Quality and Productivity*

This section summarizes the information related to quality and productivity before and after intervention using *Kaizen*.

6.2.1 Quality

For quality, a core requirement of Tier-1 firms is supply of the products that satisfy the specifications defined in the contract between Tier-1 and Tier-2 firms. This requirement can be interpreted as reduction of the defective product ratio. Accordingly, among the several topics chosen for *Kaizen* in the JICA project, reduction in defective products was one of the major issues.

In our survey information on defect rates at the customer level before and after *Kaizen* intervention and on the evaluation of Tier-2s from the quality viewpoint was collected. In the automotive industry the defect rate is expressed as the number of defective parts per million (PPM). After intervention, the defect rate was reduced substantially. Of the 15 firms that gave information, 10 reduced their defect rate by more than 40 percent or it stayed negligible (0~5 PPM) and 12 firms reduced their rates to less than 100 PPM.

There are no data on the average number of defect PPM in the Mexican auto parts industry, but 100 PPM is lower than the average number of PPM based on JETRO's database on domestic automotive parts makers in Mexico; thus we can suggest that *Kaizen* has had a positive impact on quality.

6.2.2 Productivity

In terms of productivity *Kaizen* activities were carried out in the areas of reduction of mold changing times, reduction of waiting times for production, inventory reduction, and reduction of defects in-factory. The first two items improve output through higher operation ratios, while the latter reduce inputs related to unused output.

Of the 17 Tier-2 firms supported by the project, 10 tackled reductions in mold changing time. The average reduction rate was about 54 percent and 6 out of 10 firms reduced this more than 50 percent. In the automotive industry, where around 30,000 parts are used in a vehicle and where assembly of each model is carefully controlled to minimize stock, parts makers are required to adjust production volumes of individual parts every week or so. This creates frequent changes of mold, and each change consumes hours by stopping production machines. This situation negatively affects productivity. The JICA project introduced a method to tackle this issue. It starts with an analysis of the mold changing process, eliminating unnecessary steps, shifting processes requiring stoppage of the machines to processes without stoppage, and improving efficiency in individual steps. This method has been very important in the plastic injection industry, which uses various types of molds and has achieved positive impacts as explained earlier.

Also, of the 17 firms supported by the project, the reduction in the defect rate in-factory by the 13 firms that commented was 54 percent on average, and 9 firms achieved more than 50 percent. To the best of our knowledge, there are no data on productivity improvement in the auto parts industry, so our data could not be compared with an industry average.

6.3 STEP 3: Impact of Quality and Productivity on Tier-1 Firms' Evaluation on QCD

In this section, the relationship between improvements in quality and productivity and Tier-1 firm evaluations of Tier-2 firms on quality and cost is discussed. The purpose was to check whether improvements have a positive impact on buyer's perception. Tier-1 evaluations were classified from unacceptable (level 1) to satisfactory (level 4). Indicators related to delivery were not captured in this project so the relationship between achievement in delivery and evaluation from Tier-1 firms is not analyzed here.

6.3.1 *Quality*

The relationship between the defect rate after *Kaizen* intervention and the evaluation of quality is plotted in Fig. 8.6. Of 15 Tier-2 firms, 12 reduced the defect rate to the customer to less than 100 PPM. Several firms recorded zero or one-digit defects per million products. The firms with less than 100 PPM were evaluated as at either a satisfactory level of quality

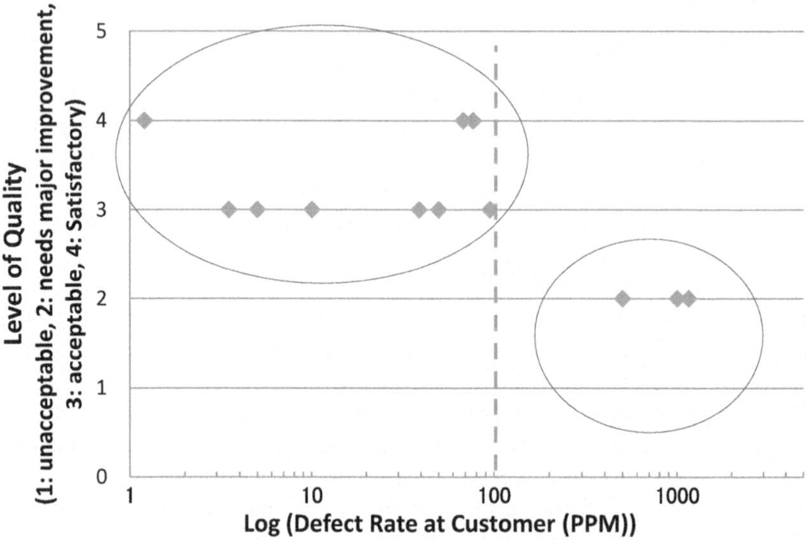

Fig. 8.6 Defect rates and Tier-1 firm evaluations of quality. Note: Four firms are plotted in the upper-left quadrant (negligible PPM and level 4 of quality). (Source: Author)

or an acceptable level of quality by the Tier-1 firms that provided feedback (circle upper left). In the three firms that recorded more than 100 PPM, this was evaluated as trouble in quality control (circle lower right).

In Fig. 8.6, plots are concentrated at upper left and lower right, and the defect rate between 100 PPM and 500 PPM is a dividing ridge between acceptable-level quality (level 3) and trouble-making quality (level 2). This relationship suggests that improvement in the quality of products measured as reductions in defect rates has a positive impact on the evaluation of quality by buyers. This idea coincides with the Tier-1 interview results in that they would like their suppliers to reduce defect rates to less than 100 PPM, and preferably down to single digits.

6.3.2 Cost

The relationship between productivity and Tier-1 firm evaluations of cost has several intermediary factors. Productivity improvement can have positive impacts on production cost reduction when other factors such as raw materials are kept unchanged. For example, if a company produces a defective product, this will require additional material costs, additional labor, opportunity costs of machine operation, and additional costs for storage. If the cost for setting up a mechanism to reduce the number of defective products is lower than the cost related to defect product, quality control should certainly reduce the total cost of production.

Then, Tier-2 firms will decide how much to quote. They might reflect the entire reduction or part of the reduction of production costs in a quotation. And finally, buyers (Tier-1 firms) will evaluate the price from their own view point. In the automotive sector, it is common practice to have a project life of around five years and car makers request suppliers to achieve reductions in price by 3 percent or so annually. This rate becomes a baseline for negotiation. The second and third steps are negotiation processes, and they are affected by competition. If Tier-2 firms have several buyers, they might be reluctant to reduce prices substantially. And if Tier-1 firms have several suppliers for a product, they might request a larger reduction.

In this survey, information related to production cost and quotation price could not be captured, but there were two findings. One was expansion of productivity improvement and the other was the Tier-1 firm evaluations from a cost point of view. There was no direct relationship observed between defect rate in-factory or reduction in mold changing times and Tier-1 firms' evaluation of costs.

Tier-2 firm interviews showed that all were expanding *Kaizen* activities to other production lines beyond that supported under the project, recognizing the benefit from those activities. This result supports the hypothesis that *Kaizen* has a positive impact on production cost. Regarding the evaluation by Tier-1 firms, 12 Tier-2 firms were evaluated as satisfactory or acceptable from a cost point of view. This result shows that Tier-2 suppliers are somehow meeting the demand for cost reduction from Tier-1 firms. There is no evidence, but one of the major sources of these cost reductions could be productivity improvement. Among the four firms rated lower in cost, three had already actively expanded their clients within the auto parts segment and the electrical industry. For them, there may have been a negotiation factor on prices.

To conclude, a positive relationship between low defect rates and Tier-1 firm evaluations of quality was observed. Regarding the relationship between productivity and Tier-1 firm evaluations on cost, while a clear and direct relationship was not seen, some information that supports the positive relationship was observed.

6.4 STEP 4: Relationship Between Evaluation of QCD and Evaluation of Positioning in the GVC

6.4.1 QCD and Positions in the GVC

It is widely understood that QCD is an important criterion for auto parts suppliers. This is understandable because, if Tier-2 suppliers can supply the required amount of high-quality product at competitive prices without delay, buyers can utilize the resulting benefits and in turn supply competitive products to car makers. Thus, buyers should be happy to contract those suppliers. To check this viewpoint, Tier-1 firms were asked to rate their suppliers in terms of QCD as well as their position in the GVC. Supplier rating was categorized from Stage 1 (non-supplier) to Stage 6 (global partner), as defined in the Hypothesis section. QCD rating was carried out from level 1 (unacceptable), level 2 (troublesome, needing major improvement), level 3 (acceptable), to level 4 (satisfactory).

The results of the evaluation for each Tier-2 firm are plotted in Fig. 8.7. By introducing a vertical line between QCD levels B & C and a horizontal line between GVC levels C & D, 11 firms are in the first quadrant where both QCD and GVC are high, 3 firms are in the third quadrant where both QCD and GVC are low, and 2 firms are in the second quadrant

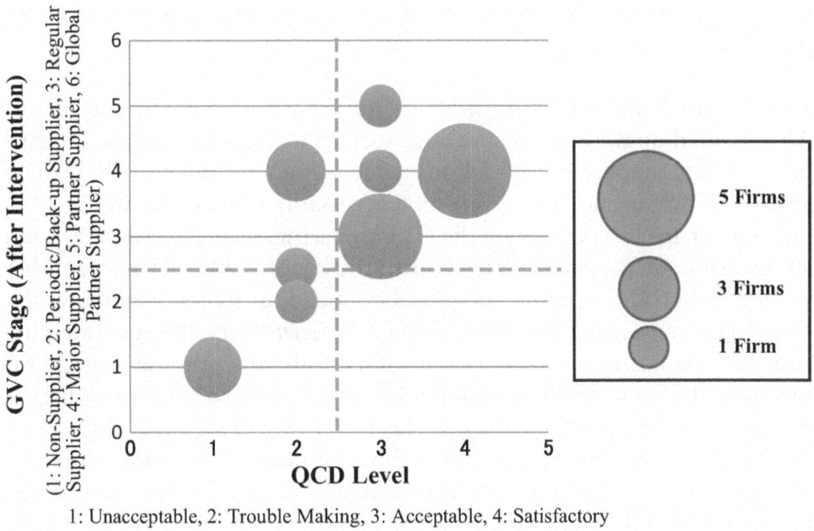

Fig. 8.7 Tier-1 firms' evaluation on QCD and position in GVC. (Source: Author)

where QCD is low and GVC is high. One firm is at the border between the second and third quadrants.

Regarding the two firms in the second quadrant, it became clear through the interviews that Tier-1s view the problem of QCD as a somewhat temporary situation for two firms. One company was a major supplier in the past and recently has been facing problems of quality control after shifting to a new factory. Tier-1 companies were observing this situation as temporary problem that could be managed. In another case, the Tier-2 was a level 5 (partner supplier) in the past and was regarded as one of the best suppliers in the segment. However, there was a change in company management, and a degradation in cash flow took place when the company was damaged by fraud. It is currently having trouble with product delivery. Nevertheless, the Tier-1 has some trust in the supplier from their relationship in the past and is hoping to bring the firm back to its original quality level.

Considering the exceptionality of the two firms in the second quadrant, we can observe a positive relationship between QCD level and position in the GVC. Also, we see that it is necessary to achieve QCD level 3 (acceptable) or higher to become a regular supplier or to be placed higher in the GVC.

6.4.2 *The Road to Partner Supplier/Role of Support for Tier-2 Firms*

An extended question in the previous section was whether it is possible to be a partner supplier if Tier-2 firms achieve higher ratings in QCD. The answer is "we are not sure," or "not necessarily." As shown in Fig. 8.7, only one firm had a position in the GVC at partner level (level 5). Through an interview with a partner Tier-1 firm, the history of the Tier-2 firm that wished to become a partner supplier became clear. At the beginning, the Tier-1 firm nominated the Tier-2 firm for *Kaizen* intervention because the supplier was facing several issues in QCD. Subsequently the Tier-2 firm introduced 5S, increased production per hour, reduced time for changing molds, and achieved the goal set by the Tier-1 firm. The Tier-1 firm found the output to be satisfactory and highly appreciated the commitment of the company to improvement. Subsequently, the Tier-1 firm considered this Tier-2 firm to have potential to be a partner firm and provided hands-on support for it to acquire the capacity to conduct the maintenance of molds and become a partner firm in the new model.

Figure 8.7 also shows that among the eight firms that improved their position in the GVC, all were either regular suppliers (Stage 3) or back-up/periodic suppliers (Stage 2) to higher positions, but none of them were major suppliers (Stage 4). This shows that even if intervention from outside facilitates improvement in the QCD capabilities of firms, it will be effective at relatively lower positions in the GVC, but it is critical to have guidance or commitment from buyers to improve to partner supplier (level 5).

6.5 *STEP 5: Improvement in GVC and Expansion of Business Volume*

The annual growth rates of sales for partner Tier-1 firms under the project as well as the annual growth rate for the auto parts segment were analyzed. Table 8.3 shows the distribution of annual growth rates. Among the growth rate from 0 to 20 percent, a division is inserted at 6 percent,[4] which was the average growth rate of auto parts in the target region. Linear approximation equations were also prepared for annual growth rate against changes in position in the GVC. If the position moved from a back-up supplier (Stage 2) to a major supplier (Stage 4), the change is recorded as two. Positive relationships between position in GVC and

Table 8.3 Annual growth rate of sales

	Annual growth rate of sales for partner Tier-1 firms		*Annual growth rate of sales for auto parts segment*	
	Number of Tier-2 firms	*Ratio (%)*	*Number of Tier-2 firms*	*Ratio (%)*
More than 20%	4	33.3	10	71.4
More than 0%	5	41.7	4	28.6
More than 6%	5	41.7	2	14.3
More than 0%	0	0.0	2	14.3
More than −20%	2	16.7	0	0.0
No business (−100%)	1	8.3	0	0.0
Total	12	100.0	14	100.0
Linear approximation equation ($Y = aX + b$)				
a	−0.9123		0.2522	
B	0.324		0.0066	
R square	0.4656		0.0013	

Source: Author

growth of sales for partner Tier-1 firms were observed and a 32 percent increase in sales can be expected for an increase of GVC position by one point. However, a relationship between positions in the GVC and sales volumes was not observed.

Based on the above we can derive two results. One is that improvement in GVC position is positively correlated with business expansion with partner Tier-1 firms. The other is a diversification effect that is exactly what Tier-2 firms are trying to achieve to avoid volatility in business. In this study, out of 15 firms, 10 successfully acquired one to four new Tier-1 clients.

7 Conclusions and Policy Implications

7.1 Conclusions

In this study, the relationships between *Kaizen* and improvements in quality and productivity and positioning in the GVC were analyzed. Seventeen Tier-2 firms were interviewed and therefore a rigorous statistical analysis could not be carried out, but some findings were derived.

First, the positive impact of *Kaizen* for improving and maintaining position in the GVC was observed in comparison with other Tier-2 suppliers for the same Tier-1 firms. Second, the introduction of *Kaizen* had a positive impact on quality and productivity (STEPS 1 and 2). Indicators of the defective product rates at the customer level were checked for quality, and indicators of mold changing times and the defect product rates in-factory were checked from the productivity point of view.

Third, any positive impacts of improvement in quality and productivity on Tier-1 firm evaluations of Tier-2 firms were analyzed (STEP 3). A positive relationship between improvement of quality in terms of defective products at customer and Tier-1 firm evaluations of quality was observed. However, a clear and direct relationship was not observed between productivity and Tier-1 firm evaluations of cost. Nevertheless, some information that supports positive relationships was observed.

Fourth, a positive relationship between Tier-1 firm evaluation of QCD levels and their evaluation of GVC position was observed (STEP 4). If a Tier-2 firm is targeting to be a major supplier, it should achieve an acceptable level 3 QCD rating by Tier-1 firms. It was also noted that becoming a partner supplier (Stage 5) requires more than QCD and should include support from Tier-1 firms.

Fifth, a positive relationship between Tier-1 firm evaluations of Tier-2 firm positions in the GVC and business volume between the two was observed (STEP 5); however, a relationship between Tier-1 firm evaluations of Tier-2 firm positions and their total sales in the auto parts segment was not observed. The major reason for this could be the diversification effort by the Tier-2 firms. It is also observed that 14 out of the 15 firms with data available expanded sales more than the industry average of 6 percent.

7.2 Policy Implications

The major policy implication of this study is that the introduction of *Kaizen* can facilitate promotion in position in the automotive industry GVC, and it should be widely recommended to Tier-2 suppliers to do this. As shown earlier, Tier-2 firms expanded *Kaizen* activities beyond the production line supported under the project and achieved business expansion higher than the industry average. These results show that the supported Tier-2 firms achieved major internal transformation for production management capabilities as well as competitiveness in the domestic market.

Second, due to the small sample size concentrating on Japanese Tier-1 firms and the absence of a control group, our ability to infer causality was negatively affected. Further studies should analyze the validity of these conclusions. Also, the relationship between improvements in quality and productivity (STEP 2) and Tier-1 firm evaluations of QCD should be further explored. For example, to explain the relationship between productivity and cost, other intermediary data such as sales price or profit ratios would be useful. The interviews with Tier-1 firms showed that they evaluate suppliers at the time of trial orders and in periodic reviews of ongoing business. They often reward superior suppliers using these data. Analysis of those evaluations might suggest additional strategies for improving position in the GVC.

Third, *Kaizen* itself may be difficult to implement in moving Tier-2 firms up to partner supplier level (Stage 5), so it may be better to focus on Tier-2 firms as either back-up/periodic suppliers (Stage 2) or regular suppliers (Stage 3) when providing technical support. For Tier-2 firms to become partner suppliers, additional features such as R&D capability or a strong relationship with Tier-1 firms might be necessary.

Finally, it is important to have collaboration with Tier-1 firms in implementing *Kaizen* and setting targets. A target of 100 PPM has been derived from the quality point of view, but it may be better to identify the requirements for improving Tier-1 firm evaluations on quality, cost, and delivery as well as position in the GVC among competitors through collaboration with Tier-1 firms.

Notes

1. https://www.nissan-global.com/EN/DOCUMENT/PDF/SR/Renault_Nissan_Purchasing_Way_English.pdf.
2. http://world.honda.com/sustainability/report/pdf/2015/Honda-SR-2015-en-087.pdf.
3. https://www.toyota-industries.com/company/procurement/policy/index.html.
4. The average growth rate of the industry is based on the interviews of the automotive cluster in Queretaro State.

References

Blalock, Garrick, and Paul J. Gertler. 2008. Welfare Gains from Foreign Direct Investment Through Technology Transfer to Local Suppliers. *Journal of International Economics* 74 (2): 402–421.

Cirera, Xavier, and William F. Maloney. 2017. *The Innovation Paradox: Developing-Country Capabilities and Unrealized Promise of Technological Catch-up*. Washington, DC: World Bank.

Cusolito, Ana Paula, Raed Safadi, and Daria Taglioni. 2016. *Inclusive Global Value Chains: Policy Options for Small and Medium Enterprises and Low-Income Countries*, Directions in Development. Washington, DC: World Bank.

Görg, Holger, and David Greenaway. 2004. Much Ado About Nothing? Do Domestic Firms Really Benefit from Foreign Direct Investment? *The World Bank Research Observer* 19 (2): 171–197.

Gorodnichenko, Yuriy, Jan Svejnar, and Katherine Terrell. 2014. When Does FDI Have Positive Spillovers? Evidence from 17 Transition Market Economies. *Journal of Comparative Economics* 42 (4): 954–969.

Guzman-Anaya, Leo. 2013. Inter-Industry Productivity Spillovers from Japanese and US FDI in Mexico's Manufacturing Sector. *Technology and Investment* 4 (4): 236–243.

Hoshino, Taeko. 2015. *Automotive Supply Chain in Mexico. Tokyo—Is It Possible to Participate for Mexican Firms* (in Japanese). Tokyo: JETRO, Institute of Developing Economies (IDE).

Japan External Trade Organization (JETRO). 2017. *Trends in the Production and Sales of Automotive Parts in Major Countries in 2016*. Tokyo: JETRO.

———. 2018. Auto Parts Industry in Mexico Still Has Large Opportunities for Expansion of Business from Japan (in Japanese). *Area Report*. Tokyo: JETRO.

Japan International Cooperation Agency (JICA). Forthcoming. *Final Report for Project for Elaboration of Industrial Promotion Plans Using Value Chain Analysis in the Republic of the Philippines*. Tokyo: JICA.

Javorick, Beata Smarzynska. 2004. Does Foreign Direct Investment Increase the Productivity of Domestic Firms? In Search of Spillovers Through Backward Linkages. *American Economic Review* 94 (3): 605–627.

Kummritz, Victor. 2016. Do Global Value Chains Cause Industrial Development? *CTEI Working Papers 01-2016*. Geneva: Centre for Trade and Economic Integration, Graduate Institute.

Kummritz, Victor, Daria Taglioni, and Deborah Winker. 2017. Economic Upgradation Through Global Value Chain Participation: Which Policies Increase the Value Added Gains. *Policy Research Working Paper 8007*. Washington, DC: World Bank.

Mizuho Financial Group. 2017. *Mizuho Research & Analysis 2017 No. 12*. Tokyo: Mizuho Financial Group.

Mudambi, Ram. 2008. Location, Control and Innovation in Knowledge-Intensive Industries. *Journal of Economic Geography* 8 (5): 699–725.

Taglioni, Daria, and Deborah Winkler. 2016. *Making Global Value Chains Work for Development*. Trade and Development. Washington, DC: World Bank. https://elibrary.worldbank.org/doi/book/10.1596/978-1-4648-0157-0.

CHAPTER 9

Enhancing Learning Through Continuous Improvement: Case Studies of the Toyota Production System in the Automotive Industry in South Africa

Keiji Ishigame

1 Introduction

Learning is one of the keys to sustained growth. Stiglitz and Greenwald (2014) insist that, compared to developed countries, developing countries have gaps in their knowledge, and learning is important in closing such gaps. With many firms in developing countries situated below global best practice levels, learning improves productivity as they catch up.

Learning also unlocks a company's potential and promotes its development as a global firm. Toyota is a global automotive manufacturer well known for its efficient production system (Womack et al. 1990; Monden 2011). Toyota has learned from global best practices to improve its productivity. In 1945, Toyota estimated that its productivity was at one-tenth of global best practice (Fujimoto 1999). It learned from US car makers[1] and developed its own production system, the so-called Toyota Production System (TPS) (Ohno 1998). The system aims at "making the vehicles

K. Ishigame (✉)
Partnership Program Division, Yokohama Center, Japan International Cooperation Agency, Tokyo, Japan
e-mail: Ishigame.Keiji@jica.go.jp

A. Hosono et al. (eds.), *Workers, Managers, Productivity*,
https://doi.org/10.1007/978-981-15-0364-1_9

ordered by customers in the quickest and most efficient way, to deliver the vehicles as quickly as possible." TPS was established "based on many years of continuous improvements (*Kaizen*)" (Toyota 2018a).[2]

Toyota also learned by exporting. As Page (Chap. 2) asserts, domestic firms build capabilities through learning. Toyota improved quality and productivity through exports to the US market in the 1960s. Initially, Toyota exported passenger cars but had to suspend exports due to quality-related problems. After developing a vehicle suitable for the US market, Toyota overcame its quality problems (Toyota Jidōsha Kabushiki Kaisha 1988).

Liker (2004) emphasized that TPS is designed to push team members to think, learn, and grow. Through relentless reflection and continuous improvement, a company can become a learning organization, as defined by Senge (1990). Hosono (2016 and chap. 3) concludes that the Toyota Way is similar to the concept of the learning firm explored by Stiglitz and Greenwald (2014).

Kaizen was first introduced into Asian countries through the business activities of Japanese companies and Japanese official development assistance programs. It was extended to Latin America and the Middle East, before finally being implemented in Africa (Ohno et al. 2009). In Ghana, based on a randomized experiment, it was demonstrated that basic-level management training including *Kaizen* improves business practices and performance (Mano et al. 2012). Ethiopia has adopted a comprehensive approach to introducing *Kaizen* nationwide at both policy and business levels (Ohno 2014; Shimada 2015). However, research measuring the impact of *Kaizen* in Africa is limited, with few case studies of specific firms apart from Kaplinsky's (1995) case study from Zimbabwe. Yan and Makinde (2011) argued that continuous improvement plays a significant role in promoting development process of new products in small- and medium-sized enterprises (SMEs) in South Africa; however, no study has ever tried to analyze *Kaizen* in TPS with local firms in Africa.

This chapter aims to measure the impact of *Kaizen*, known as TPS in South Africa, where Japan International Cooperation Agency (JICA) projects have been implemented. The objective of the research is to investigate how *Kaizen* can enhance the competitiveness of automotive suppliers in South Africa. It also aims to assess ways that *Kaizen* supports enhanced learning in companies. The research questions are as follows:

1. Does *Kaizen* enhance the competitiveness of the suppliers?
2. Does the effectiveness of *Kaizen* differ among suppliers? What factors contribute to this? and
3. Does *Kaizen* have a positive impact on learning?

Section 2 briefly outlines the automotive industry in South Africa and the JICA project. Section 3 presents the research methodology, while Sect. 4 presents the case studies. Section 5 discusses the study findings before conclusions are presented in Sect. 6.

2 Automotive Industry in South Africa and JICA Project

2.1 Automotive Industry in South Africa

The automotive industry comprises the largest manufacturing sector in South Africa, contributing 6% to the country's gross domestic product (GDP) and supporting 113,000 jobs (DTI 2018). Annual production is 599,004 vehicles, with more than 60% exported. The industry is composed of six major vehicle assemblers, thirteen assemblers of heavy and medium commercial vehicles, and approximately 360 component manufacturers (ASCCI 2017).

The industry in South Africa has developed since Ford and General Motors started operations in the 1920s (Black 2001). After the end of apartheid in 1994, the South African government incorporated the automotive industry into development policy to promote exports (Black 2017). The Motor Industry Development Program (MIDP) (1995–2012) and Automotive Production and Development Program (APDP) (2013–2020) have provided incentives to promote local production and exports.

The MIDP was aimed at supporting the development of the local vehicle assembly and component industries, with emphasis on improving the industry's exporting prospects. It implemented the following policies for economic liberalization and promotion of exports. First, local content provisions for domestic vehicle assembly were abolished. Protection tariffs were reduced from 115% for completely built-up units (CBUs) and completely knocked-down (CKD) to 40% and 30% by 2002. These were further reduced to 30% and 25%, respectively, by 2007, and finally to 25% and 20% in 2012. Secondly, original equipment manufacturers (OEMs) receive a duty-free allowance for domestic production and component manufacturers to obtain duty credits from exporting (Comrie et al. 2013).

The APDP started in 2013 as a follow-up program of the MIDP. The APDP target is the doubling of vehicle production to 1.2 million units by 2020, with the scale of production emphasized over exports. The program has four key components (AIEC 2013): stable import tariffs, a vehicle assembly allowance, production incentives, and grants delivered through the Automotive Investment Scheme.

2.2 *JICA Project*

In 2015, JICA implemented the Automotive Industry Human Resource Development Project in South Africa. The purpose of the project was to enhance the capacity of human resources in the South African automotive industry and to improve the productivity and quality of suppliers.

Two Japanese experts with rich experience in TPS worked at the Automotive Industry Development Center (AIDC) in South Africa. The experts trained AIDC trainers and provided technical advice to local suppliers along with AIDC trainers. Eight suppliers were selected and received technical advice from the experts and AIDC trainers.[3] Table 9.1 shows the summery of JICA project companies.

Japanese experts visited suppliers five to ten days per year with AIDC trainers, and the AIDC trainers visited suppliers again separately every two weeks on average. AIDC trainers and representatives from the suppliers joined a ten-day study tour to Japan to understand *Kaizen*. Box 9.1 shows the steps in the assistance provided to suppliers.

Box 9.1 Steps in Assistance to Suppliers
[1st Stage: 5S and Understanding Current Conditions]

1. Understanding material and information flows
    - Understanding production systems
    - Finding problems and outstanding issues
2. Thorough 5S
3. First in, first out (FIFO)

[2nd Stage: Making Production Management Tool]

1. Prepare operation standards
    - Operation manuals

- Quality check standards
- Machine maintenance manuals

2. Prepare abnormality management tools

- Operator placement map
- Production performance board
- Defect parts control

3. Prepare key performance indicators (KPI)

[3rd Stage: *Kaizen* Activity]

1. One-piece flow, SEIRYUKA (rectification of production flow)
2. Pull system, Fill-up system (Kanban system)
3. Heijunka production
4. Standardized work
5. Motion *Kaizen*, multi-skilled operator

Source: Project document modified by Author

Box 9.2 Glossary of *Kaizen* Activities in the Project

- First In, First Out (FIFO) is an inventory management method: the earliest items delivered are the first used. The items must be utilized before they start deteriorating.
- One-piece flow is the ideal state where parts are manufactured one at a time, and flow throughout manufacturing. It is a key concept of TPS.
- Kanban system is a system that conveys information between processes and automatically orders parts as they are used up. Every item or box of items that flows through the production process carries its own Kanban.
- Heijunka production is a technique for leveling fluctuations in performance within the assembly line. It facilitates Just-In-Time (JIT) production and smooths out production in all departments.

Source: Toyota Production System Glossary,[4] modified by Author

Table 9.1 Summary of JICA project companies

Company	*Number of staff*	*Tier*	*Capital (local/foreign)*
A	240	Tier 1	Local
B	147	Tier 1	Local
C	242	Tier 1	Local
D	45	Tier 2	Local
E	103	Tier 1 and Tier 2	Local
F	509	Tier 1	Local
G	118	Tier 1	Local
H	18,885	Others	Local

Source: Interviews and Comrie et al. (2013)

In the first stage of assistance, 5S[5] is implemented within the target suppliers. 5S creates a foundation for well-running equipment and proper material management. It also helps to identify the current situation and makes problems visible.

In the second stage, a material and information flow diagram (MIFD) is the key to analyzing the current situation and identifying problems. MIFD is a schematic drawing prepared by the AIDC trainer with suppliers that shows the flow of information and materials. It aims at detecting hidden problems in the operation of the industrial process being studied.

In the third stage, JICA experts and AIDC trainers and suppliers discuss and draft possible solutions (*Kaizen* activities) within the available resources. The activities comprise a wide range of measures that are useful for improving quality and productivity. They are one-piece flow, motion *Kaizen*, and so on. In other *Kaizen* projects, the main intervention is 5S (see Chaps. 11, 12 and 13 in SME). In this project, 5S is used for creating a foundation to implement other *Kaizen* activities in the initial stages. International experts advise not only on 5S but also on various activities related to the diagnosis of the suppliers. The trainers learned how to analyze problems and find solutions. The project aims to foster skills among trainers to plan and implement *Kaizen* independently in the auto industry. It can be said that the project supports the learning of advanced *Kaizen*.

3 Data and Research Methods

The research methods used in this study were document reviews and semi-structured interviews. The AIDC provided reports on the JICA project, including the performance of *Kaizen*. These reports were reviewed to reveal the numerical results. Interviews and factory visits were conducted with seven suppliers, with one supplier declining due to being fully occupied by intensive work at the assembler's request. Interviews were conducted between September 2017 and October 2017. As *Kaizen* involves taking into account all levels of people from managers to workers, the interviewees comprised nine managers (managing directors, plant managers, and production managers), seven engineers, two interns, and thirteen operators—thirty-one people in total. Interviews with one AIDC manager, three AIDC trainers, and two JICA experts were also conducted. Interviews with management staff, engineers, and interns were carried out using questionnaires, while those with operators focused on three to four specific questions.

4 Case Studies

The project initially covered eight suppliers. With four of these, project activities were suspended due to a lack of company resources, intensive demands by the assemblers, or a change in business focus. Table 9.2 provides a summary of each supplier's progress in the JICA project.

Among the eight target suppliers, Companies A, B, and E are presented here as case studies owing to the considerable impact of *Kaizen* activities. Table 9.3 outlines the results of interventions in the three companies. In the case of Company A, top management and an engineer played a leading role in promoting *Kaizen*. A layout change significantly improved quality

Table 9.2 Progress of JICA project companies

Company	*Progress*
Group 1 (since October 2015)	
A	Very good progress. Regional winner of Productivity South Africa Award
B	Slow and steady progress. Best performing factory award in 2016 among group companies' factories
C	Project stopped due to the assembler's intensive support
D	Project stopped due to a lack of company resources
Group 2 (since October 2016)	
E	Good progress. Involvement of the entire workforce
F	Good progress. Starting to improve
G	Project stopped due to a change in business focus (not available for interview)
H	Project stopped due to a lack of company resources

Source: Presentation material drafted by AIDC and author's survey

Table 9.3 Summary of three companies' *Kaizen* activities

Company	*A*	*B*	*E*
Product	Accessory products (side steps)	Floor carpet	Injection molding parts
Project start	October 2015	October 2015	October 2016
Main activities	5S, Layout change, One-piece flow	5S, Top management workplace walk, Kanban	5S, One-piece flow, Milk-Run
Productivity	51% lead time reduction	OEE[a]: 78–90%	50% lead time reduction
Profit	Improved (turnover up 50%)	Improved (turnover up 50%)	Not improved
Management commitment	Managing director	Managing director	Managing director & production executive
Resource allocation (HR)	Intern → Engineer	Engineer	Engineer
Resource allocation (budget)	Utilize internal resources	US $18,453[b]	Limited
Repeated training	Conducted	Conducted	Intensively conducted
Learning	Positive	Positive	Very positive

Source: Author's survey

[a]OEE: Overall Equipment Effectiveness. OEE is a framework for measuring the efficiency and effectiveness of a process, by breaking it down into three constituent components: quality (only good parts), performance (as fast as possible), and availability (no stop time)

[b]250,000 ZAR = US $18,453.9 (US $1 = 13.5473 ZAR, exchange rate on October 1, 2017)

and productivity, and sales and profits also improved. In the case of Company B, commitments and actions of both top management and an engineer led to gradual improvements. In the case of Company E, *Kaizen* is practiced by the entire workforce under the commitment and involvement of top management. Introduction of a one-piece flow system brought obvious improvements in quality and productivity in the short term. The following case studies provide further details regarding *Kaizen* activities.

4.1 *Company A*

4.1.1 *Company Profile*

Company A was founded in 1960 and has 240 employees. The company produces automotive accessory products, including nudge bars, bumper replacements, side steps, and so on, selling them to US, Japanese, and

German manufacturers. As a small business producing low volume but highly diverse parts, the company was motivated to join the JICA project because it saw the need to boost working culture and processes.

4.1.2 Process

The managing director has a strong commitment to the *Kaizen* process. He assigned an engineer, an intern from universities of technology. The engineer learned specific *Kaizen* methods from Japanese experts and AIDC trainers and implemented them. The company initially conducted 5S activities. After 5S was carried out, problems were identified by MIFD and an optimized layout was drawn up. AIDC trainers and the engineer drafted the MIFD. The MIFD showed problems in the material and information flow, with extended distances to be traveled, causing significant stagnation. In the styling bar production line, the process flow was not established properly, and the layout was not optimized. The average units-per-day production did not meet customer demand. The company decided to change its factory layout based on recommendations from experts and AIDC trainers. The managing director allocated the budget necessary to change the layout. Large-size machinery was moved into the right places and one-piece flow was implemented. Lead times were shortened and stagnation reduced according to the MIFD analysis. Quality was improved by moving from batch production to one-piece flow as the operator can identify defects during the process. The main outcomes are shown in Table 9.4. Motion was improved and cycle time and work in process were reduced.

Before *Kaizen* was introduced, processes were scattered around the factory. When one process was completed, work in process piled up on the floor. It was then moved to a rack for delivery to the next process. Operators concentrated on one specific process and did not multitask.

Table 9.4 Outcomes of optimizing layout (styling bar improvements)

Action (optimized layout)	*Improvement (%)*
Walking distances while carrying styling bar	83.3% motion improvement
Total cycle time	51.9% more efficient
Work in process (WIP[a])	67.6% reduction
Number of required operators	66% reduction

Source: Presentation material drafted by AIDC and modified by Author

[a]Work in process is partially completed goods, parts, or subassemblies that are no longer part of the raw materials inventory and not yet part of the finished products inventory

After the layout changed, the process has become a line and work in process is no longer placed directly on the floor but is put on a newly crafted rack ready for the next process. A single operator can undertake several tasks at the same point. Walking for delivery has been eliminated and the volume of work in process has been reduced. In all, the number of required operators and total cycle time has been reduced. The company utilized scrap steel to make racks and trollies. Racks were designed and fabricated for specific parts. Transportation trollies were also made and double handling was eliminated, improving productivity.

When the engineer faced difficulties, he reported them to the managing director, who provided solutions and advice in a timely manner. After the positive impact of the JICA project was observed, the company decided to accept five interns—students from universities of technology studying industrial engineering. The engineer trained them to expand *Kaizen* activities in the factory. In addition, all three production managers were sent to college to take a one-year course in industrial engineering.

4.1.3 Results

Results were very positive: monthly turnover increased by 50% and profits improved. After the company changed (optimized) its layout based on the problem analysis, it received a Productivity Award, the second in South Africa. Based on MIFD analysis, the layout changes improved quality and productivity.

4.1.4 Challenges

Changing the mindset of employees is arduous. They do not accept change easily and often mistakenly believe that improvement could increase their workloads or result in loss of their jobs. *Kaizen* training did promote a change in this mindset. However, it was not only the operators who needed repeated training to sustain *Kaizen* activities but also middle managers. Employees in South Africa are diverse, with multiple languages and cultures. Careful management is required to ensure that employees with a diverse sense of values can work together.

4.2 Company B

4.2.1 Company Profile

Company B was founded in 1998 and has 147 employees. It produces textile-based automotive acoustic and trim components like main floor carpets, floor insulators, and trunk trim. The company sells to US and Japanese manufacturers. The motivation to join the JICA project was that the plant manager had a long experience in lean manufacturing and was keen on introducing TPS.

4.2.2 Process

The plant manager assigned the industrial engineer to manage the JICA project, with the student interns providing support. First, 5S was conducted, improving productivity. Home positions for all items on the workstation were established. Lines were drawn on the floor to improve visual management. "Gemba" (workplace) walks by management were done regularly with the aim of establishing better 5S. Weekly audits were standardized and cleaning schedules were established. Accessible cleaning materials were placed at workstations. Before implementing 5S, material shortages were unpredictable, and therefore production lines ceased operations. When 5S was introduced and used to categorize each material, stocks were more easily monitored, and downtimes reduced.

The engineer and AIDC trainer drafted MIFD and identified three problems: (1) no inventory control between processes; (2) excessive work in process; and (3) unbalanced production lines. Ideas to solve issues were discussed and implemented: (1) Kanban; (2) one-piece flow; and (3) standard trolleys.

While Kanban was introduced and Kanban workflow was established, it has not been sustained because operators do not fully understand its necessity. Repeated trainings are required to ensure sustainability.

Training in one-piece flow was also conducted. The AIDC trainer and the industrial engineer showed operators a video about one-piece flow and explained its benefits. While its feasibility was confirmed after a trial, it has not been implemented to date as additional training is required.

Standard trolleys were introduced. This reduced the space needed for products, freeing up space for the accommodation of higher quantities of raw materials, and making products lighter for pushing or pulling.

Management allocated the necessary funds, although budget resources were constrained. When funding was available, it was allocated to *Kaizen* activities. In one year, about US $18,453 was spent on trolleys, signs, demarcation on the shop floor, training, machine automation, and weekend overtime for some activities.

4.2.3 Results

Although *Kaizen* activities are still being implemented, the impact has been gradual but positive. Over the past two years, with the same headcount, productivity, and quality improved, costs were reduced by about US $1.6 million,[6] and revenue increased by 25%. The lead time has also been shortened in specific production lines and overall equipment effectiveness (OEE) has improved from 78% to 90%. The company was given an award as the best performing factory in 2016 among the group's factories.

4.2.4 Challenges

Resource allocation remains a challenge. The industrial engineer is a project manager for the JICA project and is the new business manager and industrial engineer for the whole factory. The company accepted two student interns to provide support for the JICA project activities. While financial resources were constrained, management put importance on allocating funds necessary for *Kaizen* activities.

Changing operator mindsets takes a lot of time and effort as many operators do not necessarily have sufficient knowledge of math and science. The industrial engineer put a lot of effort into mentoring and coaching operators. He organized repeated 5S and one-piece flow trainings to operators. *Kaizen* activities required frequent communications between the industrial engineer and the operators, contributing to better communication among the staff. The factory staff conducts meetings in front of the team board (a visual management whiteboard), and operators are developing the knowledge to carry out operations smoothly.

4.3 Company E

4.3.1 Company Profile

Company E was founded in 1996. The number of employees is 103. The company produces plastic molded components such as automotive injection molding parts and scuba fins. The company sells them to the US and Japanese manufacturers and other clients. The destruction of their factory by fire provided the motivation for joining the JICA project, as rebuilding the factory provided an opportune time to create a new production system.

4.3.2 Process

The company promoted *Kaizen* among all levels of staff from managers to operators. The managing director showed a strong commitment, was deeply involved in all *Kaizen* activities, and monitored progress. The operation's executive and engineer were assigned to implement the JICA project.

The company production system was transformed from batch production to one-piece flow according to the MIFD analysis. 5S was implemented and the MIFD drafted by the AIDC trainer was used to identify problems. Three main problems were detected and countermeasures to solve these problems were proposed: (1) minimizing non-value-added work; (2) establishing the pull production system; and (3) establishing new standardized work. The AIDC trainer and JICA experts conducted training in the one-piece flow system. However, operators insisted that batch production is more productive than one-piece flow. Management and the engineer patiently persuaded them regarding the benefits of one-piece flow. Training programs were provided repeatedly. In each case, management was present and supported the introduction of one-piece flow. Videos were shown to employees on the principles of TPS and one-piece flow.

Managers and supervisors were also trained with operators to understand the benefits of one-piece flow. Simulation games were played to visualize possible improvements. After the training and intense discussions, operators understood the benefits of one-piece flow, and finally agreed that "one-piece flow is amazing because our life is easier." More output can be achieved with less input. Lead time has been reduced significantly and operator loads eased. One-piece flow can also allow inspections for quality into the process. Therefore, the need for four quality inspection staff at final inspection could be eliminated and utilized for other tasks. Managers are also more relaxed and can monitor production progress more easily.

The company minimized non-value-added work. Before *Kaizen* was implemented, each part was packed in a box, transferred, and unpacked before each process of molding, painting, and assembly. Under the new system such non-value-added work was eliminated and production lead time reduced from 24 hours to 1 hour. Required staff was reduced from four to two people and two staff were reassigned for other tasks. Table 9.5 provides some results from *Kaizen* activities. Lead times were shortened by eliminating waste in each step of the process.

Table 9.5 Before and after performance

Measure	*Before*	*After*	*Impact*
Introduction of one-piece flow in car cap assembly			
Car cap assembly/shift	190 products	240 products	26%
Lead time	18 hours	9 hours	1/2
Introduction of a milk-run to collect products in each shift			
Lead time for one box to move from molding section to finished goods section	420 min (7 hours)	30 min	1/14

Source: Presentation material drafted by AIDC and modified by Author

4.3.3 *Results*

The results were positive. Tangible improvements in operations were observed. However, sales and profits did not improve because of weak market demand. Participation in the JICA project was for one year, so it took time for the outcomes to indicate improved business performance. Nevertheless, factory-based improvement was considerable.

4.3.4 *Challenges*

As in the previous discussion, significant efforts and continuous training were necessary to persuade operators to overcome their initial resistance and understand the benefits of one-piece flow. The most important factor in success was the commitment of management. Management was highly involved in *Kaizen* activities and persuaded operators of their value.

The budgetary amount was not important because various activities can be implemented within limited budgets. The company spent a small amount on production tables, demarcating the floor, and fencing operations. On the other hand, allocating time for *Kaizen* activities is more important. Working harder and training is the key.

4.4 *Suspended Cases*

Clarification of suspended cases is useful for identifying contributing factors to successful implementation of *Kaizen*. The project activities were suspended in four companies.

4.4.1 *Suspended Cases Due to Assemblers' Intervention*

Two companies had to suspend involvement in the project because the suppliers became fully occupied in intensive work at the assembler's request. The company started to produce parts for a new model of car.

However, the company did not provide the parts in a timely manner to the assembler, who had to shut down their factory operations as a result. The assembler then intervened in the company's production in order to normalize production and build the new model of car as planned. With the company focusing on responding to the assembler's requests, they were unable to engage in project activities. The company, however, recognized significance of *Kaizen* through the project implementation. The assembler also promoted *Kaizen* activities. The company set up a *dojo* (*Kaizen* training room) and implemented continuous improvement. The company continued to improve and was able to produce the parts in a timely manner.

Another company also had to respond to assembler's requests due to some operational problems. Therefore, the company stopped the project and declined to participate in interviews for this research.

4.4.2 Suspended Cases Due to Lack of Management's Commitments

In the other two companies, the management neither took a positive approach to *Kaizen* nor allocated necessary resources. One company received technical advice from the experts and AIDC trainers and implemented the improvement activities such as 5S. The production manager and an intern implemented project activities. MIFD analysis discovered that layout change could reduce the lead time and save manpower resulting from the scattering of processes around the factory. AIDC trainers and experts with the production manager proposed the layout change to the top management. As the changes required the movement of large machinery, there were some significant costs involved. Consequently, management did not accept the proposal and project activities were suspended. The production manager and the intern continued to implement *Kaizen*. Incremental positive results were realized gradually.

The other company implemented 5S activity in its storage areas first. After the completion of the initial 5S activity, activity stagnated. An assigned engineer did not receive proper instructions from management to proceed with the activity. The management did not commit to the project and finally decided to withdraw.

5 Major Findings

5.1 Enhancing the Competitiveness of the Suppliers

Kaizen has enhanced the competitiveness of all four companies that continued with the project. With only a limited number of participating companies and no control group, there is insufficient evidence to determine whether *Kaizen* enhanced competitiveness. The four companies, however, reduced manufacturing lead time and improved quality and productivity. 5S activity and MIFD analysis helped to identify problems. Layout change according to the MIFD brought improvements in quality and productivity. The companies utilized scrap metal to make specialized racks and trollies for parts. Introduction of one-piece flow facilitated quality checks in each process, improved quality, and reduced manpower needs.

In terms of profitability, only two companies confirmed an improvement. Many companies were not willing to disclose their business performance, such as profits and sales revenue. As a result, the impact on business performance could not be determined. According to the limited answers available, Companies A and B increased their sales and improved their profits after the project started. The other companies did not improve their sales and profits as the automotive market in South Africa has stagnated since the project commencement. In 2015 and 2016, economic growth in South Africa was 1.30% and 0.28%, respectively. Annual automotive domestic production is 615,658 and 599,004 vehicles (OICA 2018). One condition for participation in the project was that there should be no reduction in employees resulting from productivity improvements. Although automotive suppliers in South Africa are under severe circumstances, Companies A and B increased profits. In Companies E and F, improvements in quality and productivity were observed; however, their profits did not increase during the one-year intervention. In the short term, quality and productivity improvements did not result in increased business performance. Profits were affected by market trends and assemblers' business strategies. It can be said that *Kaizen* works well for increasing a firm's capabilities, especially in the long run.

5.2 *Success Factors of* Kaizen *Activities*

The impact of *Kaizen* differed widely among the eight pilot companies. In four of the pilot companies, *Kaizen* shortened manufacturing lead times and improved quality and productivity. The remaining four companies had to suspend *Kaizen* activities. Case studies and interviews illustrate that factors contributing to *Kaizen* implementation are: (1) management commitment; (2) resource allocation; and (3) continuous training.

5.2.1 *Management Commitment*

In the interviews, 88% of the respondents identified management commitment as a crucial contributing factor in the successful implementation of *Kaizen*. Management plays a central role in supervising and implementing *Kaizen* activities as observed in the case studies. Management has to allocate resources to *Kaizen* and often needs to coax staff into implementing *Kaizen*. In Companies A, B, and E, management showed strong commitment to *Kaizen* activities.

In the two suspended cases, lack of management commitment was significant. In the two companies, management was not fully supportive; therefore, *Kaizen* activities were suspended. Management needs to understand the benefits of *Kaizen* and must allocate minimum financial and human resources for *Kaizen*. In other words, management is required to prioritize productivity and quality improvements in the long term through sufficient expenditure rather than to balk at spending on improvements to maintain current profits.

García et al. (2013) reported that management commitment is a critical success factors for *Kaizen*. The results of the case studies support their findings. Throughout the project, JICA experts emphasized the need for commitment from management when selecting a pilot company for the introduction of *Kaizen*. The results of the present study confirm this approach.

5.2.2 *Resource Allocation*

Kaizen needs specific allocations of human and financial resources. A company does not need to hire a production manager with a brilliant background. Management needs only to appoint an engineer and let him/her focus on *Kaizen*, but with the authority to conduct it. Management should set a reporting time. If they face any problems, management should intervene in a timely manner.

In the case studies of the three companies, the management assigned the engineer and allocated a designated budget to implement *Kaizen* activities. The management also supported the activities and intervened when necessary. In the JICA project, many companies took on interns from the universities of technology who had studied industrial engineering. *Kaizen* activities are simple and practical. Sophisticated statistical expertise is not necessarily required. In one of the most successful companies, an intern implements the project activities and is now a permanent member of staff.

Implementation of *Kaizen* requires a certain budget, but its size can be flexible and based on a company's resources. As discussed above, companies introduced racks and trollies made of scrap steel. Money was spent on making signs, demarcation of the shop floor, and conducting training. Such costs were limited.

Resource allocations of the eight suppliers differed, although there was no big difference in their business environments. They are in the same auto industry and all companies are locally owned. Companies A and E faced difficulties in improving profitability during the implementation of *Kaizen*. Nonetheless, these companies allocated the minimum financial and human resources. Understanding of the management made differences in resource allocation. One company had sufficient sales. Management, however, did not agree on changing the layout because the management put a high value on reducing costs in the short run rather investing in an optimized layout to improve productivity in the long run. Understanding management is important for allocating available resources.

5.2.3 Continuous Training

Continuous training, especially for operators, is a contributing factor to successful *Kaizen*. *Kaizen* needs continuation, as it is called "continuous improvement." Operators often resist introducing new approaches and insist on continuing with their current ways because it is easier for them. Repeated trainings are required to ensure understanding of *Kaizen*. Once they understand the benefits, such as the fact that the introduction of a one-piece flow system achieves increased production and reduces work through lower rejection rates, they support implementation. They will continue to implement it because the work is much easier and productive as seen in the case studies. It can be said that *Kaizen* is friendly to the operator.

5.3 Impact on Learning

In interviews with seven suppliers, 88% of the respondents answered that *Kaizen* has a positive impact on learning. Even in companies that suspended involvement, management and engineers observed positive impacts on learning.

In the case studies of the three companies, it was observed that *Kaizen* promotes learning. In Company A, the operators and other individuals who did not understand the project's value at the beginning are now seeing the benefits and starting to make suggestions on continuous improvements.

In Company B, the individual mindset is starting to change. Organizational capability grew, and staff was trying to think lean and reduce waste. The plant manager's morning onsite walk led to changes in mindsets, and individuals were motivated and strived more.

In Company E, the management insisted that *Kaizen* has had a very positive impact and helped the company to become a learning organization. *Kaizen* culture is starting to be adopted. The adoption of improvements proposed by operators is gradually increasing. Individuals understand the benefits of one-piece flow and this is a win-win situation between the company and its operators.

Through *Kaizen* activities, operators had opportunities to express their opinions, as *Kaizen* involves the entire workforce. Before the project was implemented, operators had to follow the instructions and were passive. Once the project began, the operators participated in training and learned about the benefits of 5S and one-piece flow. Management and engineers encouraged them to express their opinions. They learned to think by themselves and express their opinions and take the lead in improving factory operations. Conversely, managements and engineers learned not only *Kaizen* tools but also the importance of involving operators in quality and productivity improvement. They learned how to communicate with operators, listening to their opinions especially carefully. They understood that motivating operators was the key to improvement factories operations. In this way, *Kaizen* was implemented successfully.

6 Conclusion

This study aimed to assess the impact of *Kaizen* through the introduction of TPS to automotive suppliers in South Africa, as there are few previous studies that have assessed TPS introduction in Africa. First, it was observed that *Kaizen* enhanced the competitiveness of suppliers through reductions in lead time and improvements in quality and productivity. On the other hand, short-term profitability did not improve. Two suppliers out of the initial eight improved sales and profits. Sales of auto parts are dependent on the market and, in addition, one condition of project participation was no layoffs as a result of project assistance. Second, the impact of *Kaizen* differed among the suppliers. The contributory factors are management commitment, resource allocation, and continuous training. Third, *Kaizen* had a positive impact on learning, with operators learning how to improve productivity and quality. Managements and engineers insisted that there are positive impacts from creating continuous learning, including in the companies that suspended *Kaizen* activities. In the case studies, positive impacts on learning were observed.

Through learning *Kaizen* methods, 5S, MIFD, standardized work, one-piece flow, and so on, factory operators, engineers, and managers learn how to improve productivity and quality. Because *Kaizen* is small-step improvements, the operators and engineers acquired information on how to learn and recognized how they themselves can contribute to better factories in the short term. This incremental achievement process also produces a positive desire for a system cycle to make a better workplace.

This review of the project has implications for developing countries. Firstly, governments should utilize *Kaizen* to develop the private sector. Promoting *Kaizen* to top management is crucial in the successful implementation and expansion of *Kaizen*. Secondly, development agencies should select target companies in the *Kaizen* projects based on careful meetings with management. The project outputs will be less effective if the management do not properly understand the benefits and approach of *Kaizen*. Thirdly, *Kaizen* can have a positive impact on employees, especially when learning is emphasized. The operators have the opportunity to learn to improve quality and productivity through participation in *Kaizen* activities, creating better factories. However, in this research, the number of investigated companies was limited and no control case studies comparisons conducted. Further studies are needed in order to establish the effectiveness of *Kaizen* and its impacts on learning.

Notes

1. A Toyota management member visited Ford Motor Company in 1950, where he learned of the employee suggestion system. He adapted the idea in line with the Toyota Way, establishing the Toyota Creative Ideas and Suggestion System (TCISS), and in 1953 set the company slogan "Good Thinking, Good Product," selected through an internal contest. The slogan has been used in Toyota factories around the world (Toyota 2018c).
2. *Kaizen* is one of the core principles of the Toyota Production System and is the heart of the Toyota Way (Toyota 2018b).

3. The project supported eight suppliers in October 2017, when interviews were conducted. After that, the project added four more suppliers—in total twelve suppliers.
4. Toyota Production System Glossary, May 31, 2013, https://blog.toyota.co.uk/toyota-production-system-glossary.
5. In the project, it is called 4S instead of 5S because Shitsuke (discipline), sustaining adherence to rules is not covered in 1st stage assistance activity.
6. 22,000,000 ZAR = US $1,623,939.9 (US $1 = 13.5473 ZAR, exchange rate on October 1, 2017).

References

ASCCI. 2017. *Automotive Supply Chain Competitiveness Initiative.* http://ascci.co.za/sector-profile/.

Automotive Industry Export Council (AIEC). 2013. *Automotive Export Manual 2013, South Africa. MIDP, Motor Industry Development Programme, the Track Record 1995–2012.* Arcadia, SA: AIEC.

Black, A. 2001. Globalization and Restructuring in the South African Automotive Industry. *Journal of International Development* 13 (6): 779–796.

———. 2017. Trade Liberalization, Technical Change and Firm Level Restructuring in the South African Automotive Component Sector. *Institutions and Economies* 3 (2): 173–202.

Comrie, D., J. Terreblanche, J. Johnson, and J. Syman. 2013. *Industry Mapping and Supplier Diagnostic Report.* Gillitts, SA: B&M Analysts.

Department of Trade and Industry (DTI). 2018. *Industrial Policy Action Plan 2018/19–2020/21.* Sunnyside, Pretoria: DTI.

Fujimoto, T. 1999. *The Evolution of a Manufacturing System at Toyota.* New York: Oxford University Press.

García, J.L., D.G. Rivera, and A.A. Iniesta. 2013. Critical Success Factors for Kaizen Implementation in Manufacturing Industries in Mexico. *The International Journal of Advanced Manufacturing Technology* 68 (1–4): 537–545.

Hosono, A. 2016. Industrial Strategies: Toward a Learning Society for Quality Growth. In *Efficiency, Finance, and Varieties of Industrial Policy*, ed. A. Noman and J.E. Stiglitz, 306–352. New York: Columbia University Press.

Kaplinsky, R. 1995. Technique and System: The Spread of Japanese Management Techniques to Developing Countries. *World Development* 23 (1): 57–71.

Liker, J.K. 2004. *The Toyota Way.* Tokyo: Esensi.

Mano, Y., A. Iddrisu, Y. Yoshino, and T. Sonobe. 2012. How Can Micro and Small Enterprises in Sub-Saharan Africa Become More Productive? The Impacts of Experimental Basic Managerial Training. *World Development* 40 (3): 458–468.

Monden, Y. 2011. *Toyota Production System: An Integrated Approach to Just-in-Time*. London: CRC Press.

Ohno, T. 1998. *Toyota Production System: Beyond Large-Scale Production*. OR: Productivity Press.

Ohno, K. 2014. *Learning to Industrialize: From Given Growth to Policy-aided Value Creation*. London: Routledge.

Ohno, I., K. Ohno, S. Uesu, A. Ishiwata, A. Hosono, T. Kikuchi, and T. Uenda. 2009. *Introducing Kaizen in Africa*. Tokyo: GRIPS Development Forum.

OICA. 2018. *International Organization of Motor Vehicle Manufacturers, 2016 Production Statistics*. http://www.oica.net/wp-content/uploads/By-country.pdf

Senge, P.M. 1990. *The Fifth Discipline: The Art and Practice of the Learning Organization*. New York: Currency Doubleday.

Shimada, G. 2015. The Economic Implications of Comprehensive Approach to Learning on Industrial Development (Policy and Managerial Capability Learning): A Case of Ethiopia. In *Industrial Policy and Economic Transformation in Africa*, ed. Akbar Noman and Joseph Stiglitz, 102–122. New York: Columbia University Press.

Stiglitz, J.E., and B.C. Greenwald. 2014. *Creating a Learning Society: A New Approach to Growth, Development, and Social Progress*. New York: Columbia University Press.

Toyota. 2018a. *Toyota Production System*. http://www.toyota-global.com/company/vision_philosophy/toyota_production_system/

———. 2018b. *The Official Blog of Toyota GB*. http://blog.toyota.co.uk/kaizen-toyota-production-system

———. 2018c. *Toyota traditions: Good Thinking, Good Products*. http://www.toyota-global.com/company/toyota_traditions/quality/may_jun_2005.html

Toyota Jidōsha Kabushiki Kaisha. 1988. *Toyota: A History of the First 50 Years*. Toyota Motor Corporation.

Womack, J.P., D.T. Jones, and D. Roos. 1990. *Machine that Changed the World: The Story of Lean Production*. New York: Simon and Schuster.

Yan, B., and O.D. Makinde. 2011. Impact of Continuous Improvement on New Product Development Within SMEs in the Western Cape, South Africa. *African Journal of Business Management* 5 (6): 2220.

CHAPTER 10

Impact of *Kaizen*-like Practices in the Brazilian Manufacturing Sector

Filipe Lage de Sousa, Mauricio Canêdo-Pinheiro, Bernardo Pereira Cabral, and Glaucia Estefânia de Sousa Ferreira

F. Lage de Sousa (✉)
Department of Economics, Fluminense Federal University (UFF), Niterói, Brazil

Research Department, Brazilian Development Bank (BNDES), Rio de Janeiro, Brazil
e-mail: fl_sousa@id.uff.br

M. Canêdo-Pinheiro
Brazilian School of Economics and Finance (FGV EPGE), Rio de Janeiro, Brazil

Faculty of Economic Sciences, Center for Social Sciences, University of Rio de Janeiro State—UERJ, Rio de Janeiro, Brazil

B. Pereira Cabral
Faculty of Economics, Federal University of Bahia, Salvador, Brazil

G. E. de Sousa Ferreira
Economic Commission for Latin America and the Caribbean, United Nations/CEPAL, Rio de Janeiro, Brazil

A. Hosono et al. (eds.), *Workers, Managers, Productivity*,
https://doi.org/10.1007/978-981-15-0364-1_10

1 Introduction

Productivity has always been a relevant topic among economists and policymakers. Interest is understandable since productivity is the main factor for long-term economic growth. Krugman (1994) coined an expression that shows its importance: "Productivity isn't everything, but in the long run it is almost everything. A country's ability to improve its standard of living over time depends almost entirely on its ability to raise its output per worker." Based on this acknowledgment, economists try to understand the determinants of productivity and their effectiveness to promote sustainable development. For instance, management and innovation are considered key internal drivers for productivity growth by the literature (Syverson 2011).

The Brazilian economy has benefited substantially after the entrance of China in the international market due to the terms of trade change.[1] The abundance of resources provided opportunities to expand government support in different areas, especially on innovation. Indeed, the volume of government support to foster innovation in Brazil has increased substantially in the last years. These government policies have also reached a different spectrum of firms, as there were new financial tools to support innovation. One example is the creation of new credit lines in 2008 designed to support exclusively innovation by the Brazilian Development Bank (BNDES is its acronym in Portuguese). The surge of these policies was influenced by impact evaluation assessment of BNDES schemes. For instance, (Ottaviano and Lage de Sousa 2008) found limited impact of existent financial support on productivity from this development bank, which was explained by the lower emphasis on innovation in supported projects.[2] Additionally, there was also a shift in government policies toward more support for innovation in the private sector rather than government support for innovation activities made in universities and research centers (Cânedo-Pinheiro 2013). As an illustration, 6.4% of Brazilian manufacturing firms have received government support to innovate in 2005, while the same share reached 14.5% in 2014 (Cânedo-Pinheiro and Figueiredo 2017).

On one hand, the existent literature shows that, in general terms, these government policies to support innovation in the private sector worked reasonably well. There is evidence that, everything else constant, the public support increased the innovative efforts in the private sector, not merely crowded out other sources of private funding to innovation (Cânedo-Pinheiro and Figueiredo 2017). On the other hand, other evidence shows that these policies were not so successful. For example, outcomes regarding new products and processes do not correspond to the quantity of financial resources allocated in this period. After an initial increment between 2005 and 2008, the percentage of innovative firms in the manufacturing sector reduced from 38.4% in 2008 to 36.3% in 2014.[3] A similar trend was observed for expenditures on innovation (such as its share in terms of sales), according to the Brazilian innovation surveys.

Although there is a substantial amount of work done in terms of how innovation affects productivity, we are not aware of any research investigating how management practices can improve firms' productivity in the Brazilian economy, even more on specific management practice that requires low level of investment, as *Kaizen*. The relevance of management on productivity differences is considerable; Bloom et al. (2016) estimated that differences in management practices account for about 30% of cross-country total factor productivity differences. In the international arena, management practices of the private sector in developing countries, including Brazil, are lagging behind developed countries (N. Bloom et al. 2012). Moreover, firms with low-quality management practices are concentrated at the bottom of the productivity distribution in developing countries, which implies that improving the quality of management practices constitutes an opportunity to close productivity gaps not only between firms within a given industry in a country but also between developed and developing countries.[4]

This chapter tries to evaluate how *Kaizen* management practice has been able to improve firms' performance looking at quantitative and qualitative approaches. To the best of our knowledge, this is the first attempt to combine these two approaches to evaluate how *Kaizen* is able to boost firms' performance. This is particularly relevant in the context of an economy struggling to recover from the worst period of recession in its economic history. Not only fiscal constraints from the Brazilian government are binding any supplemental support, but also the private sector does not have sufficient resources to invest substantially in the next years. Therefore, improvements in firm's performance with low levels of investment should be a norm in the next years.

Our main findings suggest a productivity premium for implementing *Kaizen*. On average, *Kaizen* adopters show labor productivity 14.5% higher than similar non-adopters and total factor productivity 8% superior comparing with similar firms. However, investigating when this impact materializes on those starting to implement it during the investigated period, we were not able to detect it. However, we found robust evidence that *Kaizen* induces innovation, which is a catalyzer for productivity improvements in the long term. Nevertheless, it is important to emphasize that our qualitative approach corroborates our quantitative findings that productivity is achieved only in the long term and innovation is achieved immediately. Therefore, our interpretation consists of *Kaizen* as an effective tool to raise innovation in the short term and productivity in the long term.

To make this assessment, this chapter is organized as follows. Section 2 describes the dataset used in our quantitative approach, followed by how *Kaizen* might be inferred using innovation surveys in Sect. 3. Section 4 presents our empirical strategy from the quantitative approach and interpretation of the outcomes is shown in Sect. 5. Section 6 presents our qualitative methodology, including data collection and selection criteria. The outcomes of our qualitative approach are discussed in Sect. 7. Last section (Sect. 8) provides our concluding remarks.

2 Brazilian Firm-Level Datasets

For our quantitative investigation, we require firm-level dataset in order to assess whether *Kaizen* is able to impact firm's performance. The Brazilian Statistical Institute (IBGE) provides microdata at firm level from two relevant surveys: the Brazilian Innovation Survey (*Pesquisa de Inovaçao Tecnologica*—PINTEC) and the Annual Manufacturing Survey (*Pesquisa Industrial Anual*—PIA).

PINTEC is a sample survey, inspired by the Oslo Manual from Organisation for Economic Co-operation and Development (OECD), which means that it is comparable to other similar surveys worldwide. Six waves of this survey are available (1998–2000, 2001–2003, 2003–2005, 2006–2008, 2009–2011 and 2012–2014), which enables us to follow firms over a certain period if the questions related to management practices are consistent over time. PINTEC's sample is stratified with respect to firm size (number of employees), sector, state and innovation potential. Firms with less than 10 employees are not surveyed and larger firms (with 500 or more employees) are allocated in a specific stratum and selected with probability equal to one (certain stratum). Remaining firms are allocated to sampled strata, which were defined by crossing information on state and sectors. These strata (called natural strata) are then subdivided into two strata (called final strata): one with potential innovators and other with the remaining firms.[5] The sample is disproportionately allocated in these two final strata, so that approximately 80% of the firms selected for a sample, in each natural stratum, are companies very likely to be innovative.[6] Although extremely restrictive, more than 4400 firms from the manufacturing sector participated in the 2014 innovation survey.[7]

The PIA database contains information that allow us to build a measure of firm productivity and other key explanatory variables such as number of employees, investments in physical capital and others. This annual survey initiated in the 1986, but a consistent approach started only after 1996 and remains the same until 2014. PIA comprehends all manufacturing firms over 30 employees, which means a census for firms over this threshold. Firms from 5 to 30 employees are randomly surveyed in PIA. On average, around 30,000 firms are surveyed annually in the census part (over 30 employees).

Since the same institution (IBGE) elaborates these two surveys, they share similar methodological aspects, such as the identical sector classification, which follows the International Standard Industry Classification (ISIC). Since both datasets use the same firm identification, we are able to merge them.

3 *Kaizen* Identified in an Innovation Survey

From an empirical perspective, our study faces the challenge of identifying the *Kaizen* adoption because we do not have the information whether a firm has implemented this management approach. However, we are able to develop a taxonomy to identify firms adopting management practice based on *Kaizen*'s principle. This can be considered a contribution on using innovation surveys to define *Kaizen* adopters when this information is not available.

Although PINTEC provides information on whether firms have implemented management practices in all six waves of this survey, questions change overtime, hampering us to use all years available. However, the last three innovation surveys provide identical questions on management. This consistency in the questionnaires enables us to create an approach to distinguish whether firms are implementing *Kaizen* style of management practice. Nevertheless, firms need to be present in the three waves for us to define which firms are continuously implementing a management practice, as this is a requirement for being considered a *Kaizen*. Therefore, we restricted our sample to a balanced panel of firms from these three waves.

In this survey, they consider as an organizational innovation any implementation of new management practice or significant changes in the division of labor within the firm as well as in the external relations with clients or suppliers. These changes must aim to improve their knowledge, efficiency in their operations or in the quality of its goods and services. They should also be a consequence of the strategic decisions of firm's directors and a new organizational method for the firm. Although this definition seems extremely broad, they do not consider merging and acquisition as an organizational innovation, even if this is the first time.

Given this background to what is considered an organizational innovation, firms reply to the survey to whether they have implemented any new management practice to improve their routines and labor practice in the last three years. Under this concept, examples of new management practices are re-engineering, knowledge management, total quality control, training activities, enterprise resource planning and others. Therefore, replying affirmative to this question is just an indication to whether the firm could be implementing *Kaizen*, since we do not know if it involves all the employees or that it is a continuous process. Complementary information is needed to refine the identification of *Kaizen* approach.

Following this initial question on management practice, the questionnaire further asks if new methods of labor organization aiming to delegate responsibilities for achieving better decision-making, such as new managing working teams, restructuring departments or others in a similar fashion. Since *Kaizen* requires labor participation to improve their operations, we consider this as a second characteristic of this management practice.

Last, another feature of *Kaizen* is the recurrent improvements in firm's operations. In other words, it requires continuous changes in their business practice. Therefore, we define as a *Kaizen* management approach if a firm has answered affirmatively to both questions described previously in recurrent years.

Considering the definition provided in the previous paragraphs, the distribution of firms implementing or not *Kaizen* are described in Fig. 10.1. First, our balanced panel comprehends 2185 firms available in both datasets described previously. In terms of *Kaizen*, around 57% of the firms have implemented this management practice over the period investigated.[8] However, implementation of *Kaizen* occurs in distinct periods and firms are evenly distributed overtime whether they have implemented in three, two or only in the last survey year.[9]

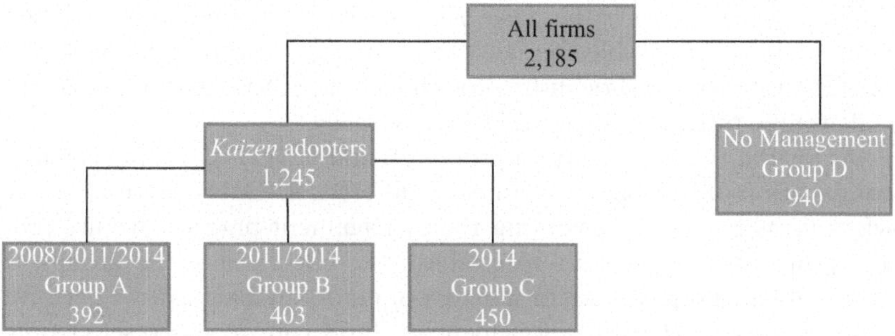

Fig. 10.1 Distribution of firms implementing *Kaizen*

4 Empirical Strategy from the Quantitative Approach

Given the distribution of firms in the categories described in the previous section, two different strategies are able to pursue. Initially, our best candidates as firms implementing *Kaizen* are those that continuously replied yes to both questions overtime. This comprehends those firms implementing *Kaizen* over the three survey years investigated (Group A). Our initial approach is to compare them with those that have not implemented any management practice (Group D).

Although Group A is the most proper group to be considered as a *Kaizen* management style, since they have implemented constantly from 2006 to 2014, we do not know when they have adopted this management method. As the gains of *Kaizen* might be when they have started this management approach, it is relevant to investigate when the firm begins the implementation of *Kaizen*. Therefore, we assume that firms carrying out *Kaizen* approach based on the last two PINTEC (Groups B and C, respectively) are also candidates to investigate the effects on firm's performance after the implementation of this management practice.

Empirical strategy to investigate the effects of *Kaizen* for Groups A, B and C cannot be identical, as they have their particularities on when they have implemented this management practice. In Group A, we are not aware of when the firm started carrying out *Kaizen*. Therefore, our strategy should be what the bonus of implementing this Japanese management practice is. Comparing the performance between groups is an initial approach, but firms from either group might be biased. Firms might have different characteristics because *Kaizen* was not randomly assigned between firms. A feasible approach to reduce this selection bias is implementing one-to-one propensity score matching (PSM) with replacement and average treatment effect (ATE) sequentially.[10]

As for the other comparison groups (B and C vs. D), we implement a combination of PSM and difference-in-differences (DID). Since we know when firms began implementing the management practice, we use pre- and post-intervention years to establish the effect. Since the groups of firms implementing *Kaizen* or not are not randomly assigned, we perform a one-to-one PSM with replacement in 2008 (pre-*Kaizen*), select only those matched firms in the control group and perform a DID for the whole period.

5 Econometric Results

As described in the empirical strategy, our results are presented using two approaches. First, our treated group consists of firms that have implemented *Kaizen* continuously during all period investigated. Based on the previous description of the empirical strategy, our first approach is to perform PSM with Groups A versus D. In order to implement the PSM, it is essential to estimate what the relevant indicators that influence the adoption of *Kaizen* are. Therefore, a Probit is estimated using a dummy for the adoption of *Kaizen* as the dependent variable and a number of characteristics as independent variables. Table 10.1 provides us the results on which indicators are relevant determinants for the implementation of *Kaizen*.

At first, most of the characteristics used are relevant determinants for the adoption of *Kaizen* and they present economic interpretation. Productivity, innovation (product and process), physical investment per worker, share of R&D workers and multinational status present a positive corresponding estimated parameter, which means that they tend to increase the probability to adopt *Kaizen*. Furthermore, firms with higher margin tend to have lower incentives to implement *Kaizen*, which is also consistent with the idea firms facing higher competition tend to implement more *Kaizen*. This evidence is further corroborated by the measure on how markets are concentrated. In sectors with higher concentration (less competition), firms have fewer incentives to improve their performance through the implementation of *Kaizen*.[11] Therefore, competition seems to be a key driver for *Kaizen* adoption.

Table 10.1 *Kaizen's* determinants (Probit)

Probit estimation—Kaizen *dummy as the dependent variable*

Variables	*Parameter*	*Standard deviation*	p-*value*
Labor productivity	0.055*	(0.033)	0.097
Costs/revenue	0.086	(0.056)	0.125
Margin	−0.138*	(0.083)	0.096
Exports/revenue	−0.001	(0.001)	0.623
Product innovation	0.493***	(0.060)	0.000
Process innovation	0.642***	(0.059)	0.000
Number of workers	0.107	(0.189)	0.571
No. of workers squared	0.018	(0.015)	0.218
Production workers/total	−0.419***	(0.133)	0.002
R&D workers/total	3.789***	(0.992)	0.000
Physical invest per worker	0.084***	(0.019)	0.000
Competition (HHI)	−0.639**	(0.322)	0.047
Multinational	0.151**	(0.071)	0.032
Firm's growth	−0.019	(0.085)	0.826
Observations	3456	Pseudo *R*-squared	0.2545
R-squared	Yes	Constant	Yes

Notes: Robust standard errors in parentheses. ***$p<0.01$, **$p<0.05$, *$p<0.1$

Source: Authors' Elaboration

Table 10.2 Results of ATE (Group A vs. Group D)

Variables	*ATE*	P-*value*
Labor productivity	0.145***	0.004
TFP Levinsohn and Petrin	0.084*	0.065
TFP Olley and Pakes	0.085*	0.100

***$p<0.01$, **$p<0.05$, *$p<0.1$

Source: Authors' Elaboration

After matching *Kaizen's* adopters and non-adopters based on these characteristics, the following procedure is to see if there is a premium for implementing *Kaizen* in different measures of productivity by ATE, see Table 10.2.[12]

Among all productivity measures considered, our outcomes suggest a premium of 14.5% in labor productivity and of 8% in total factor productivity.[13] Thus, this evidence informs us that *Kaizen's* firms tend to have a higher performance compared to other not implementing any management practice even after controlling for the important determinants of its adoption. Considering that *Kaizen* adopters are implementing this management practice for at least nine years, our initial interpretation is that productivity improvements are observed in the long term. However, we do not have information of some firms' characteristics that might be affecting our results as well as we do not know what happens after the introduction of *Kaizen* management practice.[14] These issues should be considered in order to uncover when these impacts materialize.

Our analysis shifts to those firms that we assumed that they have adopted *Kaizen* during the investigated period. First, we need to evaluate whether our matching pre-*Kaizen* shows reasonable adherence between adopters and non-adopters. A way to show that is by checking whether the distribution of *p*-score from *Kaizen* and non-*Kaizen* firms becomes similar after the matching. Figure 10.2 shows the *p*-score *K*-density before and after the matching. As observed, the distributions are similar even before the PSM, but after pairing non-adopters with *Kaizen* firms differences diminish.

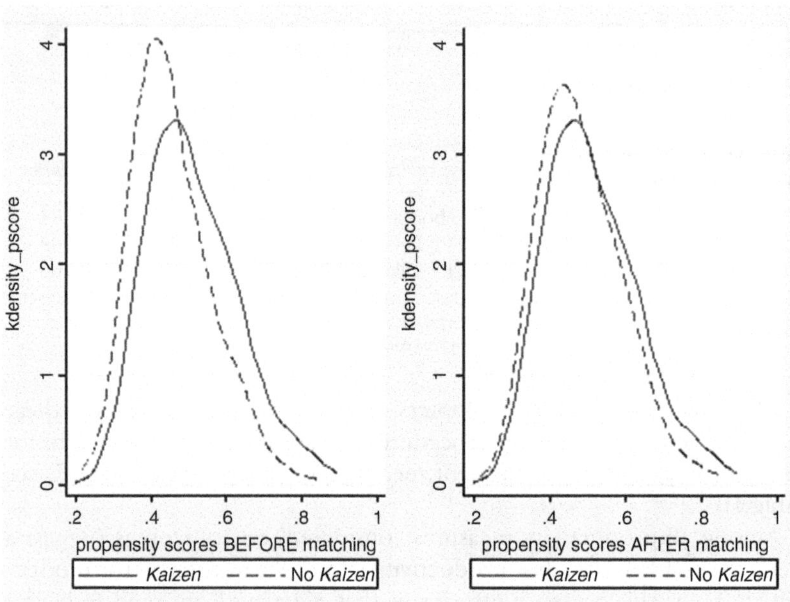

Fig. 10.2 *K*-density of *Kaizen* adopters and non-adopters groups in 2008: Groups B, C versus Group D. (Source: Authors' Elaboration)

Table 10.3 shows our DID results contrasting those treated firms against a group of matched firms that have not implemented any kind of management practice.[15] We have investigated not only productivity measures but also other indicators, yet we will present only those showing robust evidence in the DID. In other words, all other performance indicators do not show any kind of impact from implementing *Kaizen*, such as firms' growth, margin and others.[16] Therefore, our focus on the results of the DID approach is productivity (labor and Total Factor Productivity [TFP]); firm's size; product and process innovation; and share of R&D workers. Columns for each variable are first without any control followed by another considering the full set of controls and last considering only the sectors that we have interviewed in our qualitative approach.[17]

Before looking at the impact of *Kaizen*, we have selected a control to show in this table: multinational.[18] As observed, multinationals are positively related to most of our investigated variables, which is the expected result. Considering the *Kaizen's* impact, initially we observe that *Kaizen* is not able to improve firm's productivity after its implementation, neither at its labor productivity nor at its TFP. Therefore, our interpretation is: it requires a longer period to observe an impact of *Kaizen* on firm's productivity. Considering that we observed a productivity premium in the ATE while comparing Groups A and D, our interpretation is that *Kaizen* promotes productivity gains but when it materializes it is not feasible to detect in a short period, at least not during our investigated period (six years from the two last waves from PINTEC). Therefore, our conclusion is that *Kaizen* might induce higher productivity in the long term (maybe over a decade), while in the short term firms still need to adapt to this new management approach and benefits are not observed in the short run.[19] This is further corroborated by the only positive result obtained of productivity when restricting the samples to solely those sectors investigated in our qualitative approach. In this subgroup of firms, the positive impact is observed in labor productivity, which is considered a short-term productivity compared to TFP.

In other variables, we are able to see positive effects from *Kaizen* adoption. For instance, there are robust results on *Kaizen* increasing firm's size, measured by the number of employees. As the share of production workers is not impacted from the DID approach, yet share of R&D workers is, we conclude that this expansion of employees is biased toward high-skilled workers. Thus, *Kaizen* adopters tend to become larger than non-adopters by increasing the number of skilled workers. Aside number of employees,

Table 10.3 Results of Dif-in-Dif with paired firms from Groups B and C versus Group D

Variables	*Labor productivity*			*TFP (Lev and Petrin)*			*Size*		
	No controls	*With controls*	*Qualitative*	*No controls*	*With controls*	*Qualitative*	*No controls*	*With controls*	*Qualitative*
Dummy *Kaizen*	0.116**	−0.031	0.198**	0.026	0.075*	0.002	0.291***	0.203***	0.286**
	(0.046)	(0.036)	(0.093)	(0.046)	(0.041)	(0.042)	(0.052)	(0.051)	(0.132)
Kaizen impact	0.060	−0.025	0.162*	−0.004	0.022	0.052	0.222***	0.141***	0.508***
	(0.040)	(0.033)	(0.093)	(0.035)	(0.036)	(0.040)	(0.042)	(0.042)	(0.108)
Multinational		0.501***			0.213***			0.146**	
		(0.043)			(0.043)			(0.072)	
Observations	4621	4282	604	4489	4142	598	4674	4142	610
R-squared	0.012	0.406	0.085	0.001	0.203	0.037	0.044	0.160	0.092
Year FX	Yes	Yes	Yes	Yes	Yes	Yes	Yes	Yes	Yes
Controls	No	Yes	No	No	Yes	No	No	Yes	No

Variables	*Process innovation*			*Product innovation*			*R&D workers/total*		
	No controls	*With controls*	*Qualitative*	*No controls*	*With controls*	*Qualitative*	*No controls*	*With controls*	*Qualitative*
Dummy *Kaizen*	0.098***	0.034*	0.177***	0.124***	0.062***	0.232***	0.002**	0.000	0.004*
	(0.020)	(0.019)	(0.055)	(0.020)	(0.018)	(0.054)	(0.001)	(0.001)	(0.003)
Kaizen impact	0.265***	0.173***	0.227***	0.181***	0.038*	0.131**	0.006***	0.004***	0.004
	(0.024)	(0.024)	(0.059)	(0.023)	(0.022)	(0.061)	(0.001)	(0.001)	(0.003)
Multinational		−0.040**			0.070***			0.001	
		(0.020)			(0.020)			(0.001)	
Observations	4677	4142	612	4677	4142	612	4677	4142	612
R-squared	0.080	0.295	0.116	0.065	0.332	0.120	0.022	0.106	0.028
Year FX	Yes	Yes	Yes	Yes	Yes	Yes	Yes	Yes	Yes
Controls	No	Yes	No	No	Yes	No	No	Yes	No

Notes: Robust standard errors in parentheses. ***$p < 0.01$, **$p < 0.05$, *$p < 0.1$

Source: Authors' elaboration

it is also feasible to see a robust impact on product and process innovations. As *Kaizen* is a management practice with the involvement of the full workforce, in which each employee is entitled to suggest changes, an increase of innovation as a whole is a sign that *Kaizen* promotes exchange of ideas to improve firm's performance. As they are innovation outputs, both are able to induce higher productivity as described by the literature of innovation, see the model proposed by Crepon et al. (1998). So, our conclusion is that *Kaizen* can impact productivity determinants in the short term, yet productivity per se only in the long run.[20]

6 Qualitative Approach: Methodology and Data

6.1 Research Design and Methodology

Our qualitative approach aims to complement the results from the quantitative analysis regarding the effects of *Kaizen* on the performance of Brazilian firms. The specific objective is to clarify our outcomes including counterintuitive ones. We generalize our findings from case study research following the literature (Eisenhardt 1989).

We use a CAQDAS (Computer Assisted Qualitative Data Analysis Software) called NVivo to organize, manage and analyze our qualitative data. NVivo is a proprietary software commonly used for qualitative analysis like ours (Bazeley and Jackson 2013) and is referred to as an excellent tool to explore multiple meanings in the data (Richards 2002) to become aware of gaps in the collected data (Wickham and Woods 2005), to revisit data with new conceptual lens and to reflect on social construction of research evidences (Kaczynski and Kelly 2004).

NVivo offers a range of visualization possibilities that are used to better understand and analyze our interview samples. First, we use a case map to link words that were used by our interviewees—this gives us best sense of how the nodes (words) tell the history from the perspective of each participant. Then, we use a chart to compare our data and to give us an alternative view of our results. We also create relationships between the main concepts of our research and use it to better analyze the data.

Our main goal in the software is to make a qualitative matrix analysis, where information from interviewed firms is compared and analyzed. This is an efficient way to contrast data from all in-depth interviews and it helps to make sure no information is lost on the analysis process. From there, we get a set of valid statements that encompass the findings of the quantitative analysis and new specific findings from the qualitative analysis.

6.2 Selection Criteria and Data Collection

Our first step is to establish that focus is on the object (*Kaizen*) rather than the subject (firm). Therefore, chosen firms for our qualitative analysis need to meet only one criterion: use *Kaizen* in its productive activities in Brazil. There are a few *Kaizen* adopters in Brazil, but we chose three with different capital ownership and industrial activities. They are from high and medium-high technology sectors based on the OECD technological intensity and are controlled by Asian shareholders. Two of the firms adopted *Kaizen* since its creation, but the other one adopted *Kaizen* only recently—in 2015. Moreover, two firms are suppliers of the third one.

To meet our goals, the selected companies were contacted by e-mail. We took advantage of Japan International Cooperation Agency's (JICA) network of contacts and recognition in Brazil to establish contact with companies; hence, all of them have Asian ownership. We interviewed different employees from those companies and all interviews took place between March and June of 2018. The interviewees are involved with *Kaizen* taskforces in the companies, but have different working backgrounds, age and position. People responsible for the company appointed the interviewees to us. All the interviews were recorded and transcribed and average time per interview was 30 minutes.

We used a semi-structured questionnaire with open-ended questions. An interview guide was used in the meetings to assist the researchers throughout the interviews. We used a standard questionnaire and also created specific questions for each of our interviewees taking in account their position and working background in the firm. We emphasize that the aim of our qualitative approach was to complement the results found in the quantitative analysis regarding *Kaizen* activities in Brazil.

The precise object of the interview was not to explicitly answer the questions, but to get deeper impressions of *Kaizen* activities in the firm. The interviewees were encouraged to speak freely in their answers, since our questionnaire was constructed with open-ended questions. We captured information that reflected the variability needed to understand the phenomenon studied in the research (Patton 2002) and the collected cases provided relevant examples of the phenomena under scrutiny (Siggelkow 2007) with minimum of analytical generalization (Yin 2009).

7 Qualitative Outcomes and Discussion

We organize the research findings from our qualitative matrix analysis and data generated by NVivo into two different set of results: (1) those that could give us a deeper understanding of the quantitative results and (2) those that aimed to enhance our understanding of *Kaizen* practices within the firm.

7.1 Kaizen*-Adopter Firms and Their Employees*

First, it is important to share some of the main answers of our interviewees regarding what it means to work in a *Kaizen*-adopter firm. All of them stated that their work experience changed after getting more in touch with the *Kaizen* philosophy, despite their previous knowledge of this management practice. Most of the statements regarded the search for the root problem in every aspect of industrial production and for a deeper understanding of the firm's processes. *Kaizen* implies a search for permanent solutions, not only quick and short-term remedies for industrials bottlenecks.

An interesting aspect of the influence of *Kaizen* in the interviewee's daily life is related to their positions in the firm. *Kaizen* is applicable to all company's areas, but the interviewees said that they felt how it really worked only after they got in touch with the production assembly lines. Since continuous improvements are easier to see in an assembly line rather than an office space—especially because of metrics—it makes sense that *Kaizen* is seen as more important in the production area. That was the case for all the interviewees, since production assembly lines looked more suited to *Kaizen* practices than other firm's departments. This is consistent with our findings that the share of production workers of *Kaizen* adopters is lower; thus this management practice is labor saving in the production line in the long term.

7.2 Competitive Pressure and the Search for Improvements Without Increasing Expenses

An interesting discussion topic emerged when interviewees were asked why firms adopted *Kaizen*. On one hand, in the firms that carried out *Kaizen* since its creation, they were emphatic saying that *Kaizen* is intrinsically associated to their organizational culture. On the other hand, the other firm stated that *Kaizen* was adopted in order to achieve higher competitiveness and recover market share lost to other firms that previously adopted *Kaizen*. Therefore, this acknowledgment corroborates our findings in the quantitative analysis, which shows the relevance of competition as a key determinant of *Kaizen* adoption.

All our interviewees also highlight another important aspect of *Kaizen*: the search for improvements without increasing expenses. According to many of the interviewees, the main idea of *Kaizen* is to improve their performance by spending nearly nothing. Our empirical findings on the lack of impact of *Kaizen* on investment of physical capital per worker validate these qualitative assessments. One strategy for the firms is to reduce the amount of reprocessing, for example, the number of times the same process is done on the assembly line. This emphasizes the firm's concern on process innovation, which is highly associated with *Kaizen* adoption in our quantitative analysis. Product innovation is indeed less highlighted though changes in the process areas may improve the quality of the final product.

Another interesting result from our interviews is how employee participation may explain some of the continuous improvement in the firms. Employees in all firms are demanded to propose suggestions often and are rewarded financially or by recognition within the firm. Financial compensation is modest and is regarded as symbolic by our interviewees, but it is an effective way to engage employees in making suggestions. Those suggestions often result in small yet important changes in the assembly line, which correlate with process innovation improvements.

7.3 **Kaizen** ***and Brazilian Business Environment***

It is also important to situate efficacy of *Kaizen* as a management tool in Brazil's business environment considering some of the recent economic fluctuations in the domestic market. Despite using *Kaizen* for decades, employees affirm that the downturn in sales after 2008 was extremely important to improve some of the *Kaizen* techniques in the firm. For one of them, it was the perfect moment to deepen *Kaizen* practices within the firm. All firms needing to reduce costs look for *Kaizen* as a cheap and effective way to turn the tide. For the largest firm, it was also a timely moment to share these practices with its suppliers more vehemently—before 2008, these suppliers were surfing in the economic boom and did not see the need to implement *Kaizen* tools. However, after 2008, some suppliers asked for help to implement *Kaizen* and ultimately that meant a better relationship between the firm and its suppliers.

Our interviewees shared their experience working with *Kaizen* for years in their production site, but also reported experiences in other production sites—including in other countries. Cultural and business environment often changes when one is working in a different place, but our interviewees said there is always room for improvement regardless the location. *Kaizen* adapts to different scenarios and results can be seen in short, medium and long term if it is used correctly.

7.4 **Kaizen's** ***Impacts in the Companies***

An interesting result came after we asked the employees about their recent results regarding *Kaizen*. One of the interviewees told us that they canceled the contract of more than 100 professionals when assessing the implementation of a new plant, most of them from the production line. This result corroborates our empirical findings that *Kaizen* adopters tend to have lower percentage of production workers. However, as explained by the interviewee, this work created a demand for workers with higher levels of education to verify the efficiency of the plant. Given this outcome, two conclusions emerge. Although it is difficult to generalize, first, when implementing *Kaizen*, firms tend to hire more employees than others since production expands more than those not implementing *Kaizen*, because these firms present a steady growth, which confirms our empirical findings on total number of employees. Second, it provides some evidence that by implementing *Kaizen*, firms might increase demand for skilled workers rather than non-skilled workers (from production line). However, further research using more detailed information on workers' skills (such as education and experience) available in other datasets is required to investigate the impact on workers' heterogeneity.[21]

Our interviewees stated that the benefits of continuous improvements may not reflect in productivity in the short term because most of the efficiency gains are on improving the time at work from employees in the production line, which not necessarily increases the speed of producing a good. For example, one suggestion from employees to use their working time in a most efficient way could be to clean the work station after each unit of product instead of cleaning it only at the end of the work day. This change generates more organized workplaces and generates a sense of greater importance for the work. There are also many *Kaizen* practices that help diminish environment impacts but do not translate into higher profits or productivity in the short run, even being considered equally important.

At the end, we saw that most of *Kaizen* efforts affect firms in medium and long term, especially because it takes time for the employees to really believe in these tools. Our quantitative outcomes are in line with these views because a productivity premium exists (ATE), but it is not detectable after *Kaizen* implementation (DID).

8 Concluding Remarks

In this chapter, we investigate the effects of *Kaizen* on firm's performance in Brazil not only using a quantitative approach but also using a qualitative one. Overall, our argument is that *Kaizen* is an appropriate approach to improve firm's performance, especially in a context of financial constraints because it requires low levels of investments. Moreover, a more competitive environment tends to induce firms to implement *Kaizen*.

Our quantitative empirical outcomes suggest a productive premium for *Kaizen* adopters. When comparing the performance of adopters versus non-adopters, our outcomes identify a premium of 14.5% on labor productivity and 8% on TFP in Brazilian firms when estimating the average treatment effect. This evidence shows that *Kaizen* is able to improve firms' productivity not only in naïve measures (labor productivity), but also sophisticated one (TFP using (Olley and Pakes 1996; Levinsohn and Petrin 2003)). However, our evidence is not able to detect whether this improvement in productivity is observed in a short-term period (six years) when estimating the impact by difference-in-differences approach. Our conclusion is that *Kaizen* has a long-term effect that requires a reasonable period to obtain the gains of implementing this management practice.

Nevertheless, our results suggest that *Kaizen* is an important tool to enhance innovation. In our difference-in-differences approach, product and process innovation is increased after the implementation of *Kaizen*. These are innovation outputs that eventually impact productivity. Therefore, we believe that the channel for *Kaizen* impacting productivity is through the causality well established in the literature of innovation, which is innovation output leading to productivity improvement. Our interpretation in this regard is based on our results that we detect an impact of *Kaizen* on innovation on firms implementing this management practice, while the productivity premium is noticed in *Kaizen* adopters for around a decade at minimum. Another side effect of *Kaizen* is that adopters tend to increase their size after implementing it, since we observed that number of workers increase in firms implementing *Kaizen*, especially those in R&D activities.

Our qualitative approach evidenced that the impact of *Kaizen* on firms' productivity is a long-term process, since improvements might not be accounted for in the short term. However, there is a general feeling of improvement in other aspects right after implementing *Kaizen* practices that translate to better results after some time. Therefore, we believe that time horizon investigated in this chapter to verify when these effects on productivity materialize requires a long period.

Notes

1. For instance, the demand for commodities rose after the entrance of China in the World Trade Organization (WTO), as a consequence boom in commodities' price surged. Brazil, like many other developing countries, exports many commodities, which were benefited by the change of the terms of change.
2. Other papers include (Ribeiro and De Negri 2009; Lage de Sousa 2013; Negri et al. 2011; Lage de Sousa and Ottaviano 2018; Pires and Russell 2017).
3. In 2005, percentage of innovative firms in the manufacturing sector was 33.4%.
4. For a discussion on how management practice impacts innovation and productivity, see (Page 2020) and (Hosono 2020).
5. In summary, potential innovators are defined by IBGE as firms that, in the survey period, were included in the registers of beneficiaries of innovation public policies or in the Brazilian patent registers. The ones that were innovators in the previous surveys are also defined as potential innovators.
6. In natural strata where the total number of firms in the population is less than or equal to five, all firms are included in the sample with probability of selection equal to one.
7. PINTEC covers all manufacturing sector and only some from Services: telecommunications, information technology, Engineering/Architecture and Research & Development. As the number of firms in these Services is restrictive, we focus our analysis on the manufacturing sector.
8. We have excluded all firms which have answered erratically these two described questions, which means not consistent across them and/or not overtime.

9. Descriptive statistics from a wide range of indicators are available upon request.
10. As differences between adopters and non-adopters are minimal, we have chosen to implement one-to-one PSM with replacement as even the most sophisticated PSM might present outcomes similar to the chosen one.
11. We use Herfindahl-Hirschman Index (HHI) as a measure of concentration. HHI is calculated by squaring the market share of each firm competing in a market and then summing the resulting numbers.
12. Two measures of Total Factor Productivity (TFP) are considered (Olley and Pakes 1996; Levinsohn and Petrin 2003). Further details are available upon request.
13. For the ATE, we considered all variables used in the Probit model apart from productivity measures.
14. For instance, information on capital ownership, such as whether it is a family-owned firm, is not available and there is robust evidence in the literature that family-owned firms are less productive.
15. Results using only B or C groups provide similar results and are available upon request.
16. Outcomes using these other variables are available upon request.
17. As the number of observations drops dramatically, we decided to present the results without using any control.
18. Outcomes with full set of controls are available upon request.
19. As DID eliminates any time-invariant unobservable variables, such as ownership, another explanation might be that now after eliminating these unobservable factors, firms do not differ in terms of productivity.
20. Results are qualitative similar using all firms from Group D and are available upon request.
21. *Relação Anual de Informaçao Social* (RAIS) from the Ministry of Labor provide detailed information of each formal Brazilian firm.

References

Bazeley, Patricia, and Kristi Jackson. 2013. *Qualitative Data Analysis with NVivo*. 2nd ed. Sage Publications. https://doi.org/10.1080/14780887.2014.992750.

Bloom, N., C. Genakos, R. Sadun, and J. Van Reenen. 2012. Management Practices Across Firms and Countries. *Academy of Management Perspectives* 26 (1): 12–33. https://doi.org/10.5465/amp.2011.0077.

Bloom, Nicholas, Raffaella Sadun, John Van Reenen, Orazio Attanasio, Marianne Bertrand, Robert Gibbons, John Halti-wanger, et al. 2016. Management as a Technology?. *NBER Working Paper 22327* (16–133). https://doi.org/10.1017/CBO9781107415324.004.

Cânedo-Pinheiro, M. 2013. Inovação No Brasil: Panorama Geral, Diagnóstico E Sugestões de Política. In *Armadilha Da Renda Média: Visões Do Brasil E Da China*, ed. F.A.A. Veloso, L.V. Pereira, and Z. Bingwen, 81–106. Rio de Janeiro: FGV.

Cânedo-Pinheiro, M., and Paulo Figueiredo. 2017. Inovação Tecnológica E Produtividade Industrial No Brasil. In *Anatomia Da Produtividade No Brasil*, ed. Armando Pinheiro Castelar, Regis Bonelli, and Fernando Veloso, 211–240. FGV.

Crepon, Bruno, Emmanuel Duguet, and Jacques Mairessec. 1998. Research, Innovation and Productivity: An Econometric Analysis at the Firm Level. *Economics of Innovation and New Technology* 7 (2): 115–158. Routledge. https://doi.org/10.1080/10438599800000031.

Eisenhardt, K.M. 1989. Building Theories from Case Study Research. *Academy of Management Review* 14 (4): 532–550. https://doi.org/10.5465/AMR.1989.4308385.

Hosono, Akio. 2020. Kaizen Towards Learning, Transformation, and High-Quality Growth: Insights from Outstanding Experiences. In *Workers, Managers, Productivity: Kaizen in Developing Countries*, ed. Akio Hosono, John Page, and Go Shimada, 45–67. Singapore: Palgrave Macmillan.

Kaczynski, Dan, and Melissa Kelly. 2004. Curriculum Development for Teaching Qualitative Data Analysis Online. *QualIT 2004: International Conference on Qualitative Research in IT and IT in Qualitative Research*, no. November: 9.

Krugman, Paul. 1994. The Age of Diminished Expectations: U.S. Economic Policy in the 1990s. *The MIT Press* 31 (1–2): 197–201. https://doi.org/10.1016/0022-1996(91)90067-G.

Lage de Sousa, Filipe. 2013. How Can Development Banks Boost Firms' Productivity? In *Development Evaluation in Times of Turbulence*, 115–142. The World Bank. https://doi.org/10.1596/9780821398791_CH09.

Lage de Sousa, Filipe, and Gianmarco I.P. Ottaviano. 2018. Relaxing Credit Constraints in Emerging Economies: The Impact of Public Loans on the Productivity of Brazilian Manufacturers. *International Economics* 154: 23–47. https://doi.org/10.1016/j.inteco.2017.11.002.

Levinsohn, James, and Amil Petrin. 2003. Estimating Production Functions Using Inputs to Control for Unobservables Estimating Production Functions Using Inputs to Control for Unobservables. *Review of Economic Studies* 70 (70): 317–341. https://doi.org/10.1111/1467-937X.00246.

Negri, João Alberto, Alessandro Maffioli, César Rodríguez, and Gonzalo Vázquez. 2011. The Impact of Public Credit Programs on Brazilian Firms. *No. IDB-WP-293.* Washington, DC. https://publications.iadb.org/handle/11319/3826#sthash.huG2Kjk2.dpufDe.

Olley, G. Steven, and Ariel Pakes. 1996. The Dynamics of Productivity in the Telecommunications Equipment Industry. *Econometrica* 64 (6): 1263. https://doi.org/10.2307/2171831.

Ottaviano, Gianmarco I.P., and Filipe Lage de Sousa. 2008. O Efeito Do BNDES Na Produtividade Das Empresas. *Políticas de Incentivo À Inovação Tecnológica No Brasil.*

Page, John. 2020. Industrial Policy, Firm Capabilities and Kaizen. In *Workers, Managers, Productivity: Kaizen in Developing Countries*, ed. Akio Hosono, John Page, and Go Shimada, 29–44. Singapore: Palgrave Macmillan.

Patton, Michael Quinn. 2002. *Qualitative Research and Evaluation Methods. Qualitative Inquiry*, 3rd ed. ISBN: 9781412972123.

Pires, Jose Claudio, and Nathaniel Russell. 2017. *Assessing Firm-Support Programs in Brazil.* Washington, DC. https://doi.org/10.18235/0000939.

Ribeiro, Eduardo Pontual, and João Alberto De Negri. 2009. Public Credit Use and Manufacturing Productivity in Brazil. Mimeo.

Richards, Lyn. 2002. Rigorous, Rapid, Reliable and Qualitative? Computing in Qualitative Method. *American Journal of Health Behavior* 26 (6): 425–430.

Siggelkow, Nicolaj. 2007. Persuasion with Case Studies. *Academy of Management Journal* 50 (1): 20–24. https://doi.org/10.5465/AMJ.2007.24160882.

Syverson, Chad. 2011. What Determines Productivity? *Journal of Economic Literature* 49 (2): 326–365. https://doi.org/10.1257/jel.49.2.326.

Wickham, Mark, and Megan Woods. 2005. Reflecting on the Strategic Use of CAQDAS to Manage and Report on the Qualitative Research Process. *The Qualitative Report* 10 (4): 687–702.

Yin, Robert K. 2009. *Case Study Research: Design and Methods.* By Robert K. Yin. Applied Social Research Methods Series, vol. 5. https://doi.org/10.1097/FCH.0b013e31822dda9e.

PART III

Effectiveness of *Kaizen* for Micro, Small and Medium Enterprises

CHAPTER 11

Kaizen for Small- and Medium-Sized Enterprises in Vietnam

Vu Hoang Nam, Nguyen Thi Tuong Anh, and Doan Quang Hung

1 Introduction

Recent studies have found that enterprises in developing countries are more poorly managed than those in developed countries (Bloom et al. 2012). To see whether business management can be improved in the developing countries, randomized controlled trials (RCTs) have been conducted (Karlan and Valdivia 2011). McKenzie and Woodruff's (2014) survey of the literature observes that training programs are in many cases found to have marginally significant impacts on business performance. A possible explanation is that training impact varies depending on the content and other practicalities of the training program (e.g., Drexler et al. 2014).

In these studies, training content is often a certain variation of the International Labour Organization's (ILO) training curriculum "Start and Improve your Business (SIYB)," which emphasizes entrepreneurship, marketing, buying, stock control, and record-keeping. Production management and quality control, such as lean manufacturing and *Kaizen*

V. H. Nam (✉) • N. T. T. Anh • D. Q. Hung
Faculty of International Economics, Foreign Trade University,
Hanoi, Vietnam
e-mail: namvh@ftu.edu.vn; tuonganh@ftu.edu.vn; hungdq@ftu.edu.vn

A. Hosono et al. (eds.), *Workers, Managers, Productivity*,
https://doi.org/10.1007/978-981-15-0364-1_11

management, have seldom been covered. Exceptions include the training programs associated with the studies by Bloom et al. (2013) in India, Higuchi et al. (2015) in Vietnam, and Higuchi et al. (2016) in Tanzania. These studies find that training improved treated enterprises' management and business performance.

This study analyzes the impacts of *Kaizen* training on the management practices and performance of small- and medium-sized enterprises (SMEs) in Vietnam. It also addresses the issue of whether local trainers can gain sufficient skills in training enterprises. The latter is a new issue as explained shortly below. *Kaizen* and lean manufacturing have so much in common. Both start without capital investment but with what an enterprise has already had. Probably, *Kaizen* is somewhat more human-friendly and more widely adopted in the developing world (Imai 2012; Hosono 2017; Shimada and Sonobe 2017; Otsuka et al. 2018). Yet, neither *Kaizen* nor lean manufacturing is known by the majority of enterprises, especially small-scale enterprises, in the developing world. While Japan International Cooperation Agency (JICA) has had a number of projects disseminating *Kaizen*, only a very few attempts have been made to assess the effectiveness of *Kaizen* for such enterprises rigorously.

The extent to which *Kaizen* can be disseminated across the SME sector in developing countries would be limited by the availability of local trainers. It does not seem an easy task to train local trainers so that they can deliver effective training services for local enterprises on their own. This difficulty casts a shadow over the endeavor toward the quick and wide dissemination of management knowledge and skills.

Our study will shed light not only on an enterprise training program provided by local trainers but also on a trainer training (TT) program in which the local trainers are trained. To our knowledge, this study will be among the first to highlight trainer training in the literature on management training. By doing so, this study is hoped to offer some insights into a good design of trainer training.

2 Design of the *Kaizen* Training Program and the Study Site

2.1 *Trainer Training and Training Material*

2.1.1 *Trainer Training*

A trainer training (TT) was provided to five lecturers of Foreign Trade University, who are in the Faculty of Business Administration. These lecturers were all MBA holders and had advanced knowledge in management. Nevertheless, they did not have a deep understanding about *Kaizen* and skills to be a *Kaizen* trainer. We, thus, invited one Japanese expert in *Kaizen* with experiences of teaching *Kaizen* in developing countries to train these lecturers. The period of TT was from 24 April 2017 to 5 May 2017. While three out of the five local trainers could not complete the TT program, the other two could.

2.1.2 Training Material

Training material for the SMEs in Vietnam focused on key elements of *Kaizen*, of which 5S is the most important part. In addition, we provided the enterprises with basic information about business planning, book keeping, and marketing in a manner consistent with the SIYB training.

2.2 The Study Site

The study site is Trat Cau village in an outskirt of Hanoi. The production of bedding-related products in the village dates back many years ago. During the 1990s, some Korean companies came to Vietnam to produce high-quality bed matrices, blankets, bed covers, and pillows. People in the village were inspired by the success of the Korean companies and started to produce similar products.

The fine division of labor among enterprises is an important characteristic of the village. Four main groups of products, blankets, bed sheets, pillows, and bed matrices, correspond to four main groups of enterprises. Materials for production are bought from outside of the village and imported from abroad. Products of the village are sold in the domestic market and to all regions in Vietnam.

2.3 Sampling for the Survey

We obtained a list of 816 enterprises from the local government office. We selected 195 enterprises that were involved in the production of bedding-related products, of which 59 were registered enterprises and 136 were unregistered ones.[1] Out of 59 registered enterprises, there were 7 incorporated companies and 52 limited liabilities companies. Applying a stratified sampling scheme, we randomly selected 32 out of the 59 formal enterprises and 68 out of 136 informal enterprises for both the baseline and post-training surveys. We could not get complete data for three enterprises, leaving us with data for 97 enterprises in our sample.

2.4 *Questionnaire*

The baseline questionnaire asks questions about the history of enterprises to understand how enterprises were formed, and the personal information of the owners such as education, gender, age, and birthplace as these factors may affect enterprises. We are also interested in the business relationship of the owners with other business owners within their extended families, with whom they might share information, ideas, and even income following the Vietnamese culture.

We have a set of questions to collect data about business practices of the enterprises, including practices of *Kaizen*. We included questions to ask about sales revenue and costs. We designed the questionnaire to include questions to ask about networking of the owners/managers. In the post-training survey, we used the same questionnaire as the one used in the baseline survey. However, we included three additional open-ended questions to ask the owners/managers about the evaluation of the training.

3 Delivery of the *Kaizen* Training Program

3.1 *Selection of Treated-and-Control Pairs of Enterprises*

Given our small sample size, we applied the pairwise matching technique proposed by the Bruhn and McKenzie (2009). Gender of the owner of the enterprise, sales revenue, and registration status of the enterprise were used for matching the pairs of treated and control enterprises. Three enterprises, including one registered and two unregistered enterprises, were not paired leaving 94 enterprises in 47 pairs, of which 15 pairs were registered and 32 pairs were unregistered enterprises.

Due to the limited budget that only allows for *Kaizen* training provision to 40 treated enterprises, we decided to select 15 pairs of registered enterprises and randomly select 25 pairs of unregistered enterprises. This processing made our sample of 40 treated enterprises with 15 registered and 25 unregistered enterprises. Correspondingly, there were 40 control enterprises in pairs with 15 registered and 25 unregistered enterprises.

3.2 *Class-Room Seminar Training*

We conducted the class-room seminar training by inviting 40 treated enterprises to a seminar on 7 September 2017. We sent invitation letters to all 40 treated enterprises and followed by several rounds of phone calls to the owners to confirm their participation. Because owners of enterprises were busy with their daily management, only 17 came to the class-room training. For the 23 owners who could not come to the class-room seminar training, we sent our two local trainers to their enterprises to give them the training material and explained to them the content of the material.

3.3 On-site Training

The on-site training was conducted in three rounds from 11 to 30 September, from 20 to 31 October, and from 1 to 12 December. Each local trainer was randomly assigned to 20 enterprises in the treated group and the local trainers did not change the enterprises throughout three rounds of training.

For the first round of training, the local trainers spent three hours for each enterprise to analyze the production and production-related issues in the enterprise. After the analysis, the local trainers produced a report for each enterprise. The local trainers then spent two more hours to come back to each enterprise to explain to them what could be done to improve the situation of the workshop. For the second round of on-site training, the process was similar. Total hours of service provided to the enterprises were three hours. The third round of on-site training resembled the second round in terms of content of training, steps of training, and time for training. After each round of training, we sent a person to each treated enterprise to ask them to evaluate the service provided by the local trainers.

4 Post-Training Survey

The post-training survey was conducted from 15 to 30 January 2018. We managed to get information from 79 enterprises as one unregistered enterprise in the control group had closed its business before the survey and refused to participate in the survey. We could interview all 40 owners of the treated enterprises.

5 Characteristics of Sampled Enterprises and Owners

5.1 Characteristics of Sample Enterprises

According to Table 11.1, sales revenue of the 40 paired control enterprises in 2016 was higher than that of the treated enterprises. Nevertheless, the differences are not statistically significant at any conventional significant levels. There is no significant difference in gender among owners of the treated and paired control enterprises. This observation is not out of expectation as we applied the pairwise matching method to randomly select the treated and control enterprises.

Out of 35 business practices, the treated and control enterprises all performed on average about 18% of the number of business practices in 2016. Even though we have not introduced the *Kaizen* training program to the enterprises in 2016, some of them have already implemented some *Kaizen* practices in their businesses. The incidence and extension of applying *Kaizen* practices are also not statistically significantly different among the treated and control enterprises.

5.2 *Who Participated in the* Kaizen *Training Program?*

Table 11.1 also compares basic characteristics of the owners of the treated and control enterprises. On average the owners graduated from upper secondary schools. Half of the owners had prior experience in the industry before taking the management of their enterprises and few of them had training related to their production before. Almost all of the owners are indigenous people who were born in the village. Similar to other village industries in Vietnam (Vu et al. 2009, 2010), most of the owners have parents having worked in the same industry before and have their siblings and siblings-in-law who are running businesses in the industry. Only a few of the owners have been abroad for the purpose of doing business. This is not surprising because they can easily buy machine and materials in the domestic market and they only sell their products domestically.

6 Evaluation of the *Kaizen* Training Program

6.1 *Estimation Method*

We applied the treatment effect on the treated (TOT) estimation in this study. The TOT estimates show effects of the *Kaizen* training program on outcomes of the enterprises randomly selected and participated in the program. These outcomes include willingness-to-pay, business practice score, and business performance. We measure performance of enterprises by several indicators including sales revenue, value added, and gross profit. Value added is calculated as by subtracting material cost and other intermediate

Table 11.1 Mean of major characteristics of the sampled enterprises and their owners in 2016

	Treated enterprises	*Paired control enterprises*
Characteristics of the sampled enterprises		
Sales revenue (million VND)	5608.1	5757.6
Ratio of male owner	0.73	0.73
Ratio of enterprise being registered as a company	0.33	0.33
Business practice score (BSC) (out of 35)	6.57	6.43
Kaizen practice score (KSC) (out of 20)	3.63	3.83
Value of inventory	312.2	354.5
Years of operation	11.7	8.9
Initial number of workers	3.1	2.4
Initial amount of capital invested (million VND)	1022.2	524.7
Ratio of enterprises inherited from parents	0.18	0.25
Characteristics of the owners		
Age (years)	39.5	39.0
Years of education	9.5	10.0
Having prior experience in the industry	0.5	0.4
Training experience	0.175	0
Being born within the village	1.00	0.97
Having been abroad for business-related trip	0.08	0.07
Parents used to work in the industry	0.88	0.85
Number of blood siblings working in the industry	3.30	2.88
Number of siblings-in-law working in the industry	2.23	2.37
Number of enterprises	40	40

costs from sales revenue. Gross profit is equal to value added minus labor cost. As we expect that application of *Kaizen* practices will help improve productivity of the enterprises, we also measure their performance by calculating labor productivity, which is value added divided by the total number of working months of permanent workers. The calculation of labor productivity requires taking the owner and his or her spouse as permanent workers because they always participate in daily management and production of their enterprises. This inclusion also helps to avoid a problem of some enterprises that do not employ any workers. During the *Kaizen* training program, we emphasized the reduction of inventory as an important practice to reduce cost. We, thus, take the reduction in the number of products in inventory as an indicator to measure performance of enterprises. Additionally, we analyze the current value of products in inventory to see how enterprises improve management of inventory as they often have multiple kinds of products.

The estimate of the TOT can be obtained by the following regression:

$$y_{it} = \alpha_0 + \alpha_1 P_{it} + \alpha_2 S_{it} + \alpha_3 X_{it} + u_i + \gamma_t + \varepsilon_{it}, \quad (11.1)$$

where y_{it} is the outcomes of enterprise i at time t, which is before the *Kaizen* training program or after the *Kaizen* training program, containing performance of enterprises and quality of management, which will be explained below; P_{it} is the participated or treated status dummy that is equal to 1 if enterprise i participated in the *Kaizen* training program and 0 otherwise; S_{it} is a dummy variable for business communication of the owners of enterprises, which takes the value of 1 if the owner of enterprise i talked with the owner of any treated enterprise and 0 otherwise[2]; X_{it} is a vector of variables representing the characteristics of enterprise i and of the owner of enterprise i, of which many are time-invariant in our sample; u_i is the fixed effect of enterprise i; γ_t is the time effect common to all the enterprises; and ε_{it} is an error term.

To estimate Eq. (11.1), we applied the Fixed-effects or Random-effects model.[3] Our main variable of interest is P_{it}. We expect that α_1 will be statistically greater than zero, meaning that the *Kaizen* training program has positive effects on various indicators of outcomes of the treated enterprises.

Our questionnaire included a set of detailed questions about different business practices including business records, quality improvement, labor management, marketing activities, and *Kaizen*-related practices in both prior and post-training surveys. We follow Bloom et al. (2011), De Mel et al. (2012), Suzuki et al. (2014), and Higuchi et al. (2015) to construct a *Kaizen* practice score (KSC) from a subset of these indicators, which are directly related to the main content of the *Kaizen* training program. During each survey, we counted how many of the 20 *Kaizen* practices each sample enterprise has adopted by the time of the survey.[4] We used these indices to proxy for the quality of management of the enterprises.

In this study, to measure performance of enterprises apart from sales revenue, we used value added and labor productivity. Labor productivity is measured as value added divided by the total working months of all permanent workers including the owner and his or her spouse.

6.2 Effects on Willingness-to-Pay of the Owners

We collected data about willingness-to-pay for the *Kaizen* training program by asking all the owners of enterprises a question: "Are you willing to pay 3 million VND (about 132 USD using the official exchange rate as of 2017) to participate in the *Kaizen* training program" after briefly explaining the main content of the *Kaizen* training program. We asked the same question to the owners in both surveys before and after the *Kaizen* training program. This is a hypothetical question and the owner does not actually have to pay to participate in the training program if his or her answer is yes. As a result, answers to this question can exaggerate demand for the training program. We follow Blumenschein et al. (2008) and Suzuki et al. (2014) to reduce this exaggeration by further asking the respondents whether they are sure about their answer. We ask them: "Are you definitely sure about your answer?" and their answer could be either "definitely sure" or "probably sure." We took the "definitely sure" answer as the affirmative one.

Table 11.2 presents the estimation of the willingness-to-pay of the owners. We pooled the data for the regression in Column 1. Column 2 shows the intention-to-treat (ITT), which is the same as TOT, estimation with the Fixed-effects model. The coefficients of the variable for participating in the *Kaizen* training programs are all positive and significant at 1% significance level. The estimation results confirm our expectation that the *Kaizen* training program increases the willingness-to-pay of the owners. The high appreciation of the training program is not only among the owners who have never attended any other training programs but also among those who have attended other training programs before. This finding is similar to results in other previous studies in other locations in Vietnam (e.g., Suzuki et al. 2014). It, thus, confirms the unawareness of many entrepreneurs, especially of small- and medium-sized enterprises, in developing countries like Vietnam about importance of management training. Also, the finding shows that our *Kaizen* training program was successfully conducted. The program has raised awareness of the entrepreneurs about management knowledge and skills.

6.3 Effects on Kaizen Practices of Enterprises

Tables 11.3 reports the TOT impacts of the *Kaizen* training program on the *Kaizen* practice score (KSC). Columns 1 and 2 in Table 11.3 show

Table 11.2 Willingness-to-pay of the owners

	(1) *Pooled*	*(2)* *Fixed effects*
Participated in the *Kaizen* training program dummy (yes = 1)	0.485***	0.496***
	(5.90)	(6.03)
Talked with treated enterprises about *Kaizen* dummy (yes = 1)	0.029	0.033
	(0.31)	(0.35)
Registration status dummy (company = 1)	0.064	
	(1.07)	
Years of operation	0.003	
	(0.77)	
Who established the enterprise dummy (parent = 1; own=)?	0.009	
	(0.15)	
Initial number of workers	0013	
	(1.45)	
Initial capital invested	0.001	
	(0.30)	
Age of owner (years)	−0.004	
	(1.29)	
Gender of owner dummy (male = 1)	0.070	
	(1.43)	
Years of schooling of owner	−0.004	
	(0.61)	
Birthplace of owner dummy (in village = 1)	−0.104	
	(1.46)	
Prior job related to the industry dummy (Yes = 1)	−0.029	
	(0.66)	
Parents having worked in the industry dummy (Yes = 1)	−0.035	
	(0.48)	
No. of blood siblings in the industry	0.002	
	(0.14)	
No. of in-law siblings in the industry	0.001	
	(0.06)	
Having been trained about doing business in the industry dummy (yes = 1)	0.001	
	(0.00)	
Having been abroad for business-related purpose dummy (yes = 1)	−0.024	
	(0.27)	
Year dummy (2017 = 1)	0.001	−0.007
	(0.02)	(0.11)
Constant	0.893	13.663
	(0.02)	(0.11)
No. of observations	159	159
No. of groups		80
R-squared/*R*-squared overall	0.48	

Notes: Absolute values of *t*-statistics are in the brackets (robust *t*-statistics is in Columns 1 and 2). *, **, *** present 10%, 5%, and 1% statistically significant levels, respectively

that the training program significantly increased the *Kaizen* practice score by about 0.76–1.03 points (out of 20 points).

Table 11.3 additionally presents the effects of exchanging information about *Kaizen* practices among the owners. The dummy for discussing about *Kaizen* practices with the treated enterprises has positive and statistically significant coefficients in Table 11.3. The magnitude of these coefficients is similar to that of the coefficients of the variable for participation of the owners in the *Kaizen* training program. This result is not surprising as our training program focused mainly on *Kaizen* management practices. This finding suggests that good management practices not only were adopted by participation in the training program but could also be acquired through exchanging information within the network of the enterprise owners in the village. In other words, our training program has shown a spillover effect among the non-treated enterprises. Spreading of good management practices among family relatives, friends, and neighbors is an important mechanism to sustain impacts of training program in developing countries, where a dense social network exists. Such rapid spreading of *Kaizen* management practices among enterprises in this village is nothing but a result of information spillovers, which has been considered one of the advantages of enterprises being located in industrial clusters since Marshall (1920).

Column 1 in Table 11.3 provides more information about effects of the social network of the owners on their adoption of *Kaizen* management practices. The dummy variable for the enterprises having been inherited from parents has negative but not statistically significant in Column 1. The dummy variable for the owners whose parents used to work in the same industry has negative and highly statistically significant coefficients in Column 1. Similarly, the coefficient of the dummy variable for the owners having born in the village is negative and highly statistically significant in Column 1. These findings indicate that the owners who had been influenced more heavily by their parents and by their family relatives applied more traditional management style than their counterparts. In other words, having been born in the village and having been influenced by previous generations of owners including their parents is an important determinant of lower application of *Kaizen* management practices, which are more modern than traditional management practices.

In contrast, in Column 1 in Table 11.3 the variable for the number of blood siblings of the owners, who are doing similar businesses in the industry, has positive and significant effect on the adoption of *Kaizen*

Table 11.3 Effects of the *Kaizen* training program on *Kaizen* practice score (KSC)

	(1) *Pooled*	*(2)* *Fixed effects*
Participated in the *Kaizen* training program dummy (yes = 1)	0.756* (1.87)	1.025*** (2.64)
Talked with treated enterprises about *Kaizen* dummy (yes = 1)	1.222** (2.38)	0.911** (2.08)
Registration status dummy (company = 1)	3.595*** (9.70)	
Years of operation	0.042** (2.50)	
Who established the enterprise dummy (parent = 1; own=)?	−0.382 (1.07)	
Initial number of workers	0.086 (1.50)	
Initial capital invested	−0.020* (1.69)	
Age of owner (years)	−0.038** (2.31)	
Gender of owner dummy (male = 1)	−0.344 (1.21)	
Years of schooling of owner	−0.034 (0.72)	
Birthplace of owner dummy (in village = 1)	−2.150*** (3.12)	
Prior job related to the industry dummy (yes = 1)	−0.315 (1.08)	
Parents having worked in the industry dummy (yes = 1)	−0.931*** (2.63)	
No. of blood siblings in the industry	0.212*** (2.95)	
No. of in-law siblings in the industry	−0.008 (0.09)	
Having been trained about doing business in the industry dummy (yes = 1)	−0.292 (0.38)	
Having been abroad for business-related purpose dummy (yes = 1)	1.322*** (2.44)	
Year dummy (2017 = 1)	0.503* (1.83)	0.454 (1.58)
Constant	−1007.085* (1.82)	−911.572 (1.57)
No. of observations	159	159
No. of groups		80
R-squared/*R*-squared overall	0.65	0.08

Notes: Absolute values of *t*-statistics are in the brackets (robust *t*-statistics is in Columns 1 and 2). *, **, *** present 10%, 5%, and 1% statistically significant levels, respectively

practices.[5] It is also noted that the age of the owner variable is negative and significant in all regressions. The production organization of old enterprises in the village, of which many have been established by parents of the current owners, was only based on experience of the previous generation. Modern business practices in general and *Kaizen* management practices in particular were largely unknown to the owners of this old generation. Recently, together with the open and development of the economy of Vietnam, new management practices have been imported from abroad. The current generation of owners has gradually had access to such new management practices and adopted them. Therefore, these findings in Table 11.3 suggest that many of the owners in the village who inherited the businesses from their parents and are influenced by the experience and the old management style of their previous generation tend to be lacking information of and/or unaware of the value of *Kaizen* management practices.

Column 1 in this table also shows that formal or registered enterprises adopted more *Kaizen* management practices than informal or unregistered enterprises. The former had 3.5 points in the *Kaizen* practice score (out of 20 points) higher than the latter. It is reasonable to observe this finding as formal or registered enterprises tend to have better capacity to adopt *Kaizen* management practices.

In addition, the dummy variable for the owners who have attended other business-related training programs before has negative but not statistically significant coefficient in Column 1 in Table 11.3. This finding indicates that previous training programs attended by the owners might have not focused on *Kaizen* management practices. Therefore, our *Kaizen* training program was new to them.[6]

In order to qualitatively assess the impacts of the *Kaizen* training program, during the post-training survey we asked the owners open-ended questions to see how they perceived about benefits and challenges of adopting *Kaizen* management practices. As presented in Table 11.4, not all owners fully understood what *Kaizen* management practices can bring about and not all of them have actually implemented all elements of *Kaizen* yet. Nevertheless, many of them have started to apply and realize the benefits of *Kaizen* management practices for their businesses in different aspects. Particularly many of them reported that the adoption of *Kaizen* management practices helped them arrange materials, parts, and final products more neatly and more organized. As a result, they themselves and their workers could easily identify production areas. Better arrangement

Table 11.4 Summary of benefits and challenges from *Kaizen* adoption reported in 2017

Benefits	
Arranged, neat, well organized	10
Saving materials	2
Easy to know the production areas; easy for searching things; saving time and cost to search for materials, parts, tools, and products	14
Removal of unused things; more space for production	3
More production; more profit	2
Clean; saving time and cost to remove dust and waste from products	5
More responsible workers	1
Faster movement of materials and products	2
Will be very useful in the future when production is expanded	5
Challenges	
Workers do not follow instruction; workers think their experience is good enough; workers are not discipline, not responsible; frequent job quitting	13
Have not found effective ways to encourage and force workers to apply *Kaizen*	6
Characteristics of the production and need to serve orders quickly results in messy workshops and difficulty in applying *Kaizen*	4
Not enough space; small scale so that *Kaizen* application is not efficient	6
There is nobody to implement *Kaizen*	1
Shortage of capital leads to underinvestment in tools, space	2
Kaizen is useful only in some certain stages of production	1
Many workers are not in fixed shifts	1
Gradual improvement from *Kaizen* so that the effect cannot be realized immediately	2
There is no difficulty	3

Note: Numbers in the tables show the frequency of the answers

reduced time to search for materials, spare parts, tools, and final products. Also, implementation of 5S reduces waste and cost. Interestingly, 5 out of 40 owners shared their views about would-be benefits of *Kaizen* management practices by mentioning that they believe *Kaizen* management practices will be useful for them in the future when their businesses are expanded. Such awareness of the owners is a good sign of sustaining the impacts of *Kaizen* management practices.

Many difficulties in applying *Kaizen* practices have also been reported by the owners. Among these, the notable difficulty is related to the work attitude and discipline of workers. As most of workers have just quit farming and some of them are even farming part-time, they are not well trained to be industrial workers. Also, enterprises in the village are competing with each other for labor so that workers' turnover rate is high and workers' commitment is low. Additionally, lack of knowledge to motivate and control workers is considered a major weakness of many owners in the village. As a result, many owners indicated during our survey that it is not easy to implement and sustain *Kaizen* even though they are aware of benefits of *Kaizen* management practices after the training. This finding suggests that our future training (if any) to the enterprises should contain an element on labor management to be more effective. Other challenges including limited space for implementing *Kaizen* management practices, lack of capital, and gradual impacts of *Kaizen* management adoption have also been mentioned by the owners during our survey.[7]

6.4 Effects on Performance of Enterprises

We estimated the effects of participation in the *Kaizen* training program on performance of the enterprises, which are measured by sales revenue, value added, and labor productivity, for paired sample enterprises. Results of the estimation are presented in Table 11.5. According to this table, participation in the *Kaizen* training program did not help the treated enterprises to have higher sales revenue or value added. It is not out of our expectation as we conducted the post-training survey right after providing the on-site training. As such, it was too soon for the training program to have any effect on the operation size measured by sales revenue or value added of the enterprises. This finding is consistent with other previous studies (Suzuki et al. 2014; Higuchi et al. 2015).[8]

We could, however, detect that participation in the training program has positive effect on labor productivity as the coefficient of the variable for participating in the training program is positive and statistically significant in Column 6. The treated enterprises might have utilized workers more efficiently to get higher labor productivity after having participated in the training program. Another aspect we have focused on during the training program is to help the owners cut operation costs and reduce waste by lowering inventory. As the production in the village is still seasonal due to the nature of the products and weather in different locations in Vietnam, stocking products for sales during winter is often practiced by the enterprises. Given limited space for production in many enterprises, such inventory creates high costs during production. Findings in Table 11.5 suggest that the treated enterprises have adopted the idea of reducing the value of inventory after the training program more than the enterprises in the control group. Findings on the immediate significant

Table 11.5 Effects of the *Kaizen* training program on performance of paired sample enterprises

	Ln(sales revenue)		*Ln(value added)*		*Ln(labor productivity)*		*Value of inventory*	
	(1)	*(2)*	*(3)*	*(4)*	*(5)*	*(6)*	*(7)*	*(8)*
Participated in *Kaizen* training program dummy (yes = 1)	−0.166 (0.64)	−0.022 (0.21)	−0.041 (0.18)	0.023 (0.26)	0.087 (0.77)	0.091* (1.81)	−1.105 (1.58)	−1.153*** (2.58)
Talked with treated enterprises about *Kaizen* dummy (yes = 1)	−0.152 (0.50)	−0.019 (0.18)	−0.155 (0.58)	0.018 (0.17)	−0.074 (0.59)	0.004 (0.07)	−1.575** (1.99)	−1.012* (1.86)
Registration status dummy (company = 1)	0.520** (2.39)		0.503** (2.44)		0.041 (0.39)		0.683 (1.00)	
Years of operation	−0.021 (1.58)		−0.015 (1.50)		−0.012** (2.19)		−0.058** (2.11)	
Who established the enterprise dummy (parent = 1; own=)?	−0.200 (0.79)		−0.165 (0.76)		−0.068 (0.71)		0.266 (0.38)	
Initial number of workers	0.156*** (5.11)		0.158*** (5.49)		0.038*** (2.91)		0.580*** (3.78)	
Initial capital invested	−0.04** (2.11)		0.001 (0.08)		0.01** (2.37)		0.100 (1.61)	
Age of owner (years)	−0.026** (2.07)		−0.024** (2.37)		−0.009* (1.81)		−0.077 (0.24)	
Gender of owner dummy (male = 1)	0.427* (1.91)		0.498** (2.50)		0.297*** (2.95)		0.256 (0.53)	
Years of schooling of owner	0.046 (1.36)		0.052* (1.69)		0.031** (2.08)		0.175** (2.11)	
Birthplace of owner dummy (in village = 1)	0.866 (1.10)		0.690 (1.26)		0.337* (1.66)		0.268 (0.37)	

(*continued*)

Table 11.5 (continued)

	Ln (sales revenue)		*Ln (value added)*		*Ln (labor productivity)*		*Value of inventory*	
	(1)	*(2)*	*(3)*	*(4)*	*(5)*	*(6)*	*(7)*	*(8)*
Prior job related to the industry dummy (yes = 1)	−0.046		−0.066		0.007		−0.961*	
	(0.23)		(0.37)		(0.08)		(1.77)	
Parents having worked in the industry dummy (yes = 1)	1.546***		1.144***		0.542***		1.551**	
	(4.53)		(3.97)		(3.66)		(2.39)	
No. of blood siblings in the industry	0.095**		0.099**		0.016		−0.107	
	(2.21)		(2.48)		(0.89)		(0.53)	
No. of in-law siblings in the industry	−0.021		−0.011		0.006		0.459**	
	(0.34)		(0.20)		(0.23)		(2.39)	
Been trained for doing business in the industry dummy (yes = 1)	−0.026		0.014		0.090		−3.741***	
	(0.10)		(0.06)		(0.71)		(4.46)	
Having been abroad for business-related purpose dummy (yes = 1)	−0.606***		−0.725***		−0.348***		−2.183**	
	(3.00)		(3.49)		(3.22)		(2.08)	
Year dummy (2017 = 1)	0.400*	0.231**	0.327*	0.200***	0.085	0.035	0.653	0.445
	(1.85)	(2.13)	(1.73)	(2.62)	(1.17)	(1.24)	(0.94)	(1.12)
Constant	−800.806*	−458.242**	−655.592*	−395.002***	−169.904	−68.345	−1318.734	−894.156
	(1.84)	(2.09)	(1.72)	(2.58)	(1.15)	(1.18)	(0.94)	(1.11)
No. of observations	159	159	159	159	159	159	159	159
No. of groups		80		80		80		80
R-squared/*R*-squared overall	0.58	0.005	0.60	0.01	0.87	0.01	0.87	0.03

Notes: Pooled OLS in Columns 1, 3, 5, and 7; Fixed effects in Columns 2, 4, 6, and 8

effects of the *Kaizen* training program on management practices and performance of the treated enterprises, even though still limited, confirm the effectiveness and success of our training program.

7 Concluding Remarks

In this chapter, we have analyzed experimentally the impacts of a *Kaizen* management training program on management practices and performance of small- and medium-sized enterprises in a rural village in Northern Vietnam. Firstly, we showed that training of local trainers could be possible to bring *Kaizen* management practices to small- and medium-sized enterprises in the rural area in a transition economy like Vietnam. It is, thus, practically feasible to scale up and spread *Kaizen* management practices to other enterprises in other locations at a more affordable cost. Secondly, we find that the owners of the enterprises are inheriting old management practices from their previous generation and are unaware of value of management training ex ante. Our *Kaizen* training program, which was conducted by the local trainers who have attended the TOT training by a foreign expert, has changed enterprises' willingness-to-pay for management knowledge. Thirdly, we discover that the training program did indeed improve business practices of the owners in two ways, through direct participation in the training program and through exchanging ideas and discussing with their peers about the management practices. Finally, we find that the adoption of *Kaizen* management training is conditional on many factors of which labor management is important. These findings indicate that the provision of *Kaizen* management training, which is often expensive, in developing countries can be sustained through TOT training to the local trainers and through an existing dense social network where people interact and exchange information with each other.

Notes

1. In Vietnam, registered enterprises are registered under the Law of Enterprise (Ministry of Justice 2014). Registered enterprises are in the form of state-owned enterprises, incorporations, or limited liability companies and often have larger operation size. Unregistered enterprises are in the form of household enterprises with smaller operation size. Registered enterprises can export and import directly and can issue value added tax invoices when selling their products. Registered enterprises have to pay corporate income

tax, while unregistered enterprises do not. Therefore, both types of enterprises coexist.

2. Having dense social networks is an important characteristic of many village-based industrial clusters in Vietnam. The networks might be created from kinship among relatives in extended families or from friendship among people who have been living close to one another for years. We also constructed this business communication variable by further identifying whether the owner of enterprise has talked with his or her counterpart in the treated enterprises about *Kaizen*.
3. The Hausman test will be performed to select one of the two models.
4. Description of the questions used to collect data to calculate these scores is provided upon request.
5. We assume that the management practices of the current-generation owners are better than the management practices of the old-generation owners.
6. This finding is consistent with information we have obtained from interviews with the owners that almost all of them have never got any training on *Kaizen* management before. Some of them attended management training programs having been organized outside of the village on issues related to business management but not specifically on *Kaizen* management.
7. In fact, 6 owners out of 40 treated ones mentioned about limited space for *Kaizen* management adoption. These owners might have misunderstood the benefits of *Kaizen* management practices, which will create more space for production through better arrangement.
8. We are planning to conduct additional rounds of survey of the enterprises in the village to study longer-term impacts of the training program on operation size of the enterprises. We hope to be able to show positive impacts of the training program on sales revenue and value added of the treated enterprises in the near future.

References

Bloom, Nicholas, Benn Eifert, Aprajit Mahajan, David McKenzie, and John Roberts. 2011. Does Management Matter? Evidence from India. *Working Paper No. 16658*. NBER, Cambridge, MA.

———. 2013. Does Management Matter? Evidence from India. *Quarterly Journal of Economics* 128 (1): 1–51.

Bloom, Nicholas, Christos Genakos, Raffaella Sadun, and John Van Reenen. 2012. Management Practices across Firms and Countries. *Academy of Management Perspective* 26 (1): 12–33.

Blumenschein, Karen, Glenn Blomquist, Magnus Johannesson, Nancy Horn, and Patricia Freeman. 2008. Eliciting Willingness to Pay Without Bias: Evidence from a Field Experiment. *Economic Journal* 118 (Jan.): 114–137.

Bruhn, Miriam, and David McKenzie. 2009. In Pursuit of Balance: Randomization in Practice in Development Field Experiment. *American Economic Journal: Applied Economics* 1 (4, Oct.): 200–232.

De Mel, Suresh, David McKenzie, and Christopher Woodruff. 2012. Business Training and Female Enterprise Start-up, Growth, and Dynamics: Experimental Evidence from Sri Lanka. *World Bank Policy Research Working Paper No. 6145.*

Drexler, Alejandro, Greg Fischer, and Antoinette Schoar. 2014. Keeping It Simple: Financial Literacy and Rules of Thumb. *American Economic Journal: Applied Economics* 6 (2, Apr.): 1–31.

Higuchi, Yuki, E. Paul Mhede, and Tetsushi Sonobe. 2016. Short and Longer Run Impacts of *Kaizen* Management Training: The Case in Tanzania. A Paper Presented at the Annual Bank Conference on Development Economics 2016, World Bank, Washington, DC, June 20–21, 2016.

Higuchi, Yuki, Vu H. Nam, and Tetsushi Sonobe. 2015. Sustained Impacts of Kaizen Training. *Journal of Economic Behavior & Organization* 120 (Dec.): 189–206.

Hosono, Akio. 2017. Industrial Strategies: Toward a Learning Society for Quality Growth. In *Efficiency, Finance, and Varieties of Industrial Policy: Guiding Resources, Learning, and Technology for Sustained Growth*, ed. Akio Noman and E. Joseph Stiglitz. New York: Columbia University Press.

Imai, Masaaki. 2012. *Gemba Kaizen: A Commonsense Approach to Continuous Improvement Strategy.* 2nd ed. New York: McGraw-Hill.

Karlan, Dean, and Martin Valdivia. 2011. Teaching Entrepreneurship: Impact of Business Training of Microfinance Clients and Institutions. *Review of Economics and Statistics* 93 (2): 510–527.

Marshall, Afred. 1920. *Principles of Economics.* London: Macmillan, now Palgrave Macmillan.

McKenzie, David, and Christopher Woodruff. 2014. What Are We Learning from Business Training and Entrepreneurship Evaluations around the Developing World? *World Bank Research Observer* 29: 48–82.

Ministry of Justice. (2014). Luật Doanh nghiệp. Accessed June 26, 2018. http://www.moj.gov.vn/vbpq/lists/vn%20bn%20php%20lut/view_detail.aspx?itemid=30314.

Otsuka, Keijiro, Kimiaki Jin, and Tetsushi Sonobe. 2018. *Applying the Kaizen in Africa—A New Avenue for Industrial Development.* Palgrave Macmillan.

Shimada, Go, and Tetsushi Sonobe. 2017. Impacts of *Kaizen* Management on Workers: Evidence from the Central America and Caribbean Region. *JICA-RI Working Papers*, No. 173.

Suzuki, Aya, H. Nam Vu, and Tetsushi Sonobe. 2014. Willingness to Pay for Managerial Training: A Case from the Knitwear Industry in Vietnam. *Journal of Comparative Economics* 42 (3, Aug.): 693–707.

Vu, H. Nam, Tetsushi Sonobe, and Keijiro Otsuka. 2009. An Inquiry into the Transformation Process of Village-based Industrial Cluster: The Case of an Iron and Steel Cluster in Northern Vietnam. *Journal of Comparative Economics* 34 (4, Dec.): 568–581.

———. 2010. An Inquiry into the Development Process of Village Industries: The Case of a Knitwear Cluster in Northern Vietnam. *Journal of Development Studies* 46 (2): 312–330.

CHAPTER 12

Management Practices and Performance Improvement in Manufacturing Enterprises: The Case of *Kaizen* Adoption in Ghana

Charles Godfred Ackah, Richmond Atta-Ankomah, and Johnson Appiah Kubi

1 Introduction

There seem to be no controversy about the importance of industrialization for sustained growth and employment generation for developing economies. Interestingly, Rodrik (2015) argues that in spite of efforts at industrialization, sub-Saharan African (SSA) countries, with the exception of Mauritius, have suffered significant deindustrialization, whereas some of their Asian counterparts have experienced significant growth in manufacturing value added. It appears the industrial successes of these Asian countries, particularly in the case of China, are highly associated with expansion in both public and private investments in innovation capabilities, including managerial capacity (Kim 2014; Fu 2015; Bell and Pavitt 1997). Managerial capacity is particularly crucial for competitiveness in

C. G. Ackah (✉) • R. Atta-Ankomah
Institute of Statistical, Social and Economic Research, University of Ghana, Accra, Ghana
e-mail: cackah@ug.edu.gh

J. Appiah Kubi
Department of Economics, University of Ghana, Accra, Ghana

A. Hosono et al. (eds.), *Workers, Managers, Productivity*,
https://doi.org/10.1007/978-981-15-0364-1_12

the global economy (Bruhn and Zia 2013; Higuchi et al. 2015). Meanwhile, innovation and managerial capacity in Africa is comparatively low (Diop 2017) and there are a host of constraints affecting innovation in SSA, particularly firm-level innovation (Egbetokun et al. 2016). Consequently, limited innovation and managerial capabilities may constitute a key missing link in the industrialization puzzle for many SSA countries including Ghana.

Ghana's industrialization attempts date back to the early 1960s, at a time when the country's gross domestic product (GDP) per capita was equivalent to those of Malaysia and Korea. Today, Korea's GDP per capita is nearly 19 times that of Ghana, whereas Malaysia's GDP per capita is over 6 times that of Ghana (World Bank WDI online). Like many other countries in SSA, the industrialization drive in Ghana was initially being pushed through import substitution (IS) policies, meant to protect local infant industries that were mainly state owned. In the wake of a significant and continuous economic downturn in the 1970s and 1980s, the IS policy was replaced in the early 1980s with an export-oriented industrialization policy which was a component of a gamut of policies adopted under the World Bank's structural adjustment program (SAP). The change in policy however only came with a brief period of recovery particularly with regard to industrial growth, dashing off renewed hopes for a major takeoff in industrial development in Ghana. Data from the World Bank's World Development Indicators (WDI) online indicate that the value added of manufacturing and industry declined from the mid-1960s up to the early 1980s, after which a brief period of recovery ensued. Between the mid-1980s and the mid-2000s, manufacturing value added remained stymied while it has fallen continuously from the mid-2000s onward. Currently, the Ghana government has instituted a policy to establish a factory in each administrative district, in what has been dubbed "One District One Factory" program, to drive the country's industrialization agenda.

While Ghana still awaits a takeoff in industrial development, there has been a structural transformation, characterized by a leapfrogging of the manufacturing sector particularly with respect to the pattern and trends in labor movement across the major economic sectors. Available statistics from the Ghana Statistical Service (2013, 2015) show that agricultural sector's share in employment has declined while the services sector now accounts for the largest share in employment with no major change in the employment shares for industry and manufacturing sectors. The data, however, show that the majority of people in the services sector who may have moved from agriculture into services are into retail, petty trading and other informal activities. Osei and Jedwab (2016) suggest that these patterns of labor movement may be largely driven by productivity differentials between the major economic sectors. Thus, contrary to the traditional development trajectory, we observe a movement of labor from agriculture into services but not into manufacturing and this may be largely due to productivity differentials between the sectors. This means any development strategy anchored on industrialization serves as a clarion call for more attention to be paid to how to shore up productivity in the manufacturing sector. In this regard, it should be recognized that managerial capacity development is crucial for productivity growth as argued by several authors such a Bloom and Van Reenen (2007), Caselli and Gennaioli (2013) and Schmenner and Swink (1998).

In this study, we investigate the effect of training on *Kaizen*, offered to manufacturing enterprises in Ghana through a collaboration between the Japanese International Cooperation Agency (JICA) and Ghana's National Board for Small Scale Industries (NBSSI), on the firms' productivity and other performance indicators. Having been popularized by the success story of Toyota, a pioneer of *Kaizen* management technique, the impact of *Kaizen* on performance does not appear to be in dispute although the empirical evidences have largely emanated from Western countries (Humphrey 1995). A major source of contention is about the applicability of the technique to contexts other than Japan, especially in developing countries given that the *Kaizen* technique emanated from Japanese cultural philosophies. Kaplinsky (1995), however, argues that *Kaizen* may be suitable for the operating environment in developing countries due to its factor characteristics as well as the flexibility it provides in terms of descaling production and managing complexities associated with fluctuating macroeconomic conditions in developing countries.

This study contributes to the literature by providing an empirical analysis of the effect of *Kaizen* on the performance of enterprises in Ghana's stagnant manufacturing industry. We examine the impact of the training on *Kaizen* on firm productivity and other performance indicators such as profit and sales using propensity score matching (PSM)—a quasi-experimental technique. Our results show that the training has had significant effect on firm performance as well as a majority of indicators on behaviors and practices and/or process indicators. The rest of the study is organized as follows: Section 2 situates the study within the existing literature, while Sect. 3 provides a detailed outline of the methodology adopted in the study. Section 4 presents the results while conclusions are provided in Sect. 5.

2 Literature Review

In an attempt to explain the huge cross-country differences in productivity, the literature has in recent times sought for answers at the micro level, as time-persistent differences in productivity among firms within narrowly defined industries have been reported (Foster et al. 2008). Microeconomic explanations for the differences in productivity across firms particularly in the same industry focus on the differences in factor inputs (i.e. labor and capital), technological varieties and intensities, and scale of economies (Schmenner and Swink 1998). However, recent studies reveal that high productivity is owed to not only factor intensities and/or technological advantage but also allocative efficiency (Hsieh and Klenow 2009; Restuccia and Rogerson 2008) and managerial capacity as well as skill content (Bloom and Van Reenen 2007; Caselli and Gennaioli 2013; Schmenner and Swink 1998). Kaplinsky (1995) argues that the social structure within which production occurs is also a crucial aspect of the production system, which may account for a non-negligible amount of the productivity differences across firms, industries and countries, emphasizing the importance of *Kaizen* or Japanese management techniques.

Kaizen involves three main principles (Berger 1997; Brunet and New 2003). The first which focuses on gradual improvements can lead to the creation of conducive atmosphere where any innovation would easily be accepted by workers and management (Brunet and New 2003), whereas the key objective of the second principle is about improving processes and reducing waste (Humphrey 1995). Contrary to the Taylor system of management in which less or no intellectual inputs are required from workers, third principle of *Kaizen* requires involving workers at all levels in decision making about processes that lead to gradual improvement (Styhre 2001). While the above principles are important, in practice, the nature and details of *Kaizen* may vary from one firm to the other or from one context to the other. Brunet and New (2003) report different and sometimes unique patterns of *Kaizen* implementation among a number of firms in Japan. For adoption outside of Japan, cultural barriers both from within the adopting firm and in the broader local context are important (Panizzolo et al. 2012; Recht and Wilderom 1998) so are constraints around quality of infrastructure and human capital development (Kaplinsky 1995). Within the firm, the commitment of the top management, effective communication among workers and the presence of a *Kaizen* Champion are also crucial (Recht and Wilderom 1998; Maarof and Mahmud 2016).

Several authors have explored the processes by which *Kaizen* leads to productivity and performance improvement. For example, by invoking the theory of swift-even flow,[1] Schmenner and Swink (1998) argue that *Kaizen* can increase the speed at which materials pass through a production process and this can lead to productivity improvement. Brown et al. (2015) argue that *Kaizen* enhances trust building between workers and management which has been found to have positive impact on labor productivity, financial performance as well as product quality.

Kaizen's attractiveness lies in the belief that it may have a positive impact on productivity. However, there are a few empirical studies examining the effect of *Kaizen* on productivity and firm performance particularly in developing countries. Moreover, a large proportion of available empirical work are case studies, focusing on a single or a couple of establishments. A case study of a public hospital in Sri Lanka shows that adopting total quality management (TQM) and 5S (which stands for "sort," "set in order," "shine," "standardize," and "sustain") improved service quality by enhancing employee performance through good leadership and better team work (Withanachchi et al. 2007). Panizzolo et al. (2012) study four enterprises and find that *Kaizen* leads to a reduction in the amount of time needed to set up equipment for production to start. Similarly, Puvanasvaran et al. (2010) also find that *Kaizen* helps to reduce the time taken by a spare-part manufacturer in Malaysia to process sales order, with production lead falling by 15 percent. In another study on a university laboratory, Jiménez et al. (2015) report that preparation time for laboratory practicals reduces by 30 percent and risk of accidents also goes down after implementing 5S.

A few quantitative studies using experimental or quasi-experimental approaches to examine the impact of *Kaizen* in developing countries have started to emerge. Generally, these studies show that teaching *Kaizen* methods to enterprises (including micro- and small-scale ones) in developing countries shows a positive impact on productivity. For example, Higuchi et al. (2015) discuss a randomized controlled trial (RCT) of short-term management training on *Kaizen* for small manufacturers in two study sites in Vietnam and find that the training increases the value added of the participants who actually implemented the practices. Similarly, using an experimental approach to evaluate the effect of *Kaizen* on business performance of small enterprises in a metalworking cluster in Nairobi, Mano et al. (2014) report that enterprises that participated in *Kaizen* training have a significant increase in profits and value added but with no significant effect on sales revenue, compared to their counterparts that participated in other training programs. An earlier RCT study by Mano et al. (2012) to evaluate the effect of management training that involves some aspects of *Kaizen* for microenterprises was in Kumasi, also in Ghana. Significant positive impacts on performance are found. While Mano et al. (2012) focus mainly on microenterprises in a single cluster of fabricators, the current study provides more insights into the likely effect on Basic *Kaizen* on performance in that it covers firms from more manufacturing industries as well as small and medium enterprises.

3 Methodology

3.1 The Intervention Under the Study

Recognizing the critical need to develop management capabilities among small and medium-sized enterprises in Ghana, JICA in conjunction with Ghana's NBSSI has been implementing an intervention since 2012, which seeks to train small and medium enterprises (SMEs) in manufacturing to adopt *Kaizen* management techniques. Focusing mainly on four main administrative regions in Ghana (Ashanti, Northern, Brong Ahafo and Central regions), the participants received training on basic *Kaizen* principles and methods like 5S (sorting, setting, shining, standardizing and sustaining), waste reduction and visualization. Basic accounting principles like stock control, petty cash book keeping, recording of sales and accounts receivable and payables and other practices were included in the training.

The program started with a pilot, which was carried out in the Ashanti region between 2012 and 2014, after which a national project was designed to cover the other three regions but in a stepwise or cascaded fashion. The Ashanti and Northern regions' project started in 2015 and 2016 respectively, while that for firms in Brong Ahafo started in 2017 with firms in Central region expecting to receive the training in 2018. According to the implementers, the focus of the intervention on manufacturing enterprises was justified by the general belief that *Kaizen* management practices are most suitable for manufacturing firms. Hence, although the concept/practices could be applied in other business contexts, it was prudent to begin the introduction of the concept to the Ghanaian business environment by starting with manufacturing enterprises.

The training was administered to the enterprises through the NBSSI's Business Advisory Centers (BACs) in the targeted regions. The core mandate of BACs is that they provide business extension services in many areas including operational management practices. An essential feature of the training was that it involved Japanese experts on *Kaizen* (OJT) who initially delivered on-the-job-training (OJT) with NBSSI officials not only facilitating the training but also learning how to independently deliver training to their clients in the absence of Japanese experts. This was done to ensure continuity or sustainability of the program after the Japanese experts have left. In fact, between 2015 and 2017, self-implementation by the BACs has independently trained many enterprises with no direct involvement of the Japanese experts. Solely for the purpose of easily distinguishing between the firm trained by the Japanese experts and those trained by BACs, we refer to the former as OJT firms and the latter as self-implementation firms in the rest of this chapter.

3.2 Data and Analytical Approach

We set out to interview all the firms which had received the training. NBSSI/BAC officials provided us with a list of the enterprises that had received the training at the time of our survey, which took place between October and December 2017. They also provided us with a list of enterprises which had been selected for training but had not yet received the training or had just received training but yet to start actual implementation of the practices. We attempted to interview all these enterprises so they could serve as a control group for those that had received the training and started implementing the practices. We had to follow this approach because the intervention was not originally designed to allow for the use of rigorous impact assessment methods such as randomized control trials. In addition to a firm-level questionnaire which was administered to the manager of each of the firms, we also interviewed two employees (preferably a male and a female) from each firm that participated in the study. This allows us to assess the effect of the training on behavioral or process indicators from the perspectives of both the management and the employees in addition to examining the effect on firm-specific key performance indicators such as employment, output, value added, sales and profit.

Our interactions with NBSSI indicated that they approached enterprises which benefited from the training, although a few other enterprises did approach NBSSI on their own after learning about the benefits of the training from other beneficiaries. Once the enterprises meet assessment criteria, of which the details can be found in the assessment sheet provided in the Appendix to this chapter, they are admitted into the program. This means that generally the beneficiary enterprises did not only self-select into the program but their selection was also not based on any randomized process. Hence, in our attempt to assess the effect of the training on performance, we relied on propensity score matching (PSM) to examine the average treatment effect of the training by matching the treated enterprises (those which have received the training and implemented the practices) with those that have been qualified to participate in the training but are yet to receive the training and those that have just received the training but have not started implementing the practices. Using key time-invariant variables including educational background of the manager, subsector of manufacturing in which they operate, age of the manager, region and legal status of the enterprise, the treated firms were matched with the untreated ones using the nearest neighbor technique. The use of time-invariant variables was to help avoid endogeneity problems. The variables used in generating propensity scores for analyses at both management and employee levels are included in Table 12.1.

In addition to the PSM, we also used a random effect model to explore the effect of the training on the performance indicators, of which the details are presented in the Appendix. Due to some disadvantages associated the PSM methods, such as the reliance on conditional independence assumption (Bryson et al. 2002) and biasedness associated with researcher's control over selected observables for matching (King and Nielson 2018), the random effect model was used to complement the PSM results as well as serve a robustness check. Also presented in the Appendix, the results of random effect model are qualitatively similar to the PSM results.

A total of 184 enterprises were interviewed from the three administrative regions—Ashanti, Northern and Brong Ahafo regions—where *Kaizen* had been introduced.[2] Of the total interviewed, the treatment group constituted 98 firms while the remainder were in the control group. There were 110 enterprises in the Ashanti region (64 for treatment and 46 for control), 45 in the Northern region (22 for treatment and 23 for control) and 29 in the Brong Ahafo. All the enterprises in Brong Ahafo were in the control group and this was because 14 of these enterprises which had just received the training at the time of the survey were yet to start implementation of the practices while the remaining 15 had only been selected to receive the training.

Table 12.1 Description of variables and how they were generated for analysis

Variable	*Description of variables*
Wmale	Male worker = 1, female as base
w_age	Age of worker in years
Juniorstaff	Worker is a junior staff = 1, zero otherwise
Farmworker	Worker is related to manager = 1, zero otherwise
Wedusss	Worker has completed senior secondary education (SSS)
Weduhigher	Worker's education is higher than SSS = 1, zero otherwise
Wedubasic	Worker's education is basic = 1, zero otherwise
Male	Gender of the manager—male manager, female as base
Age	Age of the manager in years
proficient_eng	Manager is proficient in English = 1, zero otherwise
ashantiBA	Firm in Ashanti or Brong Ahafo regions of Ghana
Registered	Registered firm = 1, zero otherwise
sole_pro	Sole proprietor = 1, zero otherwise
Foodind	Food or water industry = 1, others zero
Wearingapparel	Wearing apparel industry = 1, others zero
Metalwork	Fabrication of metals, machine installation industry = 1, zero otherwise
Riskaverse	Manager is risk averse = 1, zero otherwise. Choose between the following two options: Receive GH¢ 100 for sure (option 1) or flip a coin and receive 0 if it's tail or GH¢ 300 if it's head (option 2)
Preferstoday	Manager is present biased = 1, zero otherwise. Choose between the following options: Receive GH¢ 1000 today (option 1) or receive GH¢ 1500 for sure one year from now (option 2)
Wriskaverse	Worker is risk averse = 1, zero otherwise. Choose between the following options: Receive GH¢ 100 for sure (option 1) or flip a coin and receive 0 if it's tail or GH¢ 300 if it's head (option 2)
Wpreferstoday	Worker is present biased = 1, zero otherwise. Choose between the following options: Receive GH¢ 1000 today (option 1) or receive GH¢ 1500 for sure one year from now (option 2)
Loutput	Log of the value of annual output
Loutputpworker	Log of annual output per worker
Lsales	Log of the value of annual sales
Lvalueaddpworker	Log of annual value added per worker
Lprofit	Log of annual profit

4 Analysis and Results

Table 12.1 provides a list of variables used in the analysis and how they were constructed. The variables used in the probit regression models which generated the propensity scores for matching the treated firms with the control firms are also included in Table 12.1. Our matching produced a strong common support between the treated and control firms with a region of common support of [0.03, 0.91] and only one treatment firm being off the common support region and not included in the analysis. We included the age of the manager in the probit regression instead of the age of the firm because our preliminary analysis revealed that the age of the manager was significantly correlated with the age of the firm. Meanwhile, a high number of the enterprises in the study are sole proprietorships whose owners' general experiences particularly from previous employment may be more relevant in this context than the age of their current firm.

Table 12.2 compares the treatment and control groups based on the characteristics of the firms and/or managers. The table shows that, in terms of the age of managers, there is no significant difference between treatment and control groups. Similarly, there is no significant difference between the two groups with respect to the gender of the manager, although the majority of the managers in both groups are males (above 70 percent). In the treatment group, 43 percent of the managers have higher than secondary education, but 29.6 percent of the control managers have attained this level of education.[3] A higher percentage of managers of the control firms (58.2 percent) have secondary education, compared to 29.1 percent for the treatment group. On the other hand, a higher percentage of the treatment group managers have basic education (27.9 percent) as

Table 12.2 Firm/manager's characteristics by whether firm is treated

Variables	*Control*	*Treatment*	*Chi²/T-test*	*P-values*
Mean age of managers	43.4	44.6	−0.745	0.457
Proportion of male managers	70.4	74.4	0.368	0.544
English proficiency of managers	33.7	57.0	10.070	0.002
Manager has basic education	12.2	27.9	7.140	0.008
Manager has sec. education	58.2	29.1	15.694	0.000
Manager has above sec. education	29.6	43.0	3.592	0.058
Proportion of firms registered	71.4	93.0	14.180	0.000
Proportion of firms with a sole proprietor	82.7	68.6	4.968	0.026
Proportion of firms in food/water industry	39.8	38.4	0.039	0.843
Proportion of firms in wearing apparel industry	26.5	9.3	9.025	0.003
Proportion of firms in metalwork industry	7.1	11.6	1.099	0.295
Proportion of risk averse managers	71.4	66.3	0.568	0.451
Proportion of present bias managers	83.7	79.1	0.644	0.422

compared to managers with basic education in the control group (12.2 percent). Registered firms constitute 93 percent of the treatment group which is statistically different from the proportion of the firms in the control group that have been registered (71.4 percent). This follows from the fact that a higher proportion of the control firms are sole proprietorships (82.7 percent) as compared to the treatment firms (69 percent).

In terms of the distribution by industry type, we observe a slight difference in the proportion of the firms for treatment and control groups in the food/water industries (38.4 percent for treatment and 39.8 percent for control), but relatively more control firms are in wearing and apparel (26.5 percent) than treatment (9.3 percent). Responses from a single hypothetical question to measure risk aversion show that there is no significant difference between the treatment managers and the control managers in terms of their tendency to take risk. About 71.4 percent of the control managers are risk averse as compared to 66.3 percent of the treatment managers. Similarly, about 83.7 percent of the control managers and 79 percent of the treatment managers prefer to receive a Ghana Cedis (GHC) 1000 today instead of GHC 1500 a year later. This implies that managers of both groups on average are highly present-bias and are impatient for returns on investment.

The mean of selected outcomes (number of workers, annual output per worker, sales, value added per worker and profit) by treatment status, gender of the manager, region of Ghana and other variables is presented in Table 12.3. These measures show the relative size of the firms. The firms trained by the Japanese experts (OJT firms) are larger than those trained by the BACs of NBSSI (self-implementation firms), which in turn are larger than the control. With the exception of value added per worker, the average values of workers, output per worker, sales and profit are higher for the treatment firms than for the control firms. Firms in the Ashanti/Brong Ahafo region of Ghana are larger than those in the Northern region. Registered firms perform better than unregistered ones, but sole proprietors do not have better measures of performance than other types of firm.

The average values of the measures of performance in Table 12.3 increase with the education of the manager of the firm. The values for firms with managers with higher than secondary education are higher than average values for firms with managers having secondary education, which are in turn higher than those with basic education. Even though the average number of workers of firms with female managers is 22 and that of male managers is 21, output per worker, sales, value added per worker and

Table 12.3 Mean of selected outcomes

	Characteristics	*Workers*	*Output per worker*	*Sales*	*Value added per worker*	*Profit*
Type of treatment	OJT	31	28.95	1061.39	12.29	397.96
	Self-implementation	29	17.95	382.17	8.98	247.33
	Treatment	31	25.05	804.93	11.12	346.54
	Control	14	20.44	323.09	14.32	203.73
Regions	Northern region	16	12.13	145.76	4.77	55.59
	Ashanti/BA region	23	25.39	662.54	15.07	338.42
Education	Manager has basic edu.	16	15.85	148.08	11.62	63.20
	Manager has sec. edu.	16	22.42	362.43	12.42	161.11
	Manager has higher edu.	31	26.04	950.73	14.08	500.35
Registration status	Not registered	12	13.93	117.08	10.05	81.93
	Registered	24	24.53	635.97	13.55	311.92
Ownership	Non-sole proprietor	40	37.29	1059.26	20.35	449.97
	Sole proprietor	16	18.06	382.47	10.63	221.16
Industry	Industry: Food	24	28.82	528.62	18.05	238.20
	Wearing apparel	15	4.41	155.24	1.50	107.93
	Wood products	20	30.19	522.68	24.27	326.50
	Metals/machines	25	33.68	1448.58	12.76	632.43
	Chemicals	39	9.43	827.79	4.07	553.81
	Paper, plastics, textiles	10	20.48	528.28	1.91	89.42
	Others	14	10.50	262.94	1.89	73.48
Gender	Male manager	21	25.80	672.53	15.52	334.44
	Female manager	22	12.74	185.92	5.27	84.39
Total	Total	21	22.54	536.67	12.89	269.95

Note: Except for the number of workers, all the variables are measured in thousands Ghana cedis

profit for firms with male managers are higher than those of female managers. In terms of the number of workers, sales and profit, firms involved with machines and metal work and those in chemicals are larger than the other industry types.

The gender distribution of the employees who were interviewed shows that there are more males (71.7 percent in treatment and 58.6 percent in control) in our sample than females. By the research design, we expected an equal distribution between males and females among the employees. However, the higher proportion of males may be due to the fact that a lot of manufacturing activities in Ghana are male dominated. Both treatment and control groups have similar proportion of junior workers (about 36.4 percent each group). There is no statistically significant difference between the treatment and control with regard to the proportion of workers who are related to the owner or manager of the enterprises. The difference in the proportions for basic and secondary education between two groups is not significant. On the contrary, a higher proportion of workers have more than senior secondary education in the treatment group (14.5 percent) as compared to the control group (5.4 percent).

The results from the PSM analysis of the effect of training on key indicators of behaviors and management practices are presented in Table 12.4 from the perspective of the managers. The nearest neighbor matching technique is used, with two nearest neighbors giving the smallest bias of 11.1. It

Table 12.4 Average treatment effect on key practices using PSM—management

Management practice	*Treated*	*Control*	*Difference*	*Std. error*	T-*stat.*
Good workers' attitude	0.624	0.235	0.388	0.086	4.5
Profited from suggestions	0.624	0.569	0.055	0.094	0.59
Cleaning	0.800	0.400	0.400	0.087	4.61
Placing tools	0.729	0.298	0.431	0.080	5.37
Kaizen committee	0.424	0.161	0.263	0.073	3.59
Floor plan	0.565	0.149	0.416	0.071	5.82
Defect reduction	0.706	0.361	0.345	0.089	3.89
Workers' attendance record	0.682	0.380	0.302	0.089	3.38
Sales record	0.647	0.490	0.157	0.094	1.66
Products record	0.859	0.486	0.373	0.087	4.26
Keeping accounts receivable/payable records	0.824	0.502	0.322	0.088	3.64
Keeping a petty cash record?	0.765	0.518	0.247	0.091	2.72
Risk averse	0.659	0.714	−0.055	0.087	−0.630
Prefers today	0.788	0.800	−0.012	0.075	−0.160
Most people in this company can be trusted (agree/strongly agree)	0.671	0.690	−0.020	0.090	−0.22
Most of my customers can be trusted (agree/strongly agree)	0.647	0.624	0.024	0.092	0.25
Most of my suppliers can be trusted (agree/strongly agree)	0.624	0.592	0.031	0.093	0.34

can be stated that most of the improved practices by the treatment firms as compared to the control can be attributed to the training on *Kaizen*. By and large, the results strongly indicate that behaviors and practices in the treatment group appear better than the situation in the control group. The differences between the two groups on the majority of the variables are not only statistically significant but are also in favor of the treatment group.

The proportion of managers reporting good workers' attitude toward work is higher in the treatment group than in the control group. A similar statement can be made about daily cleaning at the close of work, placing tools in the right place, having a *Kaizen* committee and having a floor plan/marking. The proportions of managers in the treatment group who reported that they have got measures to reduce defects as well as recording worker's attendance are significantly higher for the treatment group. The results also show that the training significantly improved the record keeping by the firms in terms of petty cash records and account receivables record. The matched difference in the proportion of firms keeping sales records is not significant, even though the unmatched is significant. This should not be surprising because most firms already keep sales records and thus only a few may have to start the practice if they were not records.

The results however show no effect of the training on risk and time preference of the managers, trust among workers and trust in customers and suppliers. We find this unsurprising as trust appears to be more embedded in a broader social system, whereas risk and time preferences are generally intransigent especially in the short term. The results from the employees' perspective largely align with those of the managers. Additionally, we find statistically significant differences in favor of the treatment group for questions or indicators that only pertains to the employees such as the perception of workers in their suggestions to management, knowledge of the firm's sales target or policies, knowledge of the mission of the firm and labeling of stock items.

In addition to the impact of the training on behavioral or process indicators discussed above, we also analyze the likely impact of the training on performance indicators using PSM and the results are presented in Table 12.5. Here, we performed the analysis using the averages of the firm's performance indicators for the period 2012–2017 or the log of the averages for the period. It is during this period that the firms were treated. In all of the performance measures, the difference between the treatment and control is statistically significant in the unmatched samples. After matching, the results from PSM show that the training has had statistically

Table 12.5 Average treatment effects after matching at the firm level

Variable	*Sample*	*Treated*	*Controls*	*Difference*	*S.E.*	T-*stat*
Mean number of workers	Unmatched	28.79	14.57	14.23	3.78	3.76
	ATT	29.11	13.09	16.02	3.99	4.01
Mean log of output	Unmatched	12.12	11.01	1.11	0.26	4.22
	ATT	12.15	11.43	0.71	0.33	2.13
Mean log of output per worker	Unmatched	9.18	8.67	0.51	0.21	2.46
	ATT	9.19	9.05	0.14	0.27	0.53
Mean log of sales	Unmatched	12.41	11.32	1.09	0.26	4.26
	ATT	12.43	11.64	0.79	0.32	2.47
Mean log of value added per worker	Unmatched	8.37	7.68	0.69	0.25	2.73
	ATT	8.39	8.13	0.26	0.34	0.76
Mean log of profit	Unmatched	11.35	9.98	1.37	0.3	4.62
	ATT	11.35	10.04	1.31	0.39	3.4

significant effects on the average number of workers, output, sales and profit, whereas the effect on value added per worker and output per worker is unexpectedly insignificant. This suggests an appreciable impact of the training on *Kaizen*. But again, since the firms were not randomly assigned into treatment and control before the training, a strict causal relationship is limited here.

5 Conclusion

Industrialization efforts by African countries, and in particular Ghana, have not yielded substantial dividends. Ghana's manufacturing value added has seen no long-term growth since political independence and has disappointingly declined in recent years while informal services sector activities have blossomed, accounting for large proportion of employment. The key question is about how to place Ghana's manufacturing sector as well as those of many SSA countries with a struggling manufacturing sector on a path of a stable and sustainable growth. Policies, programs and/or interventions that would bring about productivity growth in the manufacturing sector are likely to contribute significantly to a vitalization of SSA's struggling manufacturing sectors. In line with this call, JICA together with NBSSI has introduced *Kaizen* management techniques through training to manufacturing enterprises in Ghana, and this study sought to establish whether the intervention has had any major impact on the performance of the manufacturing firms in Ghana.

Similar to findings from empirical studies such as Higuchi et al. (2015) and Mano et al. (2014), our results show that the adoption of *Kaizen* has had significant impact on the performance of manufacturing enterprises that participated in the training and have consequently implemented the methods, practices and techniques associated with *Kaizen*. Specifically, we found evidence of a significant impact of the training on the firms' number of workers, sales, profit and output. This seems to provide some support for the argument by Kaplinsky (1995) and Schmenner and Swink (1998) that *Kaizen*, which emanated from Japanese cultural philosophy, may be applicable in context other than Japan including developing countries such as Ghana.

This study represents a contribution to the literature on the likely effect of *Kaizen* on the productivity and performance in developing countries, particularly in Africa. In terms of policy, the findings of the study suggest that extensive promotion of *Kaizen* as a management technique among a broad spectrum of manufacturing enterprises, and perhaps businesses in other economic sectors, could contribute significantly to rejuvenating manufacturing in Ghana and in SSA. We suggest that factoring *Kaizen* into Ghana's recent policy to establish a factory in each administrative district may enhance the likelihood that the policy will succeed.

Appendix

Though the survey was conducted in a one-time period, we collected information on the performance and input variables from 2011 (i.e. a year before the program started) to 2017, which allows us to model the effect of training on performance using a panel framework. We consider the following regression model:

$$y_{it} = \alpha_i + \beta_1 trt_{it} + \beta_2 treat_i + \sum_i^t \beta_{3i} year_t + \sum_i^k \beta_{4i} x_{it} + \varepsilon_{it}$$

where *y* represents the performance variable; *treat* equals 1 if the firm is in the treatment group, otherwise zero; *year* are time dummies from 2011 to 2017; and *x* are control variables. *trt* is derived from an interaction between the *treat* dummy and the year dummies, taking a value of zero for all the years before training but one for all the years from the year of training onward. α_i are the random individual-specific effects, β_i are the coefficients and ε_{it} is an idiosyncratic error. In this model, β_1, the coefficient of *trt*, measures the impact of the training on the performance variables.

We estimated the parameters of the regression equation above using random effects. Our choice of random effect over fixed effects was informed by the fact that most of our regressors in the equation are time invariant, for which fixed effects models do not provide coefficients on. Moreover, the Breusch and Pagan Lagrange Multiplier Test which compares random effects model with pooled ordinary least squares (OLS) regression showed that for all the performance variables considered, the random effect models were better than pooled OLS regression. However, the downside of the panel model is that it does not allow us to adequately address selection problems. Another problem is that the results may be affected by respondents' recall bias because the respondents had to provide information on activities that had taken place a couple of years or several years ago in some cases. Measured by the coefficient of *trt*, the regression results show that with the exception of output and value added per worker, the intervention had a positive and significant effect on four out of six performance indicators considered in this study. Qualitatively, these results generally support the PSM results about the positive impact of the intervention on the firms' performance (Tables 12.6 and 12.7).

Table 12.6 Results of random effect regression model

Variables	*(1)*	*(2)*	*(3)*	*(4)*	*(5)*	*(6)*
	Workers	*Loutput*	*Loutputpworker*	*Lsales*	*Lvalueaddpworker*	*Lprofit*
trt	5.085***	0.068	0.114**	0.126***	0.118	0.163*
	(1.901)	(0.042)	(0.047)	(0.045)	(0.074)	(0.094)
treat	11.329**	0.382*	0.247	0.433**	0.224	0.645**
	(4.573)	(0.213)	(0.222)	(0.198)	(0.266)	(0.257)
y2012	0.480	0.102**	0.125***	0.067	0.171**	0.007
	(1.844)	(0.042)	(0.048)	(0.046)	(0.077)	(0.098)
y2013	0.872	0.245***	0.273***	0.176***	0.239***	0.091
	(1.853)	(0.042)	(0.048)	(0.045)	(0.076)	(0.097)
y2014	2.743	0.341***	0.340***	0.266***	0.282***	0.086
	(1.865)	(0.042)	(0.048)	(0.045)	(0.075)	(0.097)
y2015	4.246**	0.446***	0.431***	0.380***	0.443***	0.276***
	(1.928)	(0.043)	(0.049)	(0.047)	(0.078)	(0.100)
y2016	4.586**	0.554***	0.530***	0.459***	0.515***	0.277***
	(1.995)	(0.044)	(0.051)	(0.048)	(0.081)	(0.103)
y2017	2.042	0.569***	0.547***	0.438***	0.521***	0.270**
	(2.041)	(0.046)	(0.052)	(0.049)	(0.083)	(0.107)
Workers		0.029***	−0.017***	0.036***	−0.014***	0.038***
		(0.003)	(0.003)	(0.003)	(0.005)	(0.006)
workers_squ		−0.008***	0.004***	−0.010***	0.003*	−0.013***
		(0.001)	(0.001)	(0.002)	(0.002)	(0.003)
proficient_eng	3.362	0.374	0.299	0.523**	0.504*	0.722***
	(4.899)	(0.228)	(0.237)	(0.214)	(0.281)	(0.273)
Male	−6.460	0.155	0.324	0.312	0.365	0.044

(*continued*)

Table 12.6 (continued)

Variables	*(1)*	*(2)*	*(3)*	*(4)*	*(5)*	*(6)*
	Workers	*Loutput*	*Loutputpworker*	*Lsales*	*Lvalueaddpworker*	*Lprofit*
	(5.157)	(0.246)	(0.257)	(0.229)	(0.303)	(0.297)
Age	−0.079	−0.008	−0.007	−0.006	−0.000	−0.008
	(0.195)	(0.009)	(0.009)	(0.009)	(0.011)	(0.011)
ashantiBA	9.134*	0.863***	0.635**	1.170***	0.873***	1.240***
	(5.253)	(0.246)	(0.257)	(0.229)	(0.301)	(0.293)
Registered	0.040	0.678**	0.486	0.548**	0.806**	0.262
	(6.119)	(0.287)	(0.299)	(0.269)	(0.352)	(0.352)
sole_pro	−19.902***	−0.247	−0.204	−0.032	−0.151	0.063
	(5.381)	(0.253)	(0.264)	(0.241)	(0.314)	(0.317)
Foodind	0.851	0.684***	0.641***	0.803***	0.916***	0.625**
	(4.672)	(0.218)	(0.227)	(0.205)	(0.272)	(0.262)
Metalwork	4.235	0.798**	0.587	0.782**	0.884**	1.127**
	(7.605)	(0.358)	(0.374)	(0.339)	(0.441)	(0.454)
Riskaverse	−5.285	0.300	0.305	−0.009	0.118	−0.316
	(4.905)	(0.231)	(0.241)	(0.217)	(0.282)	(0.281)
Preferstoday	1.759	−0.034	−0.093	0.362	−0.034	0.746**
	(5.619)	(0.265)	(0.276)	(0.248)	(0.324)	(0.326)
Constant	29.309**	8.853***	7.373***	8.360***	5.555***	7.421***
	(12.483)	(0.586)	(0.611)	(0.548)	(0.737)	(0.753)
Observations	1288	1100	1094	1126	990	1005
Number of qid	184	172	172	176	167	166

Notes: Standard errors in parentheses. ***$p < 0.01$, **$p < 0.05$, *$p < 0.1$

Table 12.7 Enterprise selection assessment sheet

Overall Score	Score
1. Company assessment (Point 1: Not, 2: Fair 3: Good)	
(1) Active client of BAC	1 2 3
(2) Registration with Register General Department	1 2 3
(3) Number of employees (both fully employed and part-time) (Score: 1. 1–3, 2. 4–6, 3. 7–10, 4. 11–15, 5: 16+)	1 2 3 4 5
(4) Gender balance of the organization	1 2 3
(5) Willingness to implement KAIZEN	1 3 6
(6) Growth stage of the Organization based on NBSSI ranking system	1 2 3
(7) Book and record keeping	1 2 3
(8) English literacy rate of management	1 2 3
(9) Willingness to disclose or share business information	1 2 3
(10) Activeness	1 2 3
Sub total	
2. Applicable Basic KAIZEN Menu (Point 1: Not sure 2: Applicable)	1 2
(1) 5S including Seiton board	1 2
(2) 7Wastes	1 2
(3) Factory layout change (Minor)	1 2
(4) Reduction of defects	1 2
(5) Inventory Control	1 2
(6) Code of Conduct	1 2
(7) Organization chart	1 2
(8) Line balancing (Minor)	1 2
(9) Skill map	1 2
(10) Work standard	1 2
Sub total	
3. Expectation of KAIZEN achievement (Point 1: Not sure 2: Achievable)	1 2
(1) 5S including Seiton board	1 2
(2) 7Wastes (shortening of transport)	1 2
(3) Factory layout change (Minor), shortening of transport	1 2
(4) Reduction of defects	1 2
(5) Inventory Control	1 2
(6) Code of Conduct (Absenteeism)	1 2
(7) Organization chart	1 2
(8) Line balancing (Minor)	1 2
(9) Skill map (Multi-skilled worker)	1 2
(10) Work standard	1 2
Sub total	
4. Recommendation products by GoG (Point 0: Not recommended 10: Recommended)	0 5
5. Local industry development (Applicability to many other enterprises in the same industry.) (Point 3: Somehow, 5: Fair, 8: Above average 10: Fully)	3 5 8 10

(*continued*)

Table 12.7 (continued)

6. Access to the company **(Point 1: within 30 minutes from BAC)** **(Point 3: between 30 and 60 minutes from BAC)** **(Point 5: 60 minutes+ from BAC)**	1 3 5
7. Export potential or import substitute **(Point 0: No potential Point 5: Potential)**	0 5
G. Total (100 points)	

Source: Project implementers—National Board for Small Scale Industries (NBSSI) and JICA Ghana office

Notes

1. This theory holds that the swifter and more even material flow through a process, the more productive that process is (Schmenner and Swink 1998, 102).
2. Central region was not included in the survey because no enterprise in this region had received the training.
3. The differences in educational attainment may have implications for the results particularly with regard to understanding and assimilating *Kaizen* concepts during the training. Hence, in both PSM (and regression analysis presented in the Appendix), we use the English proficiency of the manager as a matching variable in the case of PSM and a control variable in the case of the regression analysis.

References

Bell, M., and K. Pavitt. 1997. Technological Accumulation and Industrial Growth: Contrasts Between Developed and Developing Countries. In *Technology, Globalization and Economic Performance*, ed. Daniele Archibugi and Jonathan Michie, 83–137. Cambridge: Cambridge University Press.

Berger, A. 1997. Continuous Improvement and Kaizen: Standardization and Organizational Designs. *Integrated Manufacturing Systems* 8 (2): 110–117.

Bloom, N., and J. Van Reenen. 2007. Measuring and Explaining Management Practices Across Firms and Countries. *The Quarterly Journal of Economics* 122 (4, Nov.): 1351–1408.

Brown, S., D. Gray, J. McHardy, and K. Taylor. 2015. Employee Trust and Workplace Performance. *Journal of Economic Behavior & Organization* 116 (Aug.): 361–378.

Bruhn, M., and B. Zia. 2013. Stimulating Managerial Capital in Emerging Markets: The Impact of Business Training for Young Entrepreneurs. *Journal of Development Effectiveness* 5 (2): 232–266.

Brunet, A.P., and S. New. 2003. Kaizen in Japan: An Empirical Study. *International Journal of Operations & Production Management* 23 (12): 1426–1446.
Bryson, A., Dorsett, R., and Purdon, S. 2002. The Use of Propensity Score Matching in the Evaluation of Labour Market Policies. *Working Paper No. 4*. Department for Work and Pensions.
Caselli, F., and Gennaioli, N. 2013. Dynastic Management. *Economic Inquiry* 51 (1): 971–996.
Diop, M. 2017. World Bank's Vice President for Africa Institute of South–South Cooperation and Development (ISSCAD), Peking University, China: Beijing. Speech Delivered on 30 November 2017.
Egbetokun, A., R. Atta-Ankomah, O. Jegede, and E. Lorenz. 2016. Firm-level Innovation in Africa: Overcoming Limits and Constraints. *Innovation and Development* 6 (2): 161–174.
Foster, L., J. Haltiwanger, and C. Syverson. 2008. Reallocation, Firm Turnover, and Efficiency: Selection on Productivity or Profitability? *American Economic Review* 98 (1): 394–425.
Fu, X. 2015. *China's Path to Innovation*. Cambridge: Cambridge University Press.
Ghana Statistical Service. 2013. *2010 Population & Housing Census National Analytical Report*. May. Accra, Ghana: Author.
———. 2015. Annual Gross Domestic Product-September 2015 Edition. Accra, Ghana: Author.
Higuchi, Y., V.H. Nam, and T. Sonobe. 2015. Sustained Impacts of Kaizen Training. *Journal of Economic Behaviour & Organization* 120 (Dec.): 189–206.
Hsieh, C.T., and P.J. Klenow. 2009. Misallocation and Manufacturing TFP in China and India. *Quarterly Journal of Economics* 124 (4): 1403–1448.
Humphrey, J. 1995. Industrial Reorganization in Developing Countries: From Models to Trajectories. *World Development* 23 (1): 149–162.
Jiménez, M., L. Romero, M. Domínguez, and M. del Mar Espinosa. 2015. 5S Methodology Implementation in the Laboratories of an Industrial Engineering University School. *Safety Science* 78 (Oct.): 163–172.
Kaplinsky, R. 1995. Technique and System: The Spread of Japanese Management Techniques to Developing Countries. *World Development* 23 (1): 57–71.
Kim, Y. 2014. China-Africa Technology Transfer: A Matter of Technology Readiness. *CCS Commentary*. Stellenbosch: Centre for Chinese Studies. Accessed March 24, 2016. http://www.ccs.org.za/wp-content/uploads/2014/02/CCS_Commentary_China_Africa_Tech_2014_YK1.pdf.
King, G., and R. Nielson. 2018. Why Propensity Score Matching Should Not Be Used for Matching? December. Accessed February 10, 2018. https://gking.harvard.edu/files/gking/files/psnot.pdf.
Maarof, M.G., and F. Mahmud. 2016. A Review of Contributing Factors and Challenges in Implementing Kaizen in Small and Medium Enterprises. *Procedia Economics and Finance* 35: 522–531.

Mano, Y., J. Akoten, Y. Yoshino, and T. Sonobe. 2014. Teaching KAIZEN to Small Business Owners: An Experiment in a Metalworking Cluster in Nairobi. *Journal of the Japanese and International Economies* 33 (Sep.): 25–42.

Mano, Y., A. Iddrisu, Y. Yoshino, and T. Sonobe. 2012. How Can Micro and Small Enterprises in Sub-Saharan Africa Become More Productive? The Impacts of Experimental Basic Managerial Training. *World Development* 40 (3): 458–468.

Osei, R.D., and R. Jedwab. 2016. Structural Change in a Poor Country: New Historical Evidence from Ghana. In *Structural Change, Fundamentals and Growth*, ed. Margaret McMillan, Dani Rodrick, and Claudia Sepulveda, 161–196. Washington, DC: International Food Policy Research Institute.

Panizzolo, R., P. Garengo, M.K. Sharma, and A. Gore. 2012. Lean Manufacturing in Developing Countries: Evidence from Indian SMEs. *Production Planning & Control* 23 (10–11): 769–788.

Puvanasvaran, A.P., S.T. Kerk, and A.R. Ismail. 2010. A Case Study of Kaizen Implementation in SMI. National Conference in Mechanical Engineering Research and Postgraduate Studies (2nd NCMER 2010) 3–4 December 2010. Faculty of Mechanical Engineering. UMP Pekan, Kuantan, Pahang, Malaysia: 374–392.

Recht, R., and C. Wilderom. 1998. Kaizen and Culture: On the Transferability of Japanese Suggestion Systems. *International Business Review* 7 (1): 7–22.

Restuccia, D., and R. Rogerson. 2008. Policy Distortions and Aggregate Productivity with Heterogeneous Establishments. *Review of Economic Dynamics* 11 (4): 707–720.

Rodrik, D. 2015. Premature Deindustrialization. *Working Paper No. 20935.* Cambridge, MA: National Bureau of Economic Research. http://papers.nber.org/tmp/65392-w20935.pdf.

Schmenner, R.W., and M.L. Swink. 1998. On Theory in Operations Management. *Journal of Operations Management* 17 (1): 97–113.

Styhre, A. 2001. Kaizen, Ethics, and Care of the Operations: Management After Empowerment. *Journal of Management Studies* 38 (6): 795–810.

Withanachchi, N., Y. Handa, K.K.W. Karandagoda, P.P. Pathirage, N.C.K. Tennakoon, and D.S.P. Pullaperuma. 2007. TQM Emphasizing 5-S Principles: A Breakthrough for Chronic Managerial Constraints at Public Hospitals in Developing Countries. *International Journal of Public Sector Management* 20 (3): 168–177.

CHAPTER 13

Consequences of *Kaizen* Practices in MSMEs in the Philippines: The Case of the Manufacturing Productivity Extension Program (MPEX)

Nestor O. Raneses, Nelson G. Cainghog, Mili-Ann M. Tamayao, and Kristine Mae C. Gotera

1 Introduction

The micro, small, and medium enterprises (MSMEs) sector is regarded by governments as "a means to achieve a dynamic and flourishing private sector, by increasing exports and enhancing industrial competitiveness, and

N. O. Raneses
Department of Industrial Engineering and Operations Research, University of the Philippines Diliman, Quezon City, Philippines
e-mail: noraneses@up.edu.ph

N. G. Cainghog
Department of Political Science, University of the Philippines Diliman, Quezon City, Philippines

M.-A. M. Tamayao (✉)
Department of Industrial Engineering, National Engineering Center, University of the Philippines Diliman, Quezon City, Philippines
e-mail: mmtamayao@up.edu.ph

K. M. C. Gotera
University of the Philippines Diliman, Quezon City, Philippines

A. Hosono et al. (eds.), *Workers, Managers, Productivity*,
https://doi.org/10.1007/978-981-15-0364-1_13

to ensure more equitable development in terms of a broader distribution of assets, through creating jobs and increasing income, and hence improving the well-being of poor and marginalized groups" (Jeppesen 2005, 463). In the Philippines, the government through its Philippine Development Plan 2017–2022 included MSMEs in one of its outcomes in terms of access to economic opportunities in industry and services. This recognition can be traced back in 1991 when Republic Act No. 6977 or the Magna Carta for Small Enterprises was passed into law which recognizes that "small and medium scale enterprises have the potential for more employment generation and economic growth and therefore can help provide a self-sufficient industrial foundation for the country." In 2013, Republic Act No. 10644 declared that it is the state's policy "to foster national development, promote inclusive growth, and reduce poverty by encouraging the establishment of micro, small and medium enterprises (MSMEs) that facilitate local job creation, production and trade in the country."

The government's recognition of MSMEs is largely driven by the sector's impact to the economy. According to the Philippine Statistics Authority, in 2016, the sector, composed of firms with capitalization below P100 million and/or with less than 200 employees, employed 4.88 million people. This is 63 percent of the total number of jobs generated by all types of business establishments. In 2014, MSMEs contributed 35.7 percent of gross value added and 25 percent of export revenues. The manufacturing sector, with 115,748 MSME firms, employed 760,416 people or 16.1 percent of total employment. While it is not the largest sector, it is seen to have the greatest potential for upscaling because of its export potential, and has the biggest long-term value-added contribution.

Given the impact of MSMEs in the Philippine economy, their growth and expansion are of strategic importance. Government agencies have been implementing programs to assist MSMEs in realizing their potential either by making technology and financing available through low-interest loans and shared service facilities or by transferring technical know-how through extension programs or consultancies. The Department of Science and Technology's (DOST) Productivity Extension for Export Promotion (MPEX) program, renamed as Manufacturing Productivity Extension Program, is one of these government initiatives. Initiated in 1991 by the Technology Application and Promotion Institute (TAPI) of DOST, it seeks to promote increase in productivity of manufacturing firms to make their products more competitive both in price and in quality in the global and local markets (DOST 2009). It was inspired by the work of China Productivity Center in Taiwan where industrial engineers assisted industry in identifying and implementing practices that enhanced firm productivity (Badiru and Chen 1992, 53–55).

The MPEX program assists MSMEs in the manufacturing sector to attain higher productivity through improvements in the overall operation of the firm (DOST 2009). It covers the agro and food processing, furniture, gifts and holiday decorations, information technology, materials science, metals and engineering, and microelectronics sectors. The process starts with the pre-qualification of potential beneficiaries conducted by DOST regional offices and consultants from a list of firms identified or endorsed by the Provincial Science and Technology Directors, Department of Trade and Industry Provincial Offices, and other organizations in the region. After identifying firms that match the consultants' expertise and are willing to sign a commitment contract to implement consultant recommendations, an initial productivity audit is conducted to diagnose the firm's financial, management, marketing, and production performance.

MPEX consultants examine major areas like the manufacturing process, plant and equipment design, product planning and control system, materials management system, quality control and assurance system, safety and housekeeping practices, financial control system, human resource, and support services utilization. An inception report is submitted to the DOST regional office containing initial assessment, evaluation, and recommendations. At least three priority intervention areas are identified. After a period of two to three months, a validation of the finding and recommendations is conducted by the MPEX consultant to determine if the recommended improvements were implemented. Finally, a report is given to the beneficiary and the DOST regional office. The consultancy is valued at US $800 per firm and is fully subsidized by government.

While *Kaizen* is not clearly advertised, the structural foundations of MPEX are fundamentally *Kaizen* elements. The prime aim is to improve firm-level productivity and quality, and eventually promote growth. MPEX is implementing *Kaizen* at the firm level instigated by government, a shift from a purely private sector led to a public sector-driven productivity improvement program.

This chapter aims to determine the consequences of MPEX on productivity and product quality of beneficiary firms. It examines how *Kaizen* practices contribute toward this end.

2 Literature Review

2.1 Kaizen

Ohno (1988, 123–177) classified *Kaizen* as either operations, equipment, or process *Kaizen*. Operations *Kaizen* refers to improvement of specific operations in the shop floor. Equipment *Kaizen* refers to improvements in the utilization and operation of existing equipment, while process *Kaizen* refers to the reinvention or restructuring of the overall production processes. In the context of the case studies, *Kaizen* refers to any of its three kinds. *Kaizen* is further anchored on the following assumptions: it (1) requires little investment especially in terms of equipment; (2) aims to reduce waste, overburden, and unevenness; and (3) is people oriented where the welfare and the empowerment of the workers are important.

2.1.1 Kaizen *as Not Physical Capital-Intensive*

Imai (1986, 25 as cited in Ohno et al. 2009, 6) characterizes *Kaizen*, among others, as requiring little investment but great effort to maintain. It requires great effort as it needs the involvement of everyone—managers and workers. The concept of little investment (Imai 2012) is consistent with Ohno's (1988) notion of improvement using existing equipment. While managerial capital may increase firm-level productivity, *Kaizen* is relevant only in initiatives that require little expense. An obvious question emerges on the threshold of little expense. This chapter resolves this question by identifying only those that did not require the acquisition of new equipment in the production system as *Kaizen* practices. The repurposing and modification of existing machinery or tools while involving certain expense can still fall under the rubric of Ohno's equipment *Kaizen*. While expense might be incurred in equipment *Kaizen*, the assumption is that such actions are implemented to reduce the cost or waste of operating existing machinery and the expense involved is lower than acquiring a new machinery.

2.1.2 Kaizen *as Reduction of Muda, Muri, and Mura*

Another distinctive feature of *Kaizen* is that it aims to reduce waste (*muda*), overburden (*muri*), and unevenness (*mura*). *Muda* is manifested as either defects, overproduction, waiting, non-used talent, transport, inventories, motion, and excess processing or downtime. *Muri* manifests when employees and processes are subjected to unnecessary stress due to the wrong tools, wrong metrics, and wrong fit, among others. *Mura* pertains to situations where processes are inconsistent with sudden upticks that lead to excess capacity in certain times. Any low-cost improvement that reduces *muda*, *muri*, and/or *mura* can then be considered as *Kaizen* depending on its effect to the workers.

2.1.3 Kaizen *as a People-Oriented Approach*

Sonobe and Otsuka (2014, 15) believe that *Kaizen* promotes inclusive development. *Kaizen* empowers not just the employers, but the employees as well. Because of instances when workers are more knowledgeable about the production, *Kaizen* encourages the workers to come up with strategies that could improve their work. It is inclusive such that aside from the owners earning more, but *Kaizen* extends this opportunity to the workers.

Waste reducing practices that require little investment implemented in firms cannot be considered to fall within the spirit of *Kaizen* if they do not empower or would result in situations inimical to the workers' safety and well-being like layoffs. On practical terms, *Kaizen*, as implemented, will need the full cooperation of workers to be successful. Workers will not be motivated to participate if its wastes reduction and its corresponding savings will result in layoffs. Japan's postwar experience was a demonstration of *Kaizen* where firms pursued wastes reduction without jeopardizing the welfare of workers as shown in Shimada (2017) in this volume.

2.2 Factors Affecting Firm Growth

There are numerous factors that contribute toward firm growth. Nichter and Goldmark (2009, 1453–1464) reviewed researches on firm growth and found four areas that are important: individual entrepreneur characteristics like education and related work experience; firm characteristics like age, formality, and access to finance; relational factors such as social network and value chain; and contextual factors like the business environment and the situation of the larger economy. Reeg (2013) follows the same categories but conceptualizes these areas as layers in her onion model where the individual (Kaplinsky 1995, 57–71) and firm characteristics are internal factors while relational and contextual factors are considered external. Kaplinsky's (1995, 57–71) findings on the challenges in the adoption of Japanese management techniques in developing countries also fall within those areas. He identified some of these external challenges as weakness of human resource development, problems in inter-firm relations, and management and labor-management relations.

In a study by Habidin and others (2016, 512–513), follow-up activities, work area impact, and employee skill and effort were identified as *Kaizen* activities that have positive relationship to operational performances.

2.3 Kaizen *and MSMEs*

Three factors for a successful *Kaizen* implementation were determined, namely effective communication between the management and employees, a clear firm strategy, policies, and goals, and the presence of a *Kaizen* champion who pilots the activities for continuous improvement (Maarof and Mahmud 2016, 522–531). In the study of Mano et al. (2014, 25–42), the trainings on *Kaizen* did not have a statistically significant effect on sales revenue. Instead, the effect was apparent on other value-adding parameters such as reduction in waste material and activities.

Aside from improvement in productivity and quality, the introduction of the *Kaizen* training as a bottom-up approach also improved the quality of working conditions and social capital of firms through increased employees' participation in the operation of firms and better relationship among workers (Shimada and Sonobe 2018, 21–22). It resulted in the improvement of workers' attitude toward work.

In Tanzania, *Kaizen* is one of the country's interventions supporting the growth of the manufacturing sector. According to Bwemelo (2014, 85–86), participating Small Scale Manufacturing Enterprises (SSME) perceive *Kaizen* to be useful and their implementation was effective, although challenges were encountered.

Kaizen, as adopted by Japan International Cooperation Agency (JICA), does not only improve productivity of the firms, its impacts ripple beyond it. It facilitates partnership with government agencies making them adopt a pro-productivity institutional thinking which creates pro-productivity policies and outcomes. On the sectoral level, firms that apply *Kaizen* processes increase productivity and expand their market share (Lemma 2018, 24).

3 Data and Methodology

3.1 Data Sources

MPEX was implemented in all regions since its inception in 1991 from the DOST central office through TAPI. In the last five years (2013–present), however, the program was transferred to regional offices leading to uneven implementation depending on regional priorities. Based on consultations with regional directors, seven regions were considered: Region 3 (Central Luzon), Region 4-A (Calabarzon), Region 4-B (MIMAROPA), Region 6 (Western Visayas), Region 7 (Central Visayas), Region 8 (Eastern Visayas), and Region 13 (Caraga). Fieldwork pushed through in four regions (4-B, 6, 7, 8) where regional office personnel were available to assist in visiting beneficiary firms as shown in Fig. 13.1. From a population of about 300 MPEX food manufacturing beneficiaries mainly

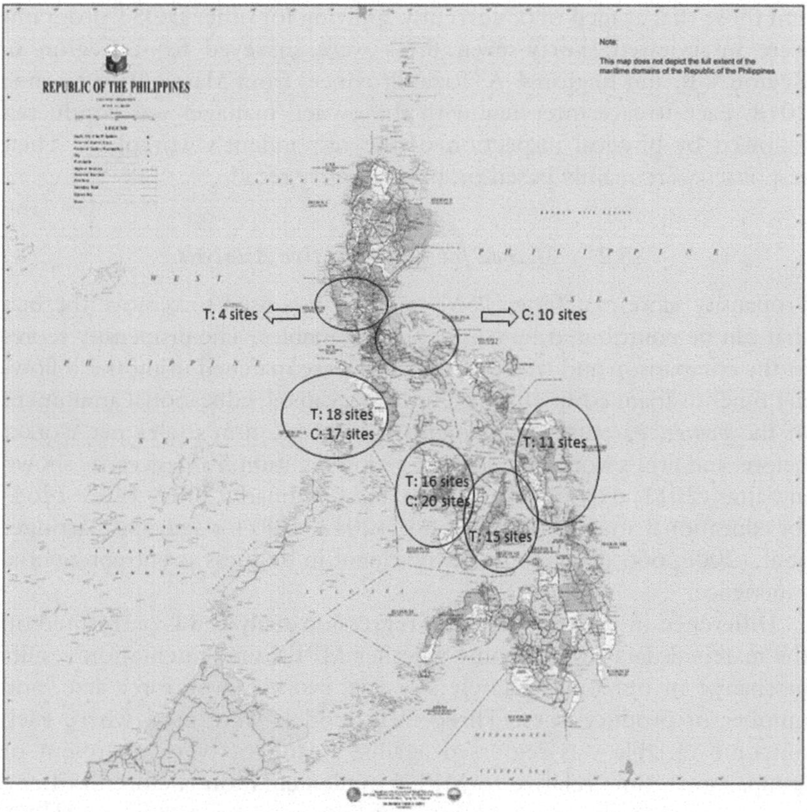

Fig. 13.1 Map of the Philippines showing the locations of respondent firms

in the bakery, cakes, and pastries sub-sector in the regions where MPEX was consistently implemented, 177 firms were culled. Seventy-four respondent firms were selected from the 177 sampling frame. They were surveyed using face-to-face interview and ocular inspection of the respondent's workplace, from September 2017 to January 2018. Of the 74 firms surveyed, 10 were eventually excluded because they were no longer operating or because of incomplete data. The remaining 64 respondent firms were analyzed. The other 113 firms were either too remote to visit, or unrelated to the bread, cakes, and pastries sub-sector, for example meat processing, catering, and others. For the comparison group, firms assisted by the Department of Trade and Industry (DTI) and those that availed of or currently applying for other DOST programs were interviewed. Forty-seven firms were surveyed from Region 6, Region 4-B, and Region 4-A (Rizal Province) from March 2018 to June 2018. Face-to-face interview with the owner/manager was conducted followed by physical inspection of the respondent's workplace. Their responses were mainly based on best memory recall.

3.2 Method for Quantitative Analysis

Propensity score matching (PSM) method was used to remove the bias that can be contributed by confounding variables. The propensity scores of the comparison and treatment groups were matched using the following time-invariant covariates: sex, firm age, capital, educational attainment of the *owner*, parents' engagement in business, firm's sales per worker before, and firm's workforce size before intervention. Evidences are shown in Sattar (2011, 64) for sex, Nichter and Goldmark (2009, 1453–1464) for educational attainment, Fadahunsi (2012, 108) for age, and Barringer et al. (2005, 666) for parents' involvement in business as entrepreneurial experience.

Difference-in-difference (DID) regression analysis was performed on the matched data to determine whether MPEX implementation results in change in outcomes namely sales per worker, workforce size, and number of product lines. Three DID models were used where each outcome variable was regressed against treatment type (treatment or comparison), time relative to MPEX implementation (before or after), and the interaction between treatment time and time relative to MPEX implementation.

3.3 *Method for Qualitative Analysis*

Two anonymized cases were examined to qualitatively identify and understand the contribution of *Kaizen* practices in firm performance. Specifically, the cases were selected based on reported positive outcomes including increase in productivity or product quality improvement, and cooperation of the owner. Representativeness was also considered in the choice of the two firms.

This qualitative analysis was done to supplement the findings from the quantitative analysis by providing context as to how observation of *Kaizen* practices is related to firm performance. Although findings may not be generalized, this analysis elucidated key insights regarding enabling conditions for *Kaizen* adoption and sustenance.

4 Findings and Analysis

4.1 *Quantitative Findings: Propensity Score Matching and Difference-In-Difference Regression Analysis*

Out of the 64 treatment firms and 47 comparison firms, 35 were matched with a match tolerance of 0.25, using the Nearest Neighbor matching method with replacement. Preliminary analysis led to the selection of the following covariates: *sex, firm age, capital, parents' engagement in business, firm's sales per worker before, and firm's workforce size before intervention.*

DID regression analysis showed mixed results when relating number of product lines, sales per worker, and number of workers to the three regressors. Details of the results are discussed further in the Appendix.

The relatively small sample size, survey responses based on memory recall, and the confounding effects on productivity of other assistance received by the MPEX firms from other government agencies inherently restricted the results of the analysis.

A study by Bloom et al. (2013) looked into the effects of management practices to firm performance of large textile industries. The study had a relatively small sample size, 14 treatment plants and 6 control plants. The interventions resulted in an 11 percent increase in productivity, decentralization of decision-making, and increased use of technology. Despite the small sample size, the statistically significant results are attributed to the data quality. The data were collected directly from machine logs and was done in a high frequency.

While most interventions in the MPEX can be considered as embodiment of the *Kaizen* philosophy, the MPEX was not conceptualized as a *Kaizen* effort. Thus, attributing MPEX implementation with increase in product lines as *Kaizen* is not straightforward. Nonetheless, the treatment group was observed to have implemented *Kaizen* methods and approaches after MPEX enrollment. About 35 percent of the firms implemented food safety and good manufacturing practices, 23 percent layout changes, 21 percent 5S and housekeeping improvement, 13 percent materials and inventory management, 13 percent process and operations efficiency, 10 percent equipment/machine upgrade, 8 percent worker/staff development/training, and 6 percent financial and recordkeeping improvement actions. Not all of the recommendations were fully implemented primarily because most of the owners' time was consumed running the enterprise and managing the daily operations (76 percent). They also have multiple responsibilities—marketing, operations and production, finance, procurement, and general management. They could not find time to delegate and involve workers in making decisions. Another reason cited was the inability to access funds to implement the improvement recommendations.

4.2 *Qualitative Findings: Comparative Case Study*

Two case studies were done to explore positive indications of relationship between *Kaizen* practices and firm-level productivity and/or product quality improvement. Each case study is organized into three parts: background of the firm; the practices embodying *Kaizen* philosophy; the productivity or product quality improvement observed in the firm; and a discussion of the insights from the case analysis.

To demonstrate how *Kaizen* practices as defined by Ohno (1988) work within specific cases, the following case studies trace how they contribute toward productivity and improved quality by achieving at least one of the four purposes of improvement: easier, better, faster, cheaper (Shingo 1988, 94). The cases chosen demonstrate at least two pathways through which *Kaizen* practices bring positive outcomes to the firms. These are faster processes and better quality through compliance with regulatory standards.

4.2.1 *Firm A:* Kaizen *Increases Productivity*

Background

Firm A, a single proprietorship, started operating as a home-based business in 2011. It sells assorted bread and cakes through an outlet and 20 deliveries within the city. It is a small enterprise with an asset size of about US $100,000. After two years of operation, the bakeshop transferred to a bigger 600-square meter plant. With a large market, it increased its outlets to 4 and supplied 36 schools. The bakeshop employs 24 bakers and a couple of administrative and finance staff.

In 2015, it availed of the MPEX program of the DOST. The MPEX consultant from a local college gave six recommendations namely:

1. Re-layout plant to minimize the risks of contamination and for systematic arrangement of work areas.
2. Replace rice hull burners with new ovens.
3. Purchase additional equipment for line balancing: one unit of spiral dough mixer (45 kg capacity) and one-unit dough roller (27 kg capacity).
4. Require all personnel to pass through the sanitary area before going to their workplaces and technical personnel to observe good manufacturing practices (GMP) inside the production area.
5. Benchmark the design of baked products of other bakeshops.
6. Benchmark the labels of baked products of other bakeshops.

Of the six recommendations, Recommendations 1 and 4 can be considered as *Kaizen* as they aim to reduce motion waste, waiting and possible defects like contamination, and do not require additional equipment. Both are also beneficial to the workers and require their sustained effort and cooperation to be realized. Recommendations 2 and 3 are capital-intensive and may not be considered pure *Kaizen* if they require buying new equipment. Recommendations 5 and 6 are marketing-related with minimal effect on the production process. The owner decided to implement Recommendations 1, 2, and 4. For Recommendation 2, the rice hull burners were replaced with new electric ovens by availing a government loan facility.

Kaizen Practices Introduced

The MPEX consultant conducted an half-day training to employees before implementing Recommendations 1 and 4. The training focused on 5S and good manufacturing practices/hygiene. As a result, the owner modified the layout and the practices of the firm. Implemented practices due to the MPEX recommendations were as follows:

1. Pre-mix ingredients a day before production. Previously, bakers themselves gather and mix ingredients on the production day. Skilled bakers were freed from the mundane act of measuring and mixing ingredients, giving them more time to spend on high-value activities like preparing the dough itself. It also prevented possible unavailability or shortage of raw materials, which could delay the production process, because required ingredients were already pre-mixed the day before.
2. Reduce the frequency of raw material delivery from once to twice a week giving them more time to pay for acquired ingredients, which they source from suppliers under a 45-day credit term. This practice did not only reduce waste, it also reduced the burden on the bakers.
3. Re-layout the existing machines according to their sequence in the production process. This reduced the distance and time traveled by the material thereby eliminating transportation waste.
4. Provide sanitary area before entering the facility to prevent contamination entering the production area.

Aside from those recommended by the consultant, additional *Kaizen* practices were also introduced by the entrepreneur, signifying adoption of the continuous improvement mindset.

One practice implemented by the owner was promoting teamwork. The production workers were grouped into two teams. Given the same production quota, the two teams engaged in a healthy daily competition of finishing the job first. Workers may leave once the quota is reached. Every fortnight, the team with the most number of wins gets US $40 bonus. This setup provides an additional incentive and introduced fun through gamification in the workplace. More importantly, it encouraged the workers to be more efficient.

Suggestions were also encouraged. Workers recommended the use of long tables instead of several short ones in the production area. This reduced the effort required to move the molded bread and shortened the move time. With long tables, trays are just pushed near the next sequence of the production process.

The entrepreneur also introduced changes in the deployment of workers for the piling of packed bread for delivery. Before, three workers pile packed breads in crates for delivery at night. This system, however, overburdened the workers and delayed the delivery. In the new system, one works during the day to immediately pile packed bread in crates and the other two work at night to pile any remaining packed bread and load the crates for delivery. The practice reduced the burden among the firm's employees, reducing *muri*, while making the process faster.

Reckoning Productivity

The *Kaizen* practices introduced, however, cannot fully account for the faster process. Other interventions had a bigger effect on the production process. These are replacing the rice hull ovens with electric ovens and the use of electric heater for proofing instead of charcoal proofing. When using rice hull oven, it took two and a half hours to bake 32 plates (an average of 0.66 kg of flour per plate). With the use of electric ovens, 36 plates can be baked in just 25 minutes. As for the heater, it takes only an hour for the dough to rise. With charcoal proofing, it took twice as much time. Overall, there has been a reduction of at least 3 hours and 5 minutes in the production of 36 plates of bread. Considering that the electric oven has 12.5 percent more capacity compared to the rice hull oven, production capacity is further increased.

Before MPEX, 18 bakers and 6 on-the-job trainees (OJTs) were able to process 1260 kilos of flour for 14 to 15 hours. Each baker was given a quota of 60 kilos, while OJTs were given 30 kilos. After MPEX, there are still 24 bakers with the 6 OJTs absorbed as regular employees. Each has a quota of 60 kilos, which translates to 1440 kilos processed for 10 hours daily. Given that the non-*Kaizen* intervention can account for decrease three hours in production time, it can be inferred that further reduction of production time by one hour can be attributed to the *Kaizen* practices implemented. The increase in oven capacity by 12.5 percent is absorbed by the increase in volume of production from 1260 to 1440 kilos, an increase of 14.2 percent.

Considering that their monthly utility costs is US $1060 for electricity and US $1378 for gas, a one-hour reduction could translate to savings of approximately US $4.60/day in gas and US $3.50/day in electricity (assuming that production is daily at ten hours per day). In four years, these amounts could pay for 80 percent of the loan amount used to acquire new equipment (US $22,383). The intervention did not only make the process efficient, it also made it cheaper. Also, a one-hour reduction in production is important given the market situation. The earlier the deliveries are made, the sooner the bread gets sold for the day.

Lessons on *Kaizen* and Productivity

The case of Firm A indicates that from the *Kaizen* approaches introduced by the MPEX consultant, the entrepreneur was able to follow through with continuous improvements causing a change in the mindset of the workers. This eventually resulted in increase in productivity that was also confounded by the acquiring of more efficient machineries.

The market pressure for breads to be delivered early and on time and the need for the entrepreneur for free time to attend to his other businesses acted as catalyst in facilitating the adoption and implementation of *Kaizen* practices that resulted in significant productivity improvement in Firm A. Additionally, as evidenced by Firm A, *Kaizen* anchors higher-order productivity and quality with the adoption of better production technology and equipment.

4.2.2 Firm B: Kaizen *Enhances Quality Through Compliance with Regulatory Standards*

Background

Firm B is a micro enterprise, originally set up as a single proprietorship with an asset size of US $40,000. It is engaged in condiments manufacturing. His business started back in 2013 when his application for distributorship to a major condiment manufacturer was met with onerous conditions. Instead of accepting the conditionalities, he formulated his own vinegar-based condiment, a mixture of natural fermented coconut sap, chilies, and other spices. The experimental vinegar got positive feedback from his friends which emboldened him to turn it into a business venture.

In 2016, he availed of the MPEX program. The MPEX consultants gave the following recommendations to improve his working area:

1. Mechanize certain processes including the chopping of spices and the filling, bottling, and sealing of condiments;

2. Institute hygienic practices including the non-use of cellphone inside the production area, putting a locker area to store personal belongings, proper flooring material and design, and re-location of the restroom outside the building;
3. Re-layout the production area to ensure continuous one-way flow of raw materials; and
4. Produce only one product at a time to ensure traceability.

The recommendations focusing on good manufacturing practices were implemented as a requirement to acquire a license to operate (LTO) from the Food and Drug Administration of the Philippines. An LTO is needed to secure a certificate of product registration (CPR) for a specific product. The CPR, in turn, is a requirement for major supermarkets before they agree to sell certain products.

The overall intervention including the purchase of machines resulted in a tenfold increase in production and sales. The purchase of a bigger blender, miller, and acetator allowed them to process a bigger volume of raw materials. The freezer enabled them to store perishable chilies when there is abundance in supply. The stainless tables and three-sink basin also facilitated their compliance with the LTO standards.

Kaizen Practices

In firm B, it is difficult to fully attribute increase in productivity to process optimization given the reconfiguration and expansion of the production area. One reconfiguration entailed a separate point of entry for raw materials and a separate point of exit for the finished product. There were also hygienic practices introduced to ensure that the raw materials are not contaminated therefore minimizing losses. However, it is difficult to ascertain any gains in productivity unless a detailed time and motion study is conducted. Their production schedule is dependent on the demand of the customers. Spoilage is not a problem because raw materials are not perishable. The owner, however, attested that production became easier after the reconfiguration of the plant layout.

Another important indicator for the presence of *Kaizen* in the firm is the empowerment of workers to run the operations of the firm and suggest innovations. Due to the multiple commitments of the owner, the workers were empowered to process orders from clients as long as the transactions are recorded. Also, the owner transformed the firm from single proprietorship to a corporation. He announced that he will eventually give stock options to his employees to encourage them to perform better.

Reckoning Quality Enhancement

The interventions especially in hygiene and the systematization of the production process allowed them to comply with the LTO standards which opened doors to bigger markets like groceries and major supermarkets. Access to new market would not have been possible without the LTO from the Food and Drug Administration. While it is difficult to quantitatively demonstrate the effect of *Kaizen* practices in the licensing process, the good practices that the employees imbibed were necessary in complying with the requirements for the LTO acquisition and granted them access to bigger markets.

It is also worth emphasizing that the decision to secure a license to operate is necessary for the firm's viability. Firm B's products are condiments. In order to attain a certain viable volume, the firm needs to expand its market reach. While Firm B is operating in a city of about a hundred thousand people, the demand is not enough to support the firm given the presence of competitors and the nature of the product. In order to be profitable, the firm needs to expand its market beyond the city and its environs, thus the need to secure an LTO.

Lessons on *Kaizen* and Quality Toward Regulatory Compliance

Increase in firm-level productivity of Firm B could not be directly assumed because of the presence of *Kaizen* practices in the workplace. However, adapting 5S, improvement in process flow, and upgrade in equipment as a part of regulatory compliance allowed the firm to have access on a bigger market. This is also consistent with the findings on the significant effect of *Kaizen* in expanding markets (Lemma 2018, 24).

Similar to Firm A, Firm B's adoption of *Kaizen* practices is driven by the need of the owner to unload some work given multiple commitments. 5S discipline gives more confidence on the manager that the firm will operate well given the established processes and practices. However, the main drive for upgrade is the requirement of the market and the market requirement of the firm. Both reinforce each other and determine whether quality upgrade driven by 5S practices is necessary.

4.2.3 Discussion of Cases

Managerial capital upgrade can be done through the enlistment of management consultant like what was done in Mexico (Bruhn et al. 2010, 629–633) and India (Bloom et al. 2013). However, increased managerial capital, it is argued, is mediated by at least two factors before certain practices are adopted. These factors include the demand of the market and the market requirement of the firm's products. Given these factors, it is possible to classify firms into at least four categories depending upon their situation: (1) demanding market environment and market scale requirement, (2) demanding market but market scale not a requirement, (3) non-demanding market and market scale requirement, and (4) non-demanding market and market scale not a requirement. Type 1 firms are more likely to adopt best practices including *Kaizen* practices because of their viability depends on meeting both the market requirement and a certain scale of the market. Type 2 firms will adopt *Kaizen* practices as practicable if it satisfies the market requirement. Type 3 firms will adopt *Kaizen* practices to expand. Type 4 firms are less likely to adopt *Kaizen* practices as there is no pressure to do so.

Based on the cases discussed above, the kind of market the business serves could influence the adoption of practices especially if adoption entails some costs. For those business requiring a license to operate (LTO) from the Food and Drugs Administration to be viable, they need to follow the recommendations especially those related to food safety and proper setup of the production area. But in cases where the market is not demanding, the recommendations may be foregone or partly implemented unless the owner deems it to be beneficial either financially or in the case studies above to reduce supervision time. In the case of Firm, A, although they can operate without an LTO, they still choose to implement the recommendations as these are beneficial to their business and reduce supervision time. But other beneficiaries did not fully implement the recommendations because the market that they serve does not demand those changes.

Hampel-Milagrosa (2014) in her study on upgrading of Philippine enterprises emphasized the importance of the entrepreneur in business upgrading. While entrepreneurial mindset is indeed important, they are more likely to implement best practices especially *Kaizen* (low-cost) practices if it is beneficial for them. Entrepreneurs are rational utility maximizing individuals who want to maximize the gains for their business. Thus, any recommendation (e.g., system waste reduction) may not be readily accepted if the cost is incurred without readily translatable significant pecuniary impact on the business.

The demands of the market could be either regulation- or customer-driven. Regulatory demands are standards imposed by government regulatory agencies that need to be complied with. The regulatory regime enforced by the Food and Drug Administration for food manufacturers is an example of this regulatory demand. To get a license to operate, the firm needs to implement good manufacturing practices which include elements of 5S. In terms of employee welfare, micro enterprises in the Philippines (those with capitalization under US $60,000) are exempted from the minimum wage law reducing the leverage of workers.

For most food manufacturers, regulatory demands need to be complied to access a larger market. Regulatory- and consumer-driven demands are thus interrelated. There are, however, small businesses with a small market that operate even without an LTO, only business registration and permits from the local government. They usually supply only the locality including gift and souvenir shops where tourists buy. Given the small volume of demand, production is usually not continuous based only on demand and can be met by relatively inefficient processes. Customer-driven demands are present in urban areas where the market is more crowded compared to rural areas where competition is not that tough.

5 Conclusion and Policy Recommendations

MPEX, a public-instigated productivity and quality improvement program directed toward MSME firm-level productivity and quality improvement, was shown to exhibit *Kaizen* applications, mindsets, methods, and practices, albeit not originally packaged or advertised as *Kaizen*.

However, due to the respondent's reliance on memory recall data and the difficulty in isolating the confounding effects of the other programs and various assistance to the MPEX firms, the study was unable to establish significant difference in productivity improvement and quality enhancement measured in terms of the number of workers and sales per worker after MPEX.

The study also underscored the role of the entrepreneur/manager in implementing *Kaizen* in MSMEs, consistent with the finding of Hampel-Milagrosa (2014) that the entrepreneur is a necessary and sufficient condition for enterprise upgrading. As shown in the case studies, the successful implementation of *Kaizen* hinges on the mindset, entrepreneurial propensity, managerial capital, and time management of the entrepreneur. Engagement and empowerment of workers were demonstrated in both cases. Regulatory compliance and customer demand requirements and entrepreneurial needs for managerial efficiency and time were catalysts for facilitating, adopting, and sustaining *Kaizen* implementation. Further study is needed to establish definitive causal relationships of *Kaizen* applications to different categories of MSMEs based on objective data.

The following are some policy recommendations to improve MPEX implementation.

1. *Introduce a* Kaizen *learning module in MPEX to entrench the* Kaizen *mindset and mastery among the entrepreneurs and their workers.*

   This will make *Kaizen* as a natural guide for the entrepreneurs and the workers.
2. *Integrate MPEX in the SET-UP program.*

   Based on the profile of the MPEX treatment firms, 88 percent of them availed of SET-UP and 72 percent of the firms availed of SET-UP before MPEX. Integrating them will eliminate redundancies and sharpen the focus on empowering the MPEX entrepreneur improve productivity and quality. Additionally, a simplified technology needs assessment (TNA) which is a requirement for SET-UP can likewise be melded in the integrated MPEX-SETUP program.
3. *Establish the Kaizen Institute in partnership with universities especially with public universities.*

   The Kaizen Institute will facilitate the inculcation of *Kaizen* principles and practices in industries and the public sector. DOST can simply expand their existing partnerships with different universities, particularly outside Metro Manila to establish the Kaizen Institute that will provide knowledge and know-how, training, joint undertakings, action research, and development on *Kaizen* that will improve productivity, quality, safety, cost, morale, and environment on a sustained basis.

Appendix: Quantitative Analysis and Results

Methodology

Propensity Score Matching was conducted in three steps—(1) Preliminary Analysis to determine the covariates that are likely to influence balance of data; (2) Estimating the propensity scores to ensure that groups are balanced; and (3) Propensity Score Matching using Nearest Neighbor method with replacement and a caliper of 0.25 (Olmos and Govindasamy 2015). In the preliminary analysis, two approaches were taken to select variables that were included in the final model. The first was an estimation of the normalized difference (i.e., difference between control and treatment group for each variable) (Imbens and Wooldridge 2009). Covariates with absolute scores greater than 25 percent were not included. This was followed by the method suggested by Hansen and Bowers (2008), resembling an omnibus test.

Three difference-in-difference models were used where each outcome variable was regressed against treatment type (treatment or comparison), time relative to *MPEX* implementation (before or after), and the interaction between treatment time and time relative to MPEX implementation. The model is mathematically shown in Eq. (13.1).

$$
\begin{aligned}
y_{ist}^{OUTCOME} &= \beta_0 + \beta_{Group} Group_{is} + \beta_{Prd} Period_{it} \\
&+ \beta_{Group \times Period} \left(Group_{is} \times Period_{it} \right) + e_{ist},
\end{aligned}
\tag{13.1}
$$

where

$y_{ist}^{OUTCOME}$ is the

$$
\begin{aligned}
OUTCOME \in & \ No.of\ Product\ Lines, Gross\ Sales\ per\ Worker \\
& and\ No.of\ Workers
\end{aligned}
$$

of firm i in group $s \in$ Treatment, Comparison for period t *After MPEX*, *Before MPEX*

$Group_{is}$ is the dummy for the group type, equal to 1 if s = *Treatment* and 0 if s = *Comparison*
$Period_{it}$ is period, equal to 1 if t = *After MPEX* and 0 if t = *Before MPEX*
β_0 is the average outcome
β_{Group} accounts for the average permanent difference between treatment and control groups

β_{Prd} captures the outcome time trends common to both treatment and control group

$\beta_{Group \times Period}$ captures the true effect of MPEX on firms, which is what we are interested in.

The description of the outcome variables is summarized in Table 13.1.

Results

DID regression analysis relating to number of product lines and MPEX implementation shows that, at 5 percent significance level, there is enough statistical evidence to indicate that there is average permanent difference between treatment and comparison groups, with treatment group having about six products more than the comparison group. However, the coefficients for *Period* and *Interaction* were not found to be significant, indicating that there is not enough statistical evidence to show that MPEX implementation caused a change in number of product lines (Table 13.2).

Meanwhile, all coefficients in the DID regression analyses for *Sales per worker* and *Number of workers* were not found to be significant. These

Table 13.1 Description of outcome variables used in the difference-in-difference regression model

Variable	*Description*
Sales per worker	Total declared sales divided by number of declared workers
Number of workers	Number of declared regular workers plus seasonal hires prorated according to number of months engaged by the firm
Number of product lines	Number of products being produced by the firm

Table 13.2 Difference-in-differences regression models results

Regressors	*1. No. of product lines*	*2. Sales per worker*	*3. No. of workers*
Group	5.9**	80,936	−1.0
Period	1.2	151,971	3.4
Interaction	−0.1	8750	−1.5

**: significant at *p*-value, $\alpha = 0.05$

results indicate that MPEX implementation did not cause change for both *Sales per worker* and *Number of workers*.

In the unmatched treatment group, the correlation between asset size and difference in sales before and after MPEX implementation is 0.760. It can be speculated that as asset size increases, firms become more capable of implementing changes that will result in increase in sales. This can be investigated further.

References

Badiru, A.B., and J.J.-G. Chen. 1992. IEs Help Transform Industrial Productivity and Quality in Taiwan. *Industrial Engineering* 24 (6): 53–55.

Barringer, Bruce R., Foard F. Jones, and Donald Neubaum. 2005. A Quantitative Content Analysis of the Characteristics of Rapid-Growth Firms and Their Founders. *Journal of Business Venturing* 20: 663–687.

Bloom, Nicholas, Benn Eifert, Aprajit Mahajan, David McKenzie, and John Roberts. 2013. Does Management Matter? Evidence from India. *The Quarterly Journal of Economics* 128 (1, Feb.): 1–51.

Bruhn, Miriam, Dean Karlan, and Antoinette Schoar. 2010. What Capital Is Missing in Developing Countries? *American Economic Review* 100 (2, May): 629–633.

Bwemelo, Gordian. 2014. KAIZEN as a Strategy for Improving SSMEs' Performance: Assessing its Acceptability and Feasibility in Tanzania. *European Journal of Business and Management* 6: 79–90.

DOST. 2009. *Memorandum Circular No. 4, s. 2009*. Memorandum Circular, Manila: DOST.

Fadahunsi, Akin. 2012. The Growth of Small Businesses: Towards A Research Agenda. *American Journal of Economics and Business Administration* 1: 105–115.

Habidin, Nurul Fadly, Hamisah Hassan, Suzaituladwini Hashim, Sharon Yong Yee Ong, and Nursyazwani Mohd Fuzi. 2016. The Relationship between Kaizen Event and Operational Performance in Malaysian Automotive SMEs. *International Journal of Academic Research in Business and Social Sciences* 6: 504–517.

Hampel-Milagrosa, Aimée. 2014. *Micro and Small Enterprise Upgrading in The Philippines: The Role of the Entrepreneur, Enterprise, Networks and Business Environment*. Bonn: Deutsches Institut für Entwicklungspolitik (DIE).

Hansen, B.B., and J. Bowers. 2008. Covariate Balance in Simple, Stratified and Clustered Comparative Studies. *Statistical Science* 23 (2): 219–263. https://doi.org/10.1214/08-STS254.

Imai, Masaaki. 1986. *Kaizen: The Key to Japan's Competitive Success*. New York: McGraw-Hill Publishing Company.

———. 2012. *Gemba Kaizen: A Commonsense Approach to a Continuous Improvement Strategy*. New York: McGraw-Hill.

Imbens, G.W., and J.M. Wooldridge. 2009. Recent Developments in the Econometrics of Program Evaluation. *Journal of Economic Literature* 47 (10): 5–86. https://doi.org/10.1257/jel.47.1.5.

Jeppesen, Soeren. 2005. Enhancing Competitiveness and Securing Equitable Development: Can Small, Micro, and Medium-Sized Enterprises (SMEs) Do the Trick? *Development in Practice* 15 (3/4, June): 463–474.

Kaplinsky, Raphael. 1995. Technique and System: The Spread of Japanese Management Techniques to Developing Countries. *World Development* 23 (1, Jan.): 57–71.

Lemma, Alberto. 2018. The Role of Kaizen in Economic Transformation. *Working Paper*. London: Overseas Development Institute.

Maarof, Mohd G., and Fatimah Mahmud. 2016. A Review of Contributing Factors and Challenges in Implementing Kaizen in Small and Medium Enterprises. *Procedia Economics and Finance* 35: 522–531.

Mano, Yukichi, John Akoten, Yutaka Yoshino, and Tetsushi Sonobe. 2014. Teaching KAIZEN to Small Business Owners: An Experiment in a Metalworking Cluster in Nairobi. *Journal of the Japanese and International Economies* 33: 25–42.

Nichter, Simeon, and Lara Goldmark. 2009. Small Firm Growth in Developing Countries. *World Development* 37 (9, Sep.): 1453–1464.

Ohno, Izumi, Kenichi Ohno, and Sayoko Uesu. 2009. Introduction. In *Introducing KAIZEN in Africa*, ed. GRIPS Development Forum, 1–12. Tokyo: GRIPS Development Forum.

Ohno, Taichi. 1988. *Workplace Management*. New York: Productivity Press.

Olmos, Antonio, and Priyalatha Govindasamy. 2015. Propensity Scores: A Practical Introduction Using R. *Journal of Multidisciplinary Evaluation* 11 (25): 68–88.

Reeg, Caroline. 2013. Micro, Small and Medium Enterprise Upgrading in Low-And Middle-Income Countries: A Literature Review. *Discussion Paper*. Bonn: Bonn: German Development Institute.

Sattar, Sarosh. 2011. *Opportunities for Men and Women: Emerging Europe and Central Asia*. World Bank.

Shimada, Go, and Tetsushi Sonobe. 2018. Impacts of Kaizen Management on Workers: Evidence from the Central America and Caribbean Region. *Working Paper*. JICA.

Shingo, Shigeo. 1988. *Non-Stock Production: The Shingo System of Continuous Improvement*. Boca Raton, FL: CRC Press.

Sonobe, Tetsushi, and Keijiro Otsuka. 2014. *Cluster-Based Industrial Development: KAIZEN Management for MSE Growth in Developing Countries*. Basingstoke and New York: Palgrave Macmillan.

Index[1]

[1] Note: Page numbers followed by 'n' refer to notes.

A. Hosono et al. (eds.), *Workers, Managers, Productivity*,
https://doi.org/10.1007/978-981-15-0364-1

M

The manufacturer's authorised representative in the EU is Springer
Nature Customer Service Centre GmbH, Europaplatz 3, 69115 Heidelberg,
Germany. If you have any concerns regarding our products, please
contact ProductSafety@springernature.com

Printed and bound by CPI Group (UK) Ltd, Croydon, CR0 4YY
25/09/2026
02222902-0012